THE EAT MORE,
WEIGH LESS™
COOKBOOK

EAT MORE, WEIGH LESS™ COOKBOOK

Terry Shintani, M.D., J.D., M.P.H.

Composition and cover design by Halpax Publishing.
Illustration by Terry Shintani, M.D., J.D., M.P.H.; Dover Publishing; Polly Baird; and Eric Uptegrove.

ISBN 0-9636117-1-2

1st printing, November 1995
2nd printing, December 1996

10 9 8 7 6 5 4

Printed in Benton Harbor, Michigan, United States of America.

DEDICATION

I dedicate this book to the memory of the following people, each of whom touched many other lives in their own special way, including my own. Their generosity and wisdom has helped shape what I am today, and I have, in a way, become an instrument to carry on some of the good that they accomplished in this world. It is my hope that a little part of them may live on in the work that I do, and that the benefits people derive from this book will be a reflection of their legacy on this Earth and the spirit of God within them all.

Dr. Fred Gilbert, physician, researcher, and one of the founders of the Pacific Health Research Institute. He helped inspire me to become a physician, helped in my transition from the field of law to medicine, and supported me in my continued efforts in research.

Dr. Frances Sydow, educator and founder of Kahumana Farm and Community. Her vision of health helped create a place where the Wai'anae Diet Program could grow. She provided much practical and spiritual support for my efforts to promote the health of the Hawaiian people.

Mr. Edward Aikala, community activist and friend. A big and powerful man, with an even bigger, more powerful heart. He shared the message of health for all Hawaiian people in his gentle, simple way. His work with the Wai'anae Diet and his personal success inspired many people to take responsibility for their own health.

Dr. Georgeda Buchbinder, physician, anthropologist, nutritionist, and my mentor in Preventive Medicine. She was always supportive of my efforts to promote health in the community. She taught me much about striving for excellence, through personal example.

Mr. Ray Brosseau, a multi-talented man in media and writing. He was the chief editor of the *Eat More, Weigh Less* ™*Diet* book. He always generously shared with me his wisdom and creative ideas on writing and on how to promote health.

"Kupuna" Katherine K. Maunakea: poet, composer, and practitioner of Hawaiian herbal medicine. She was a living example of what the spirit of Aloha truly means, through her selfless sharing of her gifts with everyone who was fortunate enough to have known her.

My grandparents, Mrs. Yukie Otoide and Mrs. Miyo Shintani, who passed on this past year; and Mr. Kansuke Shintani and Mr. Gunichi Otoide, who passed on many years ago.

My parents, Emi and Robert Shintani, whose love and support I continue to feel even years after they have left this Earth.

ACKNOWLEDGEMENTS

Producing a book always takes more effort and thought than it seems. This book required the talent and hard work of many individuals whom I would like to acknowledge and thank.

Lynne Lee headed up a group of Family and Consumer Science *(formerly home economics)* teachers including Carol Devenot and Jenny Choy, who reviewed and tested many of the recipes in conjunction with my "Way of Life"™ Program. They also involved certain members of the Hawaii Association of Family and Consumer Science Teachers to do some of the testing. Ann Tang contributed many of her recipes and also some time in the early conception of the book. Daniel Resnick was also generous with his time.

Many others contributed recipes to this book as well, including world famous athlete, Ruth Heidrich, Ph.D.; TV personality, Dick Allgire; psychologist Neal Pinckney, Ph.D.; and Chef Paul Onishi.

Janice Miller was my "ghostwriter" once again *(as she was with the Eat More, Weigh Less™ Diet)* and put in many late hours to get this book out as quickly as possible.

Jan Foster was my desktop publisher; she also proved to be an excellent editor.

Claire Hughes, M.S., R.D., Chief of Nutrition at the Department of Health, and Joda Derrickson, M.P.H., R.D., looked over the draft and made sure that my recipes and statements were reasonable from a dietitian's and a public health perspective.

Special thanks go to Maybelle Roth, Ralph Komatsu, and the Hawaii Regional Chefs, who generously and quietly made a contributions to the Wai'anae Diet Program.

Thanks also go to Down to Earth health food stores, who have been supportive of all my efforts.

I would also like to acknowledge many of my colleagues and teachers whose work has been both helpful and inspirational to me.

- The staff and Board of Waianae Coast Comprehensive Health Center – pioneers of community-based health care and, of course, my co-conspirators on the "Wai'anae Diet," which demonstrated the weight loss and health effects of traditional Hawaiian diet.

- "Na Pu'uwai," a community-based organization; Helen Kanawaliwali O'Connor; Claire Hughes, M.S., R.D.; Noa Emmett Aluli, M.D.; and Kekuni Blaisdell, M.D. – who pioneered the use of traditional Hawaiian diet on Moloka'i to control lipids.

- John McDougall, M.D. – who is a long-time friend and colleague from his days in Hawaii: for his pioneering vegetarian diets that combat heart disease and other health conditions.

- Walt Willett, M.D., Dr.P.H., Professor of Epidemiology and Nutrition, Harvard School of Public Health; Lillian Cheung, D.Sc., R.D., Principal Investigator of Eat Well and Keep Moving Project, Harvard School of Public Health; Frank Sacks, M.D.; Jelia Witschi, R.D.; William Castelli, M.D.; and Tony Schwartz of Harvard University – my teachers who were models of excellence for me.

- Colin Campbell, Ph.D., of Cornell University – who with his colleagues did pioneering research on the "China Diet Study."

- Michio Kushi and Herman Aihara of the Macrobiotic Movement – who pioneered low-fat vegan diets and the whole foods movement in the United States since the 1950's.

- Kenneth Brown; Robert Oshiro, Esq.; and the Queen Emma Foundation – who kindly supported a center to integrate modern and traditional Hawaiian medical practice, and a project to promote health through Hawaiian principles.

- Barbara Southern of Kapiolani Medical Center – visionary and marketing genius.

- Dean Ornish, M.D. – whose project demonstrated the reversal of heart disease through vegetarian diet without the use of medications.

- Neal Barnard, M.D. – who promotes vegetarian diets through the professional organization, Physicians for Responsible Medicine.

- Ruth Heidrich, Ph.D. – my radio show co-host, who I call "the no-excuses woman" and who, at age 60, still competes in triathlons.

- Nita Ilaban – my "mom" from Wai'anae.

- Auntie Myrtle Mokiao – Wai'anae Coast kupuna.

I would also like to thank the following individuals and organizations who are at the top of their fields and were kind enough to take notice of our work; Robert Arnot, M.D. and CBS; Carolyn O'Neil and CNN; Laura Shapiro and *Newsweek*; Ben DiPietro, Neki Cox, and Associated Press; Dick Allgire, Paula Akana, and KITV; Leslie Wilcox, Mary Zanakis, John Yoshimura, and KHON; Jade Moon and KGMB; Emmie Tomimbang; the TV show, "Lifestyle Magazine," Linda Tomchuck and *Encyclopedia Brittanica*; Barbara Ann Curcio and *Eating Well* magazine; *Vegetarian Times* magazine; Steven Pratt and the *Chicago Tribune*; *Tufts Newsletter*; Diana Sugg and the *Sacramento Bee*; Barbara Burke, Catherine Enomoto, Linda Hosek, Becky Ashizawa and the *Honolulu Star Bulletin*; Beverly Creamer, Chris Oliver, and the *Honolulu Advertiser*; Debbie Ward and *Ka Wai Ola O OHA*; Janice Otaguro and *Honolulu Magazine*;

Ciel Sinnex and *MidWeek Magazine*; Sally-Jo Bowman and *Aloha Magazine*; Gwen Bataad and the *Hawaii Herald*; and many others whom I have forgotten to thank.

I would like to thank my "hanai" *(adoptive)* family from Nanakuli, especially my mom Agnes Cope, and brother Kamaki Kanehele, who have provided moral and spiritual support.

Thanks also to my brother, Arthur Shintani, who is always there for me, and to the staff of his company, Trends of Hawaii, who are always courteous and professional in their work.

Thanks to my wife, Stephanie; daughters, Tracie and Nickie; and their grandparents Henry and Peggy Hong, for their support and for their patience while I was writing this book.

Finally, I'd like to thank the Lord for his blessings, because it is always God who does the healing, but too often it is only the physicians who get the credit.

PREFACE

When I presented my first *Eat More, Weigh Less*™ session in 1986, little did I know that it would evolve into the series of books that is has become or have the impact on health that it has had. When I published the original *Eat More, Weigh Less*™ *Diet* book in March 1993 *(Halpax Publishing, Honolulu, HI)*, the response was overwhelming. I have received feedback that many people have been improving their health, losing weight *(some over 50 to 100 pounds)*, and even eliminating the need for medications. This book is the sequel to the first *Eat More, Weigh Less*™ *Diet* book in response to the demand for more recipes that are both delicious and health inducing.

I hope that this book is seen as timely because since the time of the publication of my first book, our American health care system has begun to show signs of failure. For example, despite our best efforts, cancer rates are rising. Costs are spiraling out of control so much that more and more people are unable to afford basic care. The sheer magnitude of the problem is so great that it threatens the very economy of this nation.

In my opinion, part of the problem is that we have lost our fundamental understanding of what health really is. We do not have a health care system; we have a disease care system. We focus on symptoms of disease and not the cause. Because of this mindset, our system has come up with expensive designer medications and high-tech solutions to health problems, rather than simple, low-cost approaches such as diet and lifestyle. While we focus trillions of dollars on a high-tech, medication-centered approach, we fail to realize that with the exception of antibiotics, most medicines today cure nothing. And while we are in a battle for health care reform to create a healthier system, what we really need is healthier people.

If we are to win the battle to keep health care high in quality, high in accessibility, and affordable in cost, it will be won not through government action or even through the health professionals. Rather, I believe it will be won in the minds and hearts of people, in what food and lifestyle choices each of us make, and in what we teach others by our words and actions. I say this because the leading causes of death in this country are diet-related diseases such as #1 – heart disease, #2 – many cancers, #3 – stroke, and #6 – diabetes, to name but a few.

It is especially important to teach our children how to live a healthy diet and lifestyle from the very beginning. The best ways to do this are by our own example and through our schools. The focal point of teaching diet and lifestyle to our children is often in "Home Economics" class *(now called Family and Consumer Science)*. There, children are taught how to select foods and how to prepare them. In my humble opinion, here lies one of the keys to the future health in this country.

This book represents, in part, a concept which I hope will be considered revolutionary — that is, the collaboration of the medical profession, the nutrition profession, and the family and consumer science profession in an attempt to directly impact the health of the community. I have been fortunate enough to have the collaboration of three excellent family and consumer science teachers, Lynne Lee and Carol Devenot *(who have won statewide awards for their work)*; and Jenny Choy *(who has spent most of her career working with Native Hawaiians)*. I have also been blessed with the assistance of two other nutritionists Claire Hughes, M.S., R.D., and Joda Derrickson, M.P.H., R.D. They helped in production and gave me perspective on this book.

For years, I have taught that in most cases the kitchen should be our first-line pharmacy and that the use of herbs, supplements, and medications should come later and only if necessary. It is my hope that this book will help your kitchen become your pharmacy, and help to give you even more control over your health and weight. The future of your health, America's health, and perhaps even the health of the world may depend on it.

With much aloha,

Terry Shintani, M.D., J.D., M.P.H.
Honolulu, Hawaii 1995

Before You Change Your Diet and Exercise Level

Do NOT change your diet or exercise level without guidance from your medical doctor if you have health problems or are on medication. Do NOT change your medications without the guidance of your medical doctor. The information in this book is general information about your health and is NOT to be taken as professional advice; nor is it intended to serve as a substitute for medical attention. The advice in this book is directed toward reasonably healthy adults. Individual needs do vary. For those with special conditions or needs, or for children and pregnant women, modifications may be necessary and should be made under the guidance of your medical doctor or registered dietitian.

Table of Contents

Table of Contents *(continued)*

Table of Contents (continued)

Table of Contents *(continued)*

Table of Contents *(continued)*

Part One

Overview

INTRODUCTION

Dieting Is Dead
(Eat More Instead)

Have you ever dieted, lost weight, then gained it all back? Or maybe you've started a diet for the first time and you're just beginning to see how hard it is to count calories or eat smaller portions of food, in the long run.

If this is you, I have some great news.

> DIETING IS DEAD.
> EATING IS ALIVE AND WELL!

This book, the companion to Dr. Shintani's *Eat More, Weigh Less™ Diet* book, will show you how to EAT MORE and still lose weight.

The conventional approach to weight loss, through calorie restriction, may be on its way out. At least, it is being seriously challenged by some of the world's leading experts. In fact, experts at the 1993 International Congress on Obesity in Brussels, Belgium, indicated that dieting may in fact be a major cause of obesity. One expert from the University of Paris said, "In the last twenty-five years, there has been no progress in the treatment for obesity; the long-term results are miserable."[1] Another expert in nutrition from State University in Ghent, Belgium, stated that: "Dieting, the major treatment of obesity, may be the major *cause* of obesity."[2]

Eat More, Not Less

In other words, if you're having problems with your weight, *maybe it's because you've been dieting too much.* Maybe you've been eating so little that your body is responding by slowing down its metabolic rate and holding onto calories. This makes it difficult for you to lose weight. Maybe you just need to *eat more.* Does this seem like a strange idea?

Think again. Since my book, *Dr. Shintani's Eat More Weigh Less™ Diet* was published in March of 1993, thousands of people are using this approach to weight loss. In my medical practice and research, I have been using the principles behind this program with great success. You really can eat your way to a slim new you.

This concept is increasingly backed up by cutting-edge research that is forcing the old way of dieting into oblivion.[3-13] No more food deprivation for you. If meals leave you hungry, any diet is doomed to failure. With the *Eat More, Weigh Less™ Diet*, you eat as much as you want, never count calories, and never restrict portion sizes. More importantly, this approach focuses on health first and helps you achieve your optimal health level. When you're eating right, the weight comes off automatically. That's why the program works.

Eat As Much As You Want and Still Lose Weight

I receive letters from all over the world from people who tell me that they've lost anywhere from 10 to more than 100 pounds. More and more people are successfully using the *Eat More, Weigh Less*™ approach to lose weight and keep it off.

She Lost 112 Pounds . . .

Lani A. told me that the *Eat More, Weigh Less*™ *Diet* changed her life. She says: "In January 1994, I weighed over 250 pounds. I decided it was time to improve my health so I could feel better. I saw *Dr. Shintani's Eat More, Weigh Less*™ *Diet* book in the bookstore and decided to try it. He explains everything about eating from a scientific standpoint. It's all in there, food, recipes, shopping, it was very easy to understand and follow. In 15 months, I lost 112 pounds. I weigh 138 pounds now and I feel great. I'm healthy, I can exercise. It's changed my life. I plan to continue it as a healthy lifestyle, forever!"

Skeptical At First . . .

Kathy, a 48-year-old nurse, came to me feeling hopeless. She thought she'd tried everything to lose weight. I suggested the *Eat More, Weigh Less*™ *Diet*. She was skeptical at first, but she tried it. When I saw her shortly thereafter, she was afraid she was eating so much that she'd gained weight. But when I weighed her, she was surprised to find that she'd lost 11 full pounds in just two weeks.

By the end of the first two months, she lost 27 pounds and looked 15 years younger. She beamed at me. "I can't believe how my life has changed. I never thought I could feel so good and it's been like this day after day. I've been given a brand new life!"

Lost 10 Belt Sizes . . .

Bill M., age 54, says: "I weighed 213 when I first heard of Dr. Shintani's diet, and I'm only 5'9" tall. My waist had ballooned up to 42 inches, my trousers' were only 29 inches long. When people ask what motivated me to try Dr. Shintani's new approach to weight loss, I say, 'Have you ever tried to buy pants with a 42-inch waist and 29-inch length?"

At last report he had lost 57 pounds, weighed 156, and his waist size was 32.

Found It Very, Very Easy . . .

He went on to say, "I found Dr. Shintani's book in the store and did it on my own. Everything I wanted to know was in the book. When people see me now, they're amazed by what I've accomplished. But it was simple. Even now I don't think of it as a diet, but as the new, healthier, more satisfying way I eat. Very, very easy."

A Book Designed For You

Many people have asked for more recipes to enhance their new way of eating. Others want to learn more tricks to make foods fast, tasty, and healthy. That's why I felt the need to write this cookbook.

I've made the book user-friendly. It is designed for beginners as well as experienced cooks. It's simple, fun and to the point because I wanted to write the kind of cookbook I like to read and use. It is loaded with easy-to-use information about how to incorporate these ideas and recipes into your diet and lifestyle.

77 "Snacks for the Mind"

I have included 77 "*Eat More, Weigh Less* ™ Tips" to help make your *Eat More, Weigh Less* ™ *Diet* tastier and healthier. I call them "snacks for the mind." You will find that some of the ideas are so simple you can put them into practice right away. Other ideas you may want to try later, but the tips are simple so you can go right to them and know exactly what to do.

Since this book is a companion volume to my original book, *Dr. Shintani's Eat More, Weigh Less* ™ *Diet*, it is intended to be a guide for people who want to learn how to "*Eat More, Weigh Less* ™" for the rest of their lives. It also provides dozens of mouth-watering recipes that will give variety to your daily fare.

Useful Things You Will Learn In This Book

- *77 Eat More, Weigh Less™* Tips that give you specific ideas on how to lose weight while eating <u>more</u>

- How to save up to 32 grams of fat per meal without sacrificing taste

- Nine tasty sauces to make your *Eat More, Weigh Less™* foods even more delicious

- The secret to tasty low-fat gravies and sauces

- A better source of calcium than milk

- Nine tasty toppers for potatoes that are practically fat-free

- Six steps to lower your cholesterol in just 30 days

- How to "Elipidate™" *(remove the fat and cholesterol)* from your diet

77 Eat More, Weigh Less™ Tips

Here is a brief preview of some of the fascinating, easy-to-read tips you'll find in this book. Each one is a snack for the mind.

Eat More, Weigh Less™ Tip
Zing It!

Make It Tasty *(Zing It!)*

WOULD YOU BELIEVE: The best flavor enhancers are fat free and cholesterol free.

SOME FACTS: Tip #1 on the *Eat More, Weigh Less*™ Diet is to make your foods tasty so that you will stick to this way of life. Many people give up on diets because the food is too bland and tasteless. By contrast, here are some of the comments people make about this diet:

- "Absolutely delicious."
- "I didn't know eating healthy could taste so good."
- "If I could have food like this all the time, I could eat this way forever."

The recipes in this book are made to be tailored to your own personal taste. I recommend that you try these recipes and alter them to suit your preferences. There are hundreds of ways to enhance the flavor of food by using herbs, spices, sauces, and condiments without adding fat or cholesterol. This book provides you with dozens of recipes you can use and alter to your taste.

WHAT YOU CAN DO:

- Experiment with the recipes in this book by tailoring them to your tastes, i.e., increasing or decreasing, substituting or adding ingredients.

- Try using herbs and spices to flavor your foods.

- Use nonfat sauces, dressings, and gravies with your foods such as:

  - Nine zesty sauces *(Tip #45)*

  - Three gravy-making secrets *(Tip #47)*

  - Nine potato toppings *(Tip #29)*

  - Non-fat dressings *(Tip #35)*

  - Seven secrets to Asian sauces *(Tip #46)*

- Try this diet strictly for at least three weeks and you'll find that your tastes will become more sensitive, and you'll enjoy the real flavor of food even more!

Eat More, Weigh Less™ Tip
Zapf It!

2

"Elipidate™"* Your Diet *(Zapf It)***

WOULD YOU BELIEVE:

- Each gram of fat has 100% more calories than a gram of carbohydrate or protein.

- Each gram of fat has roughly 800% to 1,500% more calories than a gram of whole starchy food.

- Each fat calorie is 20% more likely to make you fat than is a starch calorie.[14-16] *(See page 21.)*

SOME FACTS: A gram is about the weight of a raisin. One gram of fat contains 9 calories. A gram of simple carbohydrate or protein has about 4 to 4.5 calories. While this makes fats undesirable enough, it is even more important to avoid fat when you realize that a gram of whole starchy

---

* Elipidate™ means to eliminate fats, oils, and cholesterol. *(See page 22).*

** Synonym for "Elipidate™." *(See page 22).*

food such as brown rice contains only 1.1 calories and a gram of potato contains only 0.6 calories. This makes fats somewhere between 8 to 15 times higher in fat *(800% to 1,500%)* when compared to whole starchy foods on a gram for gram basis.

WHAT YOU CAN DO:

- "Elipidate™" your diet *(i.e., cut fats, oils, and cholesterol out of your diet as much as possible).*

- Use nonfat or low-fat flavor enhancers such as herbs and spices, nonfat or low-fat sauces *(i.e., salsas)*, and gravies, as suggested above.

- Don't fry foods.

- Avoid oil-based dressings.

- Avoid butter, margarine, and mayonnaise.

- Try to limit your daily fat intake to approximately 10% of calories* *(22 grams of fat on a 2,000-calorie diet, 33 grams of fat on a 3,000-calorie diet, etc.).*

---

*   Remember that this is not a rigid diet and any substantial more towards a lower fat diet is helpful.

Organization

This book is divided into two parts.

The first part is an overview of the principles of the *Eat More, Weigh Less™ Diet.* Please pay close attention to the Inverted Food Pyramid and the explanation of the concept of the EMI. You should be able to lose weight effectively with this cookbook alone, but if you want to know more about how the diet works, I encourage you to obtain a copy of the original book, *Dr. Shintani's Eat More, Weigh Less™ Diet.* It makes a perfect companion to this cookbook.

The second part of this cookbook contains over 177 new recipes that will help you start and maintain your *Eat More, Weigh Less™ Diet.* It is organized into sections according to the Inverted Food Pyramid on page 27.

In each section, I have included:

1. **Basics** *(information about food)*

2. **Eat More, Weigh Less™ Tips** – these are quick "bites" of information that give you specific highlighted ideas on how to:

   - *Zing It (make it tasty)*

   - *Zip It (make it fast)*

   - *Zapf It ("Zap the fat," i.e., eliminate the fat and oil – also known as "Elipidate™" it, page 22)*

3. **Recipes** *(taste treats you can try)*

The 77 *Eat More, Weigh Less*™ Tips are distributed throughout. You will find them near to the recipes that are being discussed.

I promised this would be simple. So before we go into the recipes, I'd like to familiarize you with the concepts behind all these delicious recipes by offering you a basic summary of the amazing principles behind my *Eat More, Weigh Less*™ *Diet*.

SUMMARY OF THE

EAT MORE, WEIGH LESS™ DIET

The Anti-Diet Diet

The *Eat More, Weigh Less™ Diet* is the quintessential anti-diet diet. It turns a number of major dieting concepts upside down.

First, the *Eat More, Weigh Less™ Diet* tells you how to lose weight by eating MORE. We are now realizing that conventional dieting *(calorie restriction)* doesn't work in the long run. New research actually suggests that long-term weigh loss can be maintained even while eating more food.

This concept is supported by a number of medical and nutritional studies, including population studies that indicate that calories and obesity are not directly related,[3-4] and by intervention studies that demonstrate the effectiveness of high bulk, low-fat diets.[5-13]

Second, the *Eat More, Weigh Less™ Diet* focuses on health first and weight last.

Most weight loss programs focus on losing weight first and pay little attention to your health. By contrast,

I see obesity as an early sign of poor health. My approach to weight loss is to focus on maximizing health through diet and lifestyle. If you do this, the weight comes off automatically without calorie or food quality restriction.

Third, the *Eat More, Weigh Less*™ *Diet* inverts the conventional calorie-gram tables to create the Eat More Index, or EMI *(see below)*, which tells you how to find foods that cause weight loss.

Fourth, the *Eat More, Weigh Less*™ *Diet* inverts the USDA's Food Guide Pyramid and modifies it to make it even healthier than it is.

The result is a new "Inverted Pyramid," designed especially for the *Eat More, Weigh Less*™ *Diet*.

What the Diet **IS NOT**

This is not a "fad diet." Actually, it is **not even a "diet"** in the usual sense because there is **no calorie counting**. There are no powders, pills or magic bullets. You won't depend on portion control, and you won't need to exercise impossible self-discipline or limit the amount of food you eat. There are no gimmicks in the *Eat More, Weigh Less*™ *Diet* program. You're going to get slim and stay slim by using real food. The *Eat More, Weigh Less*™ *Diet* is a brand new, up-to-the-minute, scientifically supported plan that has worked for real people in real life situations. This book will show you how it can work for you.

It is not a rigid diet. Rather, it gives you a set of principles by which you can be creative and still stay as close as possible to the *Eat More, Weigh Less™ Diet.* At the same time, it points you toward an "ideal" diet for most people which is characterized by:

1. Whole food – based on the Eat More Index

2. Low fat – around 10% of calories

3. No cholesterol

4. Balance according to the "Inverted Pyramid"

5. Locally grown food – in harmony with your locale and not transported a great distance so it is as fresh as possible

6. In season – in sync with your climate and season so it is as fresh as possible

7. Emphasis on the whole person, whole community, whole earth approach *(see page 377)*

Techniques and Tools

The *Eat More, Weigh Less™ Diet* is based on five main techniques:

1. How to "*Eat More, Weigh Less™*" by choosing foods that satisfy your hunger while promoting weight loss. This is done by using the unique table called the "Eat More Index," or EMI. *(See Dr. Shintani's Eat More, Weigh Less™ Diet, Appendices A and B, pages 283-291.)*

2. How to avoid foods that can increase body fat using the "Fat Finder Formula."

3. How to lose weight while you sleep.

4. How to balance your diet using my "Inverted Food Pyramid."

5. How to incorporate this diet into your lifestyle.

These five techniques are described in detail in my original *Eat More, Weigh Less™Diet* book. This cookbook expands on Technique #5, "How to incorporate this diet into your lifestyle." It shows you many practical ways to make this work. It also uses the framework of Technique #4, the Inverted Food Pyramid, to present a balanced approach to Eating More in order to Weigh Less.

Three main tools are used with these techniques: the Eat More Index (EMI), the Fat Finder Formula, and the Inverted Food Pyramid. Let's take a closer look at these tools.

Tool #1 — The Eat More Index (EMI): How To Find Foods That Cause Weight Loss

Let me give you an overview of the index I devised to help you examine which foods satisfy you the most per calorie. It is a totally new way of looking at food and is one of the pillars of the Diet. The EMI number generally represents the number of pounds of food it takes to provide 2,500 calories, which is one day's worth of calories for an average active woman or average inactive man.

For example, the EMI value of corn is 6.5, which means that it takes 6.5 pounds of corn to make your daily 2,500 calories.

The Simple Logic of the EMI

Now, here's the simple logic of the EMI, the higher the EMI the better. If average people were to eat just corn for a day *(and I'm not suggesting you do that)*, they would have to eat 6.5 pounds of it to get one day's calorie requirement and maintain their weight *(based on 2,500 calorie requirement — the actual amount varies from person to person)*. Obviously, average individuals will have great difficulty eating this much corn *(30 ears!)* and will likely eat less than this amount and still be full. Thus, while eating as much as they want, they will still lose weight.

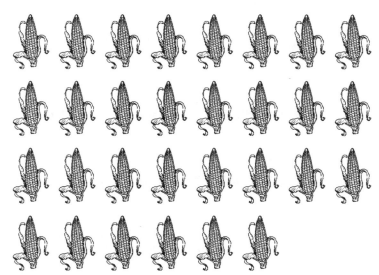

Another example is potatoes. They have an EMI value of 9.6, which means that an average person would have to eat 9.6 pounds to get one day's calories. Again, just about everyone will feel full with less than 9.6 pounds of potatoes *(that's about 24 small potatoes or 12 larger ones)* and thus would lose weight if eating just potatoes. A couple of other examples are broccoli, with an EMI value of 17.1 *(17.1 pounds of broccoli to make one day's calories)*; and apples, with an EMI value of 9.4 *(9.4 pounds of apples to make one day's calories)*, which is equal to about 31 apples! Clearly, the average person is not going to eat enough of any of these individual foods to even maintain their weight. Therefore, any combination of these foods will provide a varied diet that will naturally induce weight loss.

By sharp contrast, foods that are low in EMI can easily produce weight gain. The foods that are lowest in EMI are oils and fats.

Oils and fats have an EMI value of 0.61 *(100% fat)* and can easily be eaten in enough quantity to produce weight gain. Butter and margarine are 0.76, *(99% to 100% fat)* mayonnaise is 0.78 *(98% fat)*. Such very low EMI foods are what I consider "diet destroyers" and should be avoided or minimized.

In other words, the higher the EMI number of a food *(that is, the more pounds of food it takes to provide your daily calories)*, the more likely you are to be satisfied by eating a selected food. Choosing foods in this way emphasizes the positive aspect and encourages people to "eat more" of these foods, which helps promote automatic weight loss. In this way, the EMI allows you to select foods that will help you lose weight while you eat until you're satisfied. For a full description of the EMI, see my earlier book, *Dr. Shintani's Eat More, Weigh Less™ Diet.*

Tool #2 – The Fat Finder Formula

Now that we understand some basics about the EMI, let's talk about a second important tool of the *Eat More, Weigh Less™ Diet*, the Fat Finder Formula. One of the major problems with the American diet is fat. High fat diets are associated with heart disease, cancer, diabetes, and other diseases. And let's face it. Fat makes us fat.

All Calories Are Not The Same

There's more. For years it was believed that all calories were the same. We now know that this is only true in a test tube where the energy of food is measured by burning it to see how much heat is produced. Thus, a calorie is a calorie, and fat calories are the same as starch calories, but ONLY IN A TEST TUBE! For most people, however, what really matters is how much does a calorie count in terms of promoting fat. Recent studies indicate that fat uses only 3% of its energy to be converted to body fat, whereas starch takes 23% of its energy to turn into body fat — which means that fat calories count 20% more than starch calories in making you fat.[14-16]

"Zapf" It!

So Zapf it! In this book, I'm inventing two new words. The first is "Zapf," which I intend to mean "to remove *(Zap)* the fat *(the "f" at the end of the word)*." It is a short synonym for the word "Elipidate™," which is the second new word you need to learn and use for the rest of your life.

"Elipidate™" It!

"Elipidate™" means to <u>eli</u>minate the "<u>lipid</u>s" *(a scientific word for fats and cholesterol)* from the recipe or the diet.

When you put these two words together *("eliminate" and "lipids")*, the resulting word is "Elipidate™." Thus, "Elipidate™" means to remove the fat and cholesterol from a recipe or diet.

So, I recommend that you work towards "elipidating" your diet, and aim toward a diet that contains around 10% fat by calories. This amounts to roughly 22 grams *(from 2,000-calorie diet)* to 33 grams *(for a 3,000-calorie diet)* depending on your size, activity level and metabolism.

Where Is the Fat?

But it's hard to get rid of dietary fat when we don't know where it is. For instance, did you know that:

• The food industry has been misleading us for years?

- 2% milk is actually 35% fat by calories?

- 91% fat-free burgers are actually 49% fat by calories?

- Hot dogs are 83% fat by calories? *(They should be called "Fat dogs.")*

© *Shintani*
HOT DOGS SHOULD BE CALLED "FAT DOGS" – THEY'RE 83% FAT!

- Most salad dressings are 85% to 100% fat!

These few examples make it obvious: Food labels can often be misleading. It's up to you to learn how to identify the fats in your diet. But how can you do this when the nutrition labels on food are so confusing?

Learn the Fat Finder Formula

The Fat Finder Formula offers you a simple way to look right past the apparent nutritional content of any given product and see to the core of things. Said another way, the Fat Finder Formula is a simple calculation that allows you to determine the percentage of fat in your food.

If You Have a Standard Food Label

Most foods now carry the new FDA-required labels, which give you a little more information, but which can still be confusing. The new FDA labels have already done the first step for you by calculating how many calories per serving come from fat. Now all you have to do is divide those calories by the total calorie content per serving, and you will arrive at the proportion of fat.

$$\frac{\textcircled{40} \text{ Calories from Fat}}{\textcircled{140} \text{ Calories, Total}} = .28$$

=   proportion of calories from fat

.28 x 100   =   28% fat by calories

For example, let's calculate the percentage of fat from this label. Calories from fat = 40; calories per serving = 140. Use the formula to divide the 40 by 140, and you get .28 as the proportion of calories from fat, or about 28% fat by calories.

If You Have No Food Label

If you have no food label, then use the Fat Finder Formula. The standard formula is grams of fat per serving, multiplied by 9 *(the number of calories in each gram of fat)*, which gives you calories from fat. Then divide the answer by the total calories per serving.

$$\text{The Fat Finder Formula} = \frac{\text{Grams of Fat x 9}}{\text{Total Calories}} = \text{Proportion of Calories from Fat}$$

Your answer will give you the proportion of fat calories as a decimal figure. Then simply multiply by a hundred to find the percentage.

It's Overall Fat Intake That's Important

Remember that the important thing to look for is the overall fat intake, and that the total fat gram consumption is more than the percent fat of any particular food. For example, a teaspoon of oil is 100% fat; however, when mixed into a dish that makes 12 servings, the oil *(at 4.2 gram/teaspoon)* adds less than one-half gram per serving.

Of course, it's better to use no oil, and if you stick to medium- to high-EMI foods, you don't need to worry much about this. All high-EMI foods and almost all moderate or medium-EMI foods are low in fat; and most are fresh and unprocessed with no additives, and no cluttery labels to confuse you. Buy whole grains in bulk as much as you can, and stick to fresh fruits and vegetables. But when you must buy processed and packaged food, don't forget to take the Fat Finder Formula along so you'll know what you're getting.

Tool #3 — The Inverted Pyramid

A third tool of the *Eat More, Weigh Less™ Diet* is the Inverted Food Pyramid. As I mentioned earlier, I created this pyramid by modifying the USDA pyramid, which I turned upside down. I also rearranged the food groups to make the pyramid a little healthier.

The USDA's Food Guide Pyramid
A Guide to Daily Food Choices

Fats/Oils/Sweets Sparingly

Dairy 2-3 Servings

Meat/Beans 2-3 Servings

Vegetables 3-5 Servings

Fruit 2-4 Servings

Grains 6-11 Servings

USDA 1992

One key reason for the modification was the USDA's emphasis on dairy and meat. In my opinion *(and in the opinion of many other scientists)*, the USDA is much too liberal with dairy and meat groups from the perspective of preventing heart disease, certain cancers, and certain other chronic diseases.

Dr. Shintani's
Inverted Food Pyramid
A Guide to Healthy Food Choices

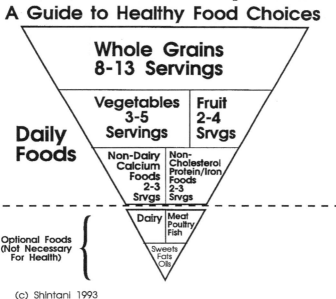

(c) Shintani 1993

By contrast, the Inverted Pyramid, used in conjunction with the Eat More Index™, addresses both health and weight loss, in a simple and practical way.

Understanding the Inverted Food Pyramid

The Inverted Food Pyramid is a diagram which provides a way to help you ensure that the nutrients you obtain from food are adequate. The following table shows how the Inverted Food Pyramid differs from the USDA pyramid. I recommend the modified "Inverted Food Pyramid" for daily use.

Food Groups	USDA Food Guide Pyramid Guidelines (servings)	Inverted Food Pyramid Guidelines (servings)
Grains	6 – 11	8 – 13
Vegetables	3 – 5	3 – 5
Fruit	2 – 4	2 – 4
Non-Dairy Calcium Foods *(replaces dairy)*		2 – 3
Non-Cholesterol Protein/ Iron Foods *(replaces meat)*		2 – 3
Dairy	2 – 3	never or rarely
Meat/Fish/Poultry	2 – 3	never or rarely
Fats/Oils/Sweets	sparingly	never or rarely

What is a "Serving?"

A "serving" an amount of selected food which is an average person might serve at a single sitting. This is actually a somewhat arbitrary definition because how much a person may serve of certain foods varies a great deal. Nonetheless, the term provides a starting point. Here are examples of "servings":

Cereal and Grains Group

1/2 cup of cooked cereal, pasta, or brown rice; 1 slice of bread; or 1 ounce of ready-to-eat cereal

Vegetable Group

1 cup of raw leafy greens; 1/2 cup of cooked, chopped, raw, or other vegetables

Fruit Group

1 medium fruit; 1/2 cup of chopped, cooked, or canned fruit

Dairy Group

1 cup of milk, yogurt, or ice cream; 1-1/2 ounce cheese; or 2 ounces processed cheese

Beans, Fish, Poultry, Meat Group

1/2 cup of cooked beans; 2 to 3 ounces of cooked fish, chicken, or meat; 1 egg.

What's New?

Notice the changes in the pyramid. I have made the fats/oils/sugar section smaller. Then I minimized the dairy and meat foods and moved them downward into the bottom of the Inverted Food Pyramid as optional/occasional foods. In place of the Dairy Group, I created a Non-dairy Calcium Group. In place of the Meat Group, I created a Non-cholesterol Protein/Iron Group.

Vegetarian Diet is Ideal

Notice also that the Inverted Food Pyramid is separated by a dotted line at the apex. The foods below the line are foods not necessary for good health for most people. It is preferable not to use them except in certain circumstances or health conditions. And if you do use them, do so sparingly and with the knowledge that they are not ideal for optimal health. This reflects the fact that animal foods were not eaten on a daily basis among Mediterranean and Asian people, who rarely suffer from the diseases that plague us today, such as heart disease. It is consistent with modern literature, which indicates that a vegetarian diet is typically healthier than a diet with daily animal product consumption.[19] It also reflects my opinion that a vegetarian, whole food, very low-fat diet is generally ideal.

In summary, the body of the pyramid above the dotted line represents foods that promote good health and should be used on a daily basis. The foods below the dotted line are not necessary for good health. Avoid them, as much as possible, if you want to make the *Eat More, Weigh Less™ Diet* work for you.

For those who have health conditions that might affect their digestion, absorption, metabolism or otherwise affect their nutrition, please consult your own physician while making your decision about using or giving up these foods.

DIET FOR
YOUR HEALTH

A Diet For Your Health

There isn't room here to describe all the disease conditions that may be improved with this diet. In my practice I have seen hundreds of people partly or fully recover from diseases they have had for years. In doing so, they have had the added benefit of losing weight.

What is important is that your health comes first. This diet will likely move you towards your optimal health. In doing so, many of your excess pounds will probably disappear. Try it and see.

A Diet to Reverse Heart Disease

THE #1 KILLER of Americans is heart disease. Over 32% of us will die from this disease. The leading cause of heart disease is the American diet with its high fat, *(36% to 42% of calories)* high cholesterol, high animal product content. The *Eat More, Weigh Less™ Diet* is an excellent antidote for heart disease because when done strictly, it is low in fat *(around 10% of calories)*, has no cholesterol *(0 milligrams)*, and has no animal products. There is even evidence that this diet may reverse heart disease and ameliorate its risk factors, such as high cholesterol and high blood pressure.

I have been using this approach to heart disease in my private practice since 1987. In addition, my colleagues and I have demonstrated the dramatic improvement of high cholesterol and blood pressure with a 10% fat diet.[6] A number of my patients no longer need their blood pressure or cholesterol medication. Some have even eliminated their need for bypass surgery. There is even evidence that good diet alone can reverse atherosclerotic placques.[18]

If you already have heart disease or are on medications for any disease, check with your doctor before changing your diet. But take "heart" in the good news that a change in diet will usually help.

A Diet to Lower Cholesterol

For people who specifically have the early signs of risk for heart disease, e.g., high cholesterol, the EMWL Diet is helpful for a number of reasons. My recommendations for lowering cholesterol can be summarized in the following list. The EMWL Diet automatically incorporates steps 1 to 4.

Six steps to lowering cholesterol:

1.   **Avoid Cholesterol Intake.** *(0 mg. is best – all dietary cholesterol contributes to your cholesterol level.)*

2. **Limit Fat Intake** to about 10% of calories. *(10% fat diets have been shown to reverse heart disease and their risk factors.)*

3. **Eat More Whole Foods** *(i.e., whole and medium to high EMI foods. These satisfy your hunger and have a full array of micronutrients and anti-oxidants. They also have more fiber, including soluble fiber that helps lower cholesterol.)*

4. **Avoid** or **Limit Saturated Fat Intake**. *(Saturated fat raises cholesterol.)*

5. **Avoid Smoking**. *(Smoking promotes atherosclerosis, high blood pressure, and raises cholesterol.)*

6. **Exercise Regularly**. *(This helps raise HDL cholesterol, also known as "high density lipoprotein," which is considered to be "good cholesterol.")*

Part Two

Eat More, Weigh Less™ Tips and Recipes

EAT MORE, WEIGH LESS™

THE EASY, TASTY WAY

This section will be fun. Food is not only tasty, it's interesting. And the more you understand what you're doing and why you're doing it, the more effective your *Eat More, Weigh Less™ Diet* will be.

Get Ready —

The recipes in this book are arranged in sections according to the Inverted Food Pyramid, rather than in the conventional manner *(appetizers, soups, salads, entrées, desserts, etc.)*. This will allow you to pick and choose your *Eat More, Weigh Less™* menus to suit your own taste. But more importantly, it will allow you to easily match the recipes to the pyramid's suggested food groups.

You're stepping into a world of delightful, delicious foods that will soon have you trying all the tasty possibilities. And remember, you can eat all you want so long as you follow the principles in the *Eat More, Weigh Less™ Diet*. As a bonus, you're going to learn 77 *Eat More, Weigh Less™* Tips that will make selecting and preparing foods easier than ever before.

Many of the tips you're about to learn are paired with recipes and topics that illustrate how the tips work in practice. Each separate section has a brief introduction that will familiarize you with the type of food: that is, grains, vegetables, fruits and so on. Then you will learn some delicious ways to prepare those foods.

In addition, in all likelihood you'll soon be healthier than you ever thought possible. That's an extra benefit to eating right. You can start spending your time counting those pounds as they melt off instead of wasting time counting calories.

So go ahead, get excited. This program can change your life in ways you won't believe until you see the results.

About Vegetarianism

Every year, one million new people decide to try the vegetarian way of life. I encourage you to try it, too. If you choose to eliminate the bottom tip of the "Inverted Pyramid" from your diet, you will have a strict vegetarian diet also known as a "vegan diet." I believe that a vegan, whole-food diet based on the principles in the *Eat More, Weigh Less™ Diet* is ideal for most people. A strict vegetarian diet has the great benefit of containing no cholesterol which already makes it superior to most diets in at least this one very important aspect. There are also spiritual and environmental reasons to adopt such a diet.

About B$_{12}$

If you decide to try a strict vegetarian diet with no dairy or eggs *(also known as a "vegan diet")* for an extended period of time, be careful about the B$_{12}$ in your diet, particularly if you are pregnant or nursing. Vitamin B$_{12}$ is necessary for the health of the nervous system and the blood system. The daily requirement for B$_{12}$ is extremely small and most of us have about a three-year supply on board so it is not easy to become B$_{12}$ deficient. B$_{12}$ is found in small amounts in some fermented foods such as miso. There is controversy surrounding whether or not this is an adequate amount. A B$_{12}$ supplement of at least 5 micrograms per day is recommended if you are pregnant or nursing or if you are strictly vegetarian for over a year.

Caution With Infants and Small Children

Be especially careful with the diets of infants and small children as their nervous systems are developing and are in special need of B$_{12}$. In addition, THEY DO REQUIRE MORE FAT THAN THE 10% FROM CALORIES. In general, the recommendations in this book should be considered pertinent to adults and older children.

Caution If You Are Ill Or Are On Medications

Do NOT change your diet or exercise level without guidance from your medical doctor if you have health problems or are on medication. Do NOT change your medications without the guidance of your medical doctor. The information in this book is general information about your health and is NOT to be taken as professional advice or to serve as a substitute for medical attention. The advice in this book is directed toward reasonably healthy adults. Individual needs do vary. As I said in the front of this book, for those with special conditions or needs, for children and pregnant women, modifications may be necessary and should be made under guidance of your medical doctor or registered dietitian.

Let's Start Cooking!

It's time to take a look at the recipes, and decide what you'd like to try first. Start with something simple, and something that looks especially good to you. For your convenience, at the end of each recipe, I've noted the calories and fat grams. I've also noted percent of protein, carbohydrates, and fat as a percentage of calories *(rather than as a percentage of weight)*.

You may want to get the companion book to this recipe book and spend some time familiarizing yourself with the EMI, even though the recipes are all spelled out for you. Remember, if the foods are medium to high in EMI, you can eat as much of it as you want, so enjoy yourself and get creative. Once you understand the principles of the *Eat More, Weigh Less™ Diet*, you can even start adapting some of your own favorite recipes.

Eat More, Weigh Less™ Tip
Zapf It!

$$\underset{3}{\nabla}$$

How To Find Foods That Cause Weight Loss

WOULD YOU BELIEVE: There are foods that can actually help you lose weight.

SOME FACTS: Cutting the fat out of your diet is not enough. It is important to replace the calories from fat by eating MORE of the right food rather than less food. Only by filling up your stomach consistently will you be able to satisfy your hunger in the long run. The trick is to find food that fills you up before you have too many total calories or fat calories. The simple way to do this is to use the EMI table. For example, the EMI value of broccoli is 17.1, which means that it takes 17.1 pounds of broccoli to provide 2,500 calories or about one days's worth. You know that you can't eat 17.1 pounds of broccoli daily so you know this is a food that will help cause weight loss. There are thousands of such foods. This is explained briefly in this book on page 20, and in detail in *Dr. Shintani's Eat More, Weigh Less™ Diet* book.

If you don't have a table handy, just remember to eat whole, plant-based foods — not parts of foods or foods from animal sources. If you do this, the foods generally wind up being medium to high on the EMI scale. Remember that it is better to eat whole wheat berries rather than whole wheat flour, and better to eat whole wheat flour than white flour. Remember that it is better to eat the whole apple than applesauce, and better to eat applesauce than apple juice. By doing this, you not only take in foods that help you lose weight, but you also are using foods that are high in micronutrients and fiber that may help you prevent cancer and heart disease.

WHAT YOU CAN DO:

- Eat whole, medium- to high-EMI foods.

- "Elipidate™" your diet. This invariably raises the EMI value of the food you eat so you can *Eat More, Weigh Less™.*

- Learn to use the EMI as a guide to helping you find foods that cause weight loss.

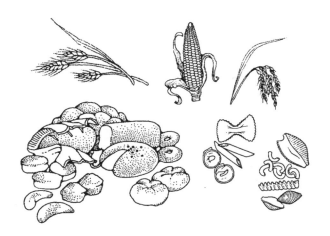

GRAINS AND OTHER
PRINCIPAL FOODS

Basic Grains

Whole grains have been humanity's primary food throughout history. The Inverted Food Pyramid is consistent with this concept. It positions the grain group as the largest part of the diet *(8 to 13 servings per day)* and places it on top of the pyramid. These foods are the heart and soul of the *Eat More, Weigh Less™ Diet*. Because some root vegetables such as potatoes and taro have been the main staples of many populations, these foods are also included in this group.

Whole Grains

In this section, you'll learn simple ways to cook each grain. You'll also learn ways to zing up your whole grain dishes by adding beans, mushrooms, sliced vegetables, and more. There are dozens of new combinations. You'll enjoy that full, satisfied feeling when you've finished each grain-centered meal.

A Delicious Variety of Whole Grains

There are literally hundreds of different grains in the world. The following list will acquaint you with some common and not-so-common varieties. I have selected only those grains which you're likely to find in your supermarket or health food store. With the specific whole grain recipes, you'll learn the basics about each grain and how to prepare it. All grains should be stored in a cool, dry, dark place for maximum shelf life, which can be months.

Whole Grains Are Best

While this group includes a number of grain products, including white and whole grain flour products, whole, unprocessed grains are best. In fact, unprocessed whole grains are the only grains I recommend to be used on an unlimited basis. Whole wheat flour products should be used less frequently, and white flour products should be used rarely, if at all.

A Note About Whole Grain Flour

When whole grains are milled or processed into white flour, valuable nutrients, such as the B vitamins and vitamin E, are lost. In addition, the grains become more compacted and the "fullness" value is diminished. This means they become lower on the EMI.

When whole grains are milled into whole grain flour, not quite so many of the valuable nutrients are lost. However, the EMI value is still diminished.

In other words, stick to whole grains as much as possible. If you need to use flour, try to use only whole grain. Use white processed flours only sparingly, and you'll get the maximum nutritional and EMI value from your whole grains. The following table can help you in making your choices in this food group.

Unlimited Use	Moderate Use	Rare Use
Brown Rice	Whole wheat Bread	White Bread
Corn	Whole Wheat Pasta	White Flour Pasta
Barley	Whole Wheat Pita Bread	White Flour
Millet	Whole Wheat Chapati	Tortillas
Whole Oats	Whole Wheat Bagels	White Flour Bagels
Buckwheat	Whole Wheat Muffins	White Flour Muffins
Wheat Berries	Buckwheat Noodles	White Flour
Potatoes	Instant Oatmeal	Noodles
Taro	White Rice	
Poi	Corn Tortillas	

Cooking Grains Made Easy

Many people don't eat whole grains because they're not sure how to prepare them. As you have just seen, whole grain is best prepared as close to its natural state as possible. The following cooking chart will you get off to a fast, simple start with your new whole grain dishes:

Cooking Chart for Grains

Regular Pot			Pressure Cooker	
1 Cup of Grain	Cups Water	Time	Cups Water	Time
Rolled Oats	2-2.5*	20-25 min.	n/a	n/a
Brown Rice	2	40-55 min.	1.5-1.75	30-40 min.
Buckwheat	2-2.5*	2-2.5 hrs.	n/a	n/a
Pearled Barley	2	25-30 min.	1.25	15 min.
Hulled Barley	2.5-3*	1.5-1.75 hrs.	2.5	20-25 min.
Bulgur Wheat	1.5-2*	20 min.	n/a	n/a
Whole Wheat	2	1.5-2 hrs.	1.5	20-25 min.
Oats, Rye	2	1-2 hrs.	1.5	20-25 min.
Millet	2	25-35 min.	1.5	15 min.

* Lower number will yield a slightly chewier grain.
  Higher number will yield a slightly softer grain.

If you'd like to try some delicious whole grain dishes right away, turn to page 66. There, and in the following recipes, you'll find something just right for your dinner tonight.

Eat More, Weigh Less™ With Whole Grains and Other Principal Foods

Now it's time to look at the delicious whole grain recipes that will make up the bulk of your foods. Remember, you're going to be eating from 8 to 13 servings a day. It's also time to learn some exciting new *Eat More, Weigh Less*™ Tips that will make cooking simple and quick.

Most of us are used to meals that are centered around a meat, poultry, and seafood entrée. The *Eat More, Weigh Less*™ *Diet* centers the diet around the whole grain food group instead. The whole grain dishes you'll find here can make wonderful entrées and will stimulate your creativity with regard to high-EMI menus. You can also plan your meals around an entrée of pasta or another starchy food, such as potatoes, corn, or noodles. These are not only delicious, but they'll also help you lose weight while staying healthy.

Eat More, Weigh Less™ Tip
Zip It!

∇ 4

The Best Grain for Weight Loss

WOULD YOU BELIEVE: It takes 6.5 pounds of corn to give you one day's worth of calories.

SOME FACTS: Corn has long been the staple grain of the Americas. It is also one of the best grains for weight control. The EMI value of corn is 6.5, which means it takes 6.5 pounds of corn kernels to provide 2,500 calories. This is the highest EMI value of all grains. In terms of corn on the cob, this translates to 30 ears of corn per day. You can see why this grain will help you lose weight.

There are a lot of simple ways to dress up corn into delightful dishes that you might not even recognize. Let's start by getting back to the basics. Too often corn on the cob is forgotten as a grain and a main dish. Maybe it just seems too easy. But if you're in the mood for a delicious, easy-to-prepare food, try some plain, steamed corn on the cob. If you want to spice it up a little, sprinkle it with some herb powder, pepper or salt, or umeboshi plum vinegar *(available in health food stores that sell macrobiotic foods)*. You can even use Butter Buds®, if you miss that old buttery taste. If you've been eating your corn on the cob with butter, you're in for a surprise. By getting rid of the taste of the butter, most types of corn are absolutely delicious especially if they're cooked quickly and eaten fresh or flavored with different toppings.

WHAT YOU CAN DO:

- Eat corn on the cob or off the cob, plain or with toppings.

- Try Japanese umeboshi plum vinegar to drizzle on your corn on the cob.

- Use herb, garlic or onion powder, or vegetarian Spike®.

Corn on the Cob

6 ears Fresh corn, husked and cleaned
1 C Water

Place 1-1/2 inches of water in a saucepan, add corn. Bring water to a boil, cover, reduce flame to low. Cook for 3 to 5 minutes, turning ears twice to ensure even cooking. Move corn to a platter and serve. Makes 6 portions. *(1 portion = 83.2 calories, 0.1 grams fat, 11% protein, 80% carbohydrates, 9% fat)*

> ▽ You can eat it plain, or sprinkle with salt, an herb condiment such as Spike®, or other favorite condiments. But stay away from margarine or butter, which are 99% fat. They'll scuttle your diet. ▽

Creamed Corn

6 ears Corn, precooked
2 Tbsp. Water, hot

Cook the corn as above *(corn on cob)*, cool, and scrape kernels off the cob. Place kernels and water in a blender. Blend quickly, to create a creamy texture *(parts of kernels still visible)*. Makes 6 portions. *(1 portion = 83.2 calories, 0.1 grams fat, 11% protein, 80% carbohydrates, 9% fat)*

> ▽ Delicious as a side dish or as a baked potato topper *(see Eat More, Weigh Less™ Tip #29)*. ▽

Corn Polenta

1 C	Cornmeal, coarsely ground
3-4 C	Water
pinch	Sea salt

In a skillet, toast cornmeal over medium heat until it smells nutty and sweet.

Move to small nonstick pot, over low heat. Pour boiling water over toasted cornmeal, stirring to dissolve lumps and eliminate sticking. Pour in a bit more water if needed.

Simmer, covered, for 45 minutes to 1 hour, until the dish has a light and fluffy consistency. Makes 4 portions.

(1 portion = 221 calories, 2.2 grams fat, 9% protein, 9% carbohydrates, 9% fat)

Polenta Mushroom Pilaf

2 C	Corn polenta *(cooked as in previous recipe)*
1 tsp.	Sea salt, or to taste
1 tsp.	Olive oil
3	Shallots or green onions, chopped small
2 cloves	Garlic, minced
1 lb.	Fresh mushrooms, cleaned and sliced *(1/2 lb. button, 1/2 lb. shiitake)*
1	Zucchini, diced

▽ Use button, oyster, shiitake, or whatever other types may be available. You can mix and match these. ▽

Sauté mushrooms and zucchini over medium heat. When they're almost done, add shallots/onions and garlic, using a tiny bit of water to prevent sticking if the oil isn't enough. Continue to sauté until onions are translucent. Salt and pepper to taste.

When sautéed mixture is well done, mix into polenta, saving out one cup. Top polenta with saved cup of mixture, top that with parsley, and serve. Makes 6 portions.
(1 portion = 182.5 calories, 2.6 grams fat, 11% protein, 77% carbohydrates, 12% fat)

Eat More, Weigh Less™ Tip
Zapf It!

▽5▽

Save 70 gm. fat!

Fat-Free Popcorn

WOULD YOU BELIEVE: A medium bucket of buttered theater popcorn can contain as much as 71 grams of fat and 910 calories![17]

SOME FACTS: Most popcorn products are popped in a fair amount of oil, and often butter is added. This turns a healthy, low-fat product into an unhealthy low-EMI item. An average 12-cup tub of popcorn can contain 37 grams of fat and 655 calories. Add a couple of ladles of "butter," and you can easily double the fat and raise the calories by 50%. You can get around this by air-popping your popcorn, and leave off the oil and butter. This will popcorn essentially fat free with only 160 calories per 12 cups.

If you buy microwave popcorn, be careful that you purchase the type that is "oil free." Even some health food stores sell microwaveable popcorn that is supposedly low in fat. If it is not "oil free," it may have a wad of grease or partially hydrogenated oil in the bag to allow it to cook or to have a certain flavor.

The best way to make sure that you have a healthy popcorn is to buy the grain in bulk, perhaps at a health food store. Invest in an air popper, or put the popcorn in a paper bag and microwave it.

There are also prepackaged microwave varieties, usually in health food stores, that specifically say "No Oil Added." But your best bet is organic, air-popped popcorn.

WHAT YOU CAN DO:

The one problem you might have with eliminating the oil is that salt doesn't stick very well to the popcorn without it. A simple solution is to add crumbled, flavored rice cakes or popcorn cakes *(found in health food stores)*, or you can try mixing in handfuls of Japanese "mochi crunch" *(found in health food stores or Oriental food markets)*. This adds a slightly salty flavor without adding fat and adds some character to the popcorn as well.

Rice Dishes

Rice is the main food for more people in the world than any other grain. Brown rice has been the staple of Asia for millennia, and it is increasingly popular in the rest of the world. It is the quintessential whole grain because it is the one common grain that is usually eaten in its whole form. It is a hearty source of satisfying complex carbohydrates with a nice healthy dose of fiber, B-complex, and other nutrients that will make you feel very good.

There are many varieties of brown rice including long grain, short grain, and medium grain. Some examples of other varieties include basmati rice, both brown and white; jasmine rice, arborio, plain brown, Thai black, long-grain wild rice, and the rissotto used in Italian dishes. You'll want to experiment with many simple rice dishes. You can find most types of rice in health food stores or Asian groceries. But be sure you stick with the brown and darker colors. Any form of brown rice is better than refined white rice. The rice is brown because it is the whole, unprocessed grain, which accounts for its rich, nutty color and chewy texture. That means none of the nutrition has been processed out and the grain contains its full compliment of nutrients, such as vitamin B complex, vitamin E, and fiber.

Eat More, Weigh Less™ Tip
Zing It!

$$\boxed{6}$$

The Easiest
Gourmet Rice

WOULD YOU BELIEVE: There is a simple way to make rice taste like a "gourmet" rice. It takes no extra time at all.

SOME FACTS: Basmati brown rice is a rich and aromatic grain from India. It is known as the "King of Rice" and is eaten by India's elite. I strongly urge you to try this grain. While there are hundreds of different types of rice in the world, this is my personal favorite. Even people who have never tried brown rice generally like this particular variety. You can find it in most health food stores. All you have to do is prepare it as you would prepare any other brown rice.

WHAT YOU CAN DO: Here are two delicious basmati rice recipes: one is a basic, the other is a gourmet dish that is still easy to prepare.

Basmati Brown Rice

2 C	**Basmati** *(or other brown Rice)*
3-1/2-4 C	**Water**
2 pinches	**Sea salt**

Gently wash rice until water rinses clear. If possible, soak for 2 to 6 hours.

Place in 2-quart pot *(stainless steel is best)*. Cover rice with water and add sea salt. Cover, bring to a boil, reduce flame then simmer for 45 minutes to one hour. *(Do not uncover rice while cooking.)* When done, remove from flame and let sit for 10 more minutes before serving. Makes 6 cup portions. *(1 portion = 216 calories, 1.8 grams fat, 9% protein, 83% carbohydrates, 7% fat)*

▽ You may also prepare basmati in a rice cooker or pressure cooker. See *Eat More, Weigh Less™ Tip #7 and Tip # 8.* ▽

Thai Rice

2 C	**Brown basmati rice**
1 stalk	**Lemon grass** *(optional, available at your Asian grocery or health food store)*
1/4 C	**Sweet yellow onion, chopped medium fine**
1/4 C	**Golden raisins** *(optional)*
3 Tbsp.	**Brewed jasmine tea** *(prepared from tea bag)*
2 Tbsp.	**Lime zest** *(finely grated lime peel)*
2 Tbsp.	**Fresh lime juice**

(continued next page)

Thai Rice (continued)

several	**Sprigs of fresh mint**
several	**Sprigs of fresh parsley**
	Lime wedges, to garnish

Cook rice, steaming if possible until fluffy and soft. *(See recipe previous page.)*

Chop onion into medium fine pieces.

Prepare lime zest, juice, and lime quarters.

Finely chop lemon grass, mint, and parsley.

Lightly sauté onions, lemon grass, and lime zest together over high heat, in jasmine tea. This is the same process as sautéing in water.

▽   Remember: To water sauté, you simply place several tablespoons of water in a heated skillet in place of oil, and watch a bit more closely so the food doesn't stick. ▽

Add precooked rice to skillet and mix well, just until heated through and steaming. Be careful not to cook it too long. Turn off heat and quickly fold in chopped mint, parsley and golden raisins, mixing well. Place in serving dish and garnish with lime wedges, mint, and parsley sprigs. Serve hot. Makes 5 portions. *(1 portion = 307.3 calories, 2.6 grams fat, 8% protein, 85% carbohydrates, 7% fat)*

▽   Excellent served with another Thai treat, minted summer rolls *(see page 280).* ▽

Eat More, Weigh Less™ Tip
Zip It!

∇ 7

A Simple Way to Cook 25% Faster

WOULD YOU BELIEVE: There is a simple way to cut 25% off the time it takes to cook grains.

SOME FACTS: Pressure cooking is about 20% to 25% faster than other types of cooking. It is also one of the best ways to cook grains, beans and vegetables, but it has become a forgotten art. The reason pressure cooking is so good is that it cuts down the time required for cooking and it seals the flavors and nutrients in because the pot itself has a pressure seal which allows the pressure to build up in the pot.

Pressure cooking seems to make all foods taste a little better. The newer pressure cookers are much safer because they have pressure safety locks.

WHAT YOU CAN DO: Try the pressure cooked brown rice recipe and see how it tastes.

Pressure Cooked Brown Rice

Ratio:

1-1/3-1-3/4 C	**Water per**
1 C	**Brown rice**
pinch	**Sea salt**

Rinse rice. Soak 2 to 6 hours, if you have time. Rice will take a little longer to cook if not presoaked.

Place rice and water into a pressure cooker *(stainless steel if possible)*. Add salt, cover with lid as directed by manufacturer of pressure cooker.

Bring to pressure on high heat then lower to low heat and cook for 30 to 40 minutes. Let pressure come down, then let stand for 5 to 10 minutes, stir and serve. Makes 2 portions. *(1 portion = 216 calories, 1.8 grams fat, 9% protein, 83% carbohydrates, 7% fat)*

Eat More, Weigh Less™ Tip
Zip It!

$\nabla 8$

The Lazy Way to Cook Rice

WOULD YOU BELIEVE: There is a way to make rice without having to watch the pot.

SOME FACTS: Automatic rice cookers are convenient for people who frequently cook rice and other grains, because they are designed to cook rice without having to watch the pot. Ordinarily, cooking rice requires that you bring the rice to a boil then simmer it at a low temperature, and watch it carefully so that it does not cook longer than it should.

Automatic rice cookers turn themselves off when the rice is done. You just put in rice and water, turn it on, and it cooks the rice perfectly every time, provided the proper amount of water is added. The cooker can also be used as an automatic steamer. The directions will come with the appliance, and it's always easy to use.

Rice-Cooker Rice

Ratio:

2 C	Water
1 C	Brown rice
pinch	Sea salt

Wash and rinse rice, add the water and turn on the cooker. Adjust the water to your liking. *(See appliance instructions for cooking times.)* Makes 2 portions. *(1 portion = 216 calories, 1.8 grams fat, 9% protein, 83% carbohydrates, 7% fat)*

▽ Steamed vegetables may be cooked in much the same way as rice. ▽

Eat More, Weigh Less™ Tip

Zing It!   ▽9▽   *Zip It!*

A No-Effort Way to Make Whole Grain Interesting

WOULD YOU BELIEVE: There's a simple way to make whole grains more interesting with no additional effort.

THE TRICK IS: Simply add different grains to your rice or other whole grains. For starters, just try wheat berries or wild rice, and toss a handful into your brown rice before cooking. Any of the following grains could be added to rice to make a wonderful whole grain dish.

Try the following: wheat berries, wild rice, rye, bulgur wheat, millet, quinoa, and amaranth.

To really dress up your cooking, add your own favorite vegetables and try some of the sauces and gravies beginning on page 240. Or try the following recipe for a simple way to cook another wonderful dish.

Wheat Berry Rice

2 C	**Long grain brown rice**
4 C	**Water** *(or 3-1/3 if using pressure cooker)*
1/4 C	**Wheat berries**
2 pinches	**Sea salt**

Rinse rice in water and drain. Place in a pot. Add water, sea salt, and wheat berries. Bring to a boil on high heat and then simmer on low heat for 45 minutes *(or 35 minutes in a pressure cooker)*. Makes 6 portions. *(1 portion = 225.5 calories, 1.8 grams fat, 10% protein, 83% carbohydrates, 7% fat)*

Variation: Try wild rice or quinoa instead of wheat berries.

Eat More, Weigh Less™ Tip
Zing It! $\boxed{10}$

Pleasing Pilafs

A pilaf was initially a Persian dish made of rice and raisins, with meats or fowl and a variety of light sauces. Today, pilafs have been adapted to showcase every great cuisine in the world. Some examples are Spanish Rice Pilaf, Indian Saffron Rice Pilaf, and American Lentil Rice. Making rice pilaf is one of the fastest, most delicious ways to become a "gourmet" cook. You can accomplish this by simply adding various chopped vegetables, and/or prepackaged spice and condiment seasonings to the rice. This will make it more festive and interesting.

WHAT YOU CAN DO:

- Here are some delicious pilaf recipes. Once you get the hang of it, you'll soon be designing your own.

- If you're in a hurry, try prepackaged pilaf mixes *(leave out butter and oil)* for convenience.

Stovetop Rice Pilaf

1/8 C	Mild yellow onion, finely chopped
1/8 C	Green onion or shallot, finely chopped
1/8 C	Celery, chopped *(about 1/4" pieces)*
1/2 C	Carrots, julienned
1/2 C	Vegetable broth
1 C	Brown rice, presteamed till fluffy *(see Tip #6)*
1/2 C	Wheat berries, presteamed with rice
1/8 tsp.	Black pepper, ground

In a large, non-stick skillet, sauté onion in 2 tablespoons of vegetable broth until tender.

Add remaining vegetable broth, heat, then add other ingredients *(except celery)* and sauté, stirring constantly, until carrots are hot through and slightly tender *(about 5 minutes)*. Add celery to skillet at the very end, leaving a lot of crunch to the celery.

Add precooked rice and wheat berries to the skillet mixture, mix well while cooking a few more minutes, to blend the flavors. Fluff and serve. Makes 5 portions. *(1 portion = 76.3 calories, 0.5 grams fat, 12% protein, 83% carbohydrates, 5% fat)*

▽ Wheat berries take longer to cook than does the rice, so should come out softened but still crunchy.

Pilafs and stir-frys are best when they offer a variety of textures. ▽

Baked Wild Rice Pilaf

3 C	Vegetable broth or konbu broth
1 med.	Mild yellow onion, diced *(about 1/4 to 1/3 cup)*
3 cloves	Garlic, minced
1 stalk	Celery, diced *(about 1/2 cup)*
1-1/2 C	Fresh mushrooms, thinly sliced
1 C	Wild rice
1-1/2 tsp.	Tamari
1/2 tsp.	Sesame seeds, toasted
pinch	Sea salt

▽ To make konbu broth, soak one 3" x 3" piece of konbu in mineral water for 1 hour. ▽

In a nonstick skillet, sauté onions, garlic, celery, and mushrooms in a little vegetable broth until onions are translucent.

Add water only if this mixture begins to stick to pan, though it shouldn't if you stir constantly and turn to medium heat.

In a saucepan, bring konbu stock to a boil. Pour into skillet with other ingredients, mix well, then place all in a casserole or baking dish.

Cover and bake at 350° F. for 1-1/2 hours. Remove cover and bake another 15 to 20 minutes to remove any excess liquid. Makes 3 portions. *(1 portion = 264.9 calories, 1.3 grams fat, 20% protein, 76% carbohydrates, 4% fat)*

▽ Serve with a leafy green salad, for a well-rounded meal. ▽

Stovetop Spanish Rice

1 can	Whole tomatoes, stewed *(15 oz.)*
1/2 C	Green pepper, diced
1 C	Water
3/4 C	Vegetable broth
3/4 C	Brown rice, uncooked
1/2 tsp.	Sea salt
2 tsp.	Chili powder *(or to taste)*

Combine tomatoes, pepper, water, salt, and chili powder in medium saucepan. Boil over medium heat. Add rice.

Reduce heat to low, cover, and simmer until most of the liquid has been absorbed, about 45 minutes.

Fluff rice, replace cover, and let stand 5 minutes before serving. Makes 4 portions. *(1 portion = 174.1 calories, 1.5 grams fat, 11% protein, 82% carbohydrates, 7% fat)*

▽ You may also garnish this dish with finely diced uncooked tomatoes and green pepper, for extra texture and fresh taste. To be really creative, add a tiny bit of chopped fresh cilantro to the top of your served mounds of rice. Ole! ▽

Quinoa Pilaf

1/2 C	Mushrooms, sliced
1/2 C	Onion, finely chopped
2 C	Vegetable broth
1 C	Quinoa, toasted *(see below)*
1/2 C	Celery, chopped *(about 1/2" segments)*
1/2 C	Carrot, shredded
1/3 C	Green bell pepper, finely chopped
1/3 C	Red bell pepper, finely chopped
1/3 C	Yellow bell pepper, finely chopped
dash	Sea salt, to taste

Toasted Quinoa: Rinse thoroughly under cool running water. Place in a 10" to 12" skillet over medium heat; cook, shaking pan occasionally, until quinoa dries and turns golden brown, about 15 minutes. Pour toasted quinoa from pan and let cool. Makes 1 cup.

Water-sauté onions and mushrooms in a large *(10" to 12")* skillet over medium heat, until onions are caramelized and mushrooms are golden brown.

> ▽ To water sauté, simply put a few tablespoons of water in a skillet, let it heat, then add onions and mushrooms. Stir often. If it begins to stick, add a bit more water. ▽

Add broth, quinoa, and all vegetables, bring to a boil, lower heat, cover then simmer until liquid is absorbed, about 15 minutes, stirring often. Makes 6 portions. *(1 portion = 133.6 calories, 1.8 grams fat, 17% protein, 72% carbohydrates, 12% fat)*

Eat More, Weigh Less™ Tip
Zing It!   \11/

Try One-Dish Meals

One of the best ways to make a brown rice dish more interesting is to simply add some fast-cooking beans. This is a delicious strategy for creating "one-dish meals." For example, you can add lentils to brown rice and stir in a little spice, perhaps some chopped onions, and you will have a delicious lentil-rice as a main complex carbohydrate for your meal. Or you can be a bit more extravagant and try the pilaf dish on the next page. In Japan, it is common to use azuki beans with rice. These have an interesting reddish tint when cooked with brown rice. The forthcoming azuki rice or "sekihan" recipe is delicious. You can also try azuki beans instead of lentils in the following dish, for a totally unique yet delicious flavor.

What You Can Do:

- Add beans and your favorite vegetables, herbs, and spices to your rice.

- Try the following recipes.

American Lentil Rice Pilaf

2 C	Brown rice, cooked
1 C	Lentils, cooked *(see bean cooking chart, page 318)*
2-1/2 C	Water
1 C	Tomatoes, ripe, chopped into small cubes
1 large	Onion, sliced
2 stalks	Celery, diced
2 C	Carrots, julienned
1/2 C	Parsley, chopped
1/4 C	Onion, chopped
1/4 tsp.	Sea salt

Sauté vegetables in tiny amount of oil for about 5 minutes.

Mix heated, cooked lentils and rice together. Stir into sautéed vegetables. Garnish with sliced tomato and parsley. Serve hot, with a wave of the flag! Makes 6 portions. *(1 portion = 166.3 calories, 1.1 grams fat, 15% protein, 79% carbohydrates, 6% fat)*

Mung Bean Surprise

1-1/2 C	Basmati or long grain brown rice
1/4 C	Whole mung beans, shelled and split
1 med.	Onion, chopped
1 C	Corn
1-1/2 C	Peas and carrots, frozen
2 tsp.	Cumin
1 tsp.	Ground cardamom
1 tsp.	Sea salt
2-1/2 C	Water
	Canola oil cooking spray

You'll be surprised by how well all the flavors blend together in this special dish. Wash basmati rice and soak in cold water for 20 minutes. *(Enriched long grain rice should not be washed.)* Drain rice.

Wash split mung beans, dry, and roast in a skillet until crisp. Spray nonstick skillet with cooking spray, add onions, cumin, and sauté on moderate heat for a few seconds.

Add spices, vegetables, and salt. Stir in rice and mung beans. Add water, bring to a boil, reduce to low heat and cook about 45 minutes. For crisper vegetables, drop them into the pan after the rest has cooked for about 30 minutes, cook the dish for 15 minutes more. Let entire dish steam for 10 minutes before serving. Makes 5 portions. *(1 portion = 270.4 calories, 3.790 grams fat, 10% protein, 81% carbohydrates, 9% fat)*

(Sekihan) Azuki Rice

1/2 C	**Azuki beans**
1-3/4 C	**Liquid** *(azuki stock plus water)*
1-1/2 C	**Brown or whole grain mochi** *(sticky)* **rice**
1/2 C	**Brown rice**

Soak all rice in cold water for 15 minutes, to soften.

Rinse beans, cover with water, place in saucepan over high heat. Let beans come to a rapid boil, lower heat, and cook for 45 minutes. The cooked beans should be whole. Drain and save liquid. Put beans in a bowl to cool.

Wash rice and drain well. Measure liquid from cooked beans, add water to equal 1-3/4 cups of liquid. Mix rice and azuki with liquid and cook in rice cooker or in a pot. When done, turn off and let stand for 10 minutes.

Serve rice plain or garnish to taste. Makes 6 portions. *(1 portion = 277.3 calories, 0.7 grams fat, 11% protein, 8% carbohydrates, 2% fat)*

> ▽ For an excellent garnish, try a mixture of salt and toasted black and white sesame seeds. To make this, mix 2 teaspoons salt with 1 tablespoon of black and white toasted sesame seeds. Serve in a small dish. A tiny spoon should be used to ladle out the salt. ▽

Other Whole Grain Recipes

On this and the following pages, you will find more whole grain recipes that will make wonderful entrées, or meals in their own right. I strongly urge you to try each and every one, to see how tasty your *Eat More, Weigh Less™ Diet* can be.

Quinoa

2 C	Water or vegetable broth
1 C	Quinoa, rinsed
1/4 tsp.	Salt, or to taste

Boil broth in a 3- to 4-quart pan; add quinoa, salt to taste. Cover and simmer gently on low heat until liquid is absorbed and grain is tender. Cool, then serve. Makes 6 portions. *(1 portion = 117.4 calories, 1.7 grams fat, 17% protein, 71% carbohydrates, 13% fat)*

▽ Use as side dish, or as base for your own special pilafs. ▽

"Fried" Rice Roll-ups

1	Mild yellow onion, finely chopped
2	Carrots, finely julienned
2 bunches	Broccoli florets, chopped *(3-4 cups)*
1 bunch	Chinese cabbage *(bok choy)*, chopped in 1/2" pieces
1 block	Firm tofu, drained and cut in 1/2" pieces
6 C	Brown rice, steamed
2 Tbsp.	Low-sodium soy sauce
1 Tbsp.	Tamari
2 cloves	Garlic, sliced thin
1/2 tsp.	Sesame oil
1/4 C	Green onions, chopped fine, with tops
1/4 C	Cilantro, chopped
	Lettuce leaves
	Canola oil cooking spray

Heat pan, spray, add sesame oil for flavor only. Add garlic and round onions, sauté till translucent.

Add carrots, broccoli and Chinese cabbage, sauté on high till tender. Add rice and mix with vegetables. Add soy sauce, tamari, green onions and mix into rice.

Cook on low for 5 to 10 minutes, stirring occasionally. Add tofu to rice and mix. Cook on low heat for another 5 minutes. Clean and lay out lettuce leaves. Place 2 heaping tablespoons of mixture inside each lettuce leaf, or more to taste. Roll up like a burrito. Hold with toothpick if necessary. Serve as side dish, appetizer, or a special snack. Makes 48 portions. *(1 portion = 40.9 calories, 0.5 grams fat, 18% protein, 71% carbohydrates, 11% fat)*

Brown Rice Sushi

Wrapping:

8 sheets	Nori
3 C	Brown sushi rice, cooked *(see below)*
1/4 C	Rice vinegar, or to taste
2 Tbsp.	Mirin

Fillings: *(your choice, mix and match)*

Brown miso
Cucumbers, thinly sliced
Fresh daikon or Japanese turnip, sliced thin
Avocado, sliced
Carrots, sliced

1/4 C	Black sesame seeds, roasted
1/2 C	Turtle *(black)* beans, cooked and mashed
1/4 C	Radish sprouts
1 Tbsp.	Umeboshi plum paste

First cook rice until tender and fluffy, yet slightly glutinous so it will stick together.

▽ Cooking time will depend on the cooking method, though steaming is especially good for this dish and will take about 30 minutes. ▽

When rice is done but still hot, place in bowl and add rice vinegar and mirin, mixing thoroughly and fanning until room temperature.

(continued next page)

Brown Rice Sushi (continued)

Use sushi maker if you have one; directions will be included. If not, use a bamboo sushi roller, or a simple cloth tea towel. Put the bamboo roller or towel on a cutting board. On it, place a sheet of nori, shiny side down. Start with about 1/4 cup of brown rice for each nori sheet. Layer across the full sheet. Then, in center, spread 1 teaspoon miso or umeboshi, for your base.

▽ Some people also use hot green mustard, but be careful if you're not familiar with this dish. ▽

Add other ingredients to the center of the rice-topped sheet, to your own taste. In sushi bars, a variety of sushi is served. Try one sheet of plum/cucumber, one of miso/radish sprouts/green onions, one with sliced carrots/sesame seeds, and so on. Be creative.

An especially good sushi can be made by placing 1 to 2 tablespoons of mashed turtle black beans over miso. Then sprinkle sesame seeds and green onions over beans.

After you have designed your sushi, roll it up something like a very tight burrito, using a bamboo sushi-roller or towel. Cut into serving pieces. Makes 16 portions. *(1 portion = 71.7 calories, 1.9 grams fat, 12% protein, 64% carbohydrates, 23% fat)*

Moroccan Bulgur

1/2 C	Dry beans, cooked *(about 1 cup)*
1-1/4 C	Raw bulgur
1 #2 can	Tomatoes
1 clove	Garlic, minced
1/2 C	Green onions, chopped
1/4 C	Green pepper, diced
1 tsp.	Paprika
1 tsp.	Salt
1/8 tsp.	Ground pepper
dash	Cayenne pepper
2 Tbsp.	Vegetarian broth
	Olive oil cooking spray

Precook beans.

Spray skillet with olive oil cooking spray. Sauté garlic and onion in vegetarian broth or water, then add bulgur and toast lightly *(respraying pan, in necessary)*. Add paprika, salt, pepper, and cayenne. Add canned tomatoes, beans, and pepper.

Cover, bring to boil, reduce heat, then simmer 15 minutes or until liquid is absorbed and bulgur is tender *(adding more liquid if necessary)*. Makes 5 portions.
(1 portion = 198 calories, 1.7 grams fat, 16% protein, 76% carbohydrates, 8% fat)

Breakfast Tips (With Recipes)

Morning Energy

Breakfast should be something to look forward to. There are many simple ways you can enhance your morning meal. Delicious Breakfast Tips follow, along with simple, tasty breakfast recipes.

Stick with fresh foods whenever possible. Try to find products that are in season and grown in your locality. This will help ensure freshness. Sometimes it isn't possible to have a perfect diet, especially in the morning. In this case, do the very best you can. For instance, it is better to eat oats cooked from scratch rather than instant oats. It is better to eat brown rice than crispy rice cereal. But if you don't have the time, it is far better to eat instant or dry cereal than to eat bacon and eggs from a fast food restaurant. There is evidence that eating such a high fat breakfast *(usually over 50% fat)* is likely to sludge the capillaries in your brain and cause you to be less than optimal in your performance in whatever you do for most of the day. In addition, eating breakfast makes it less likely that you'll overeat later in the day.

Breakfast can set the tone for the entire day to follow. So treat yourself good at breakfast time. Integrate the following ideas into your morning schedule and your life and start enjoying the morning again.

Breakfast Grains

Grains are a great way to *Eat More* and *Weigh Less*. And they are especially good in the morning. Grains are our key source of complex carbohydrates and fiber. Whole complex carbohydrates give us steady, long-term energy and help keep our bodies running efficiently. When you skip breakfast, you're taking off without refueling. When you treat yourself to a whole grain dish for breakfast, you're giving your body the best fuel it can get, to start the day right. Oatmeal is an especially good way to start the day, but try to eat the oat groats *(the whole oats)*, rather than heavily processed and instant cereals. These do take a while to cook, but you can prepare them ahead of time and reheat them in the morning. Buckwheat is another delicious morning treat. The processed form of this grain is known as kasha. Try the following hot cereal for a rich morning treat. You can dress it up with chopped apples or sliced bananas, use soy milk or nut milk.

Hot Cereal

1 C	Buckwheat, whole oats, or cornmeal
1 tsp.	Vanilla
1 tsp.	Salt
4 C	Water

Bring water to a boil, add grains, whisk until grains are tender but still well defined, about 10 to 15 minutes at medium flame. Drain, scoop into bowls, serve as cereal.

The amount of water you use will determine the texture of the cereal. For a thicker cereal use less water; for a thinner consistency use more water, to taste. Makes 4 portions. *(1 portion buckwheat = 149.4 calories, 1.4 grams fat, 14% protein, 78% carbohydrates, 8% fat) (1 portion oats = 155.4 calories, 2.7 grams fat, 17% protein, 68% carbohydrates, 16% fat) (1 portion cornmeal = 114.2 calories, 1.1 grams fat, 9% protein, 83% carbohydrates, 9% fat)*

Eat More, Weigh Less™ Tip
Zing It!

$\boxed{12}$

Good Breakfast Taste Without Milk, Butter, or Sugar

You've seen that starting your day with oatmeal or another whole grain cereal is an excellent way to Eat More and Weigh Less. Unfortunately, many people are used to adding milk and/or sugar to their cereal grains. I do not recommend either milk or sugar for reasons that I have explained in the *Eat More, Weigh Less™ Diet* book. You don't need sugar and dairy anyway. Whole grains can be tasty without them. Simply dry-roast the grains in a hot skillet before cooking in water. This "dextrinizes" the grain and give a rich aromatic flavor that will enhance your enjoyment. Little tips like this and the other simple ones that follow can make any simple breakfast food a delight.

WHAT YOU CAN DO: Try dry roasting your grain before you cook it. This will add a rich, nutty flavor to it.

Toasty Cooked Cereal

1 C   **Dry oatmeal, bulgur wheat or other whole grain breakfast cereal**

Dry-roast grains by putting them in a nonstick skillet. Roast over a low flame or heat, shaking and tossing a little until it browns lightly and emits a nutty aroma.

Next simply cook the whole grains with water, as described in the whole grains cooking chart on page 46. Makes 4 portions. *(1 portion oatmeal = 145.0 calories, 2.4 grams fat, 16% protein, 69% carbohydrates, 15% fat) (1 portion bulgur = 152.0 calories, 0.4 grams fat, 14% protein, 84% carbohydrates, 2% fat)*

Eat More, Weigh Less™ Tip
Zip It!/Zapf It!   ⟨13⟩   *Save 18 gm. fat!*

Quick Breakfast

WOULD YOU BELIEVE: Granola cereal can be up to 34% fat or 19 grams of fat per cup.

SOME FACTS: Most of us grew up eating dry cereals for breakfast because they're quick and tasty. Unfortunately, many of these dry cereals are over-processed, extremely high in sugar, and sometimes high in fat.

Today, we are blessed with an entire range of healthy, whole-grain, dry cereals, from corn flakes to toasted oats to shredded wheat. As consumers become more health conscious, these products become more available. But when you're selecting your dry cereals, make sure you read the labels and use the "Fat Finder Formula" *(page 26)* or select cereals with less than 1 gram of fat. As with so many other products, the big words blazed across the labels may well be misleading. Be especially careful of those granolas, which may be up to 34% fat, or 19 grams per cup.

With that warning in mind, enjoy the new range of cereals you'll find on your supermarket and health food store shelves. They'll make a nice break on a morning when you're in a hurry.

Just don't use them all the time, at the expense of cooking your own whole grains. Anything you cook from scratch will be far, far better for you than something processed, and unprocessed grains are also higher on the EMI. Also, be careful what you put on the cereal. A cup of whole milk has over 8 grams of fat in it.

Here are some reasonably good choices:

Nabisco®:   Shredded Wheat®

Post®:   Grape Nuts®

Kelloggs®:   Nutrigrain®

Health Valley®:   Raisin Bran®
                     Oat Bran Flakes
                     Low-Fat Granola

Arrowhead   Corn Flakes
Mills®:   Bran Flakes
                     Wheat Flakes

Eat More, Weigh Less™ Tip
Zapf It!   14   *Save 8 gm. fat!*

Try Milk Substitutes

WOULD YOU BELIEVE:

- Whole dairy milk is 55% fat, with 150 calories *(8.1 grams of fat)* per cup.

- Even "2%" milk is 35% fat *(by calories)*, and has 4.6 grams of fat per cup.

- Skim milk is 0% fat and has essentially 0 cholesterol. Unfortunately, it still has 100% of its protein and all dairy protein has the potential to cause allergies and other health problems *(see "Concerns About Dairy," page 265).*

SOME FACTS: In general, I don't recommend any calorie-containing beverages, including dairy. If you want to put milk on your breakfast cereal, consider some substitutes, such as soy or rice milk.

The primary advantage of milk substitutes is that they have no cholesterol or dairy protein. They also contain far less saturated fat than dairy milk. Still, the higher fat versions of the soy, rice and nut milks can contain up to 4.5 grams per cup. This is about half as much as whole dairy milk, but similar to 2% milk *(4.1 grams)*. This varies greatly, depending upon the type of milk and whether or not it is a low-fat product. So read labels when you select milk substitutes and try to choose nonfat variations of soy or rice milk.

Also, be aware that milk substitutes like dairy milk have some sugar in them. And unlike dairy milk, these substitutes don't have the high calcium content of dairy milk, so remember to use non-dairy sources of calcium instead.

WHAT YOU CAN DO: Try nonfat rice milk or soy milk *(found at health food stores)* on your cereal instead of milk.

Eat More, Weigh Less™ Tip
Zapf It! 15 *Save 8 gm. fat!*

Fruit Juice On Cereal?

WOULD YOU BELIEVE: When you add a cup of whole milk to cereal, you add more fat and cholesterol than there is in 2-1/2 strips of bacon.

SOME FACTS: Another nonfat milk substitute to put on cereal is fruit juice. Simply pour it over your cereal and eat to your heart's delight. I know it may sound a little strange, but you're in for a nice surprise. For some  people, apple juice and cereal tastes just like apple pie. Apple juice has practically no fat at all. You'll save about 8.1 grams of fat every time you substitute a cup of apple juice for a cup of whole milk, and about 4 grams of fat when you substitute it for 2% cow's milk or low-fat soy milk. For some perspective, realize that a strip of crispy bacon is a little over 3 grams of fat. So try juice on your cereal for a change.

Other Breakfast Tips

If you start your day by eating right, chances are good that you'll continue eating right all day long. Except for meats and egg yolks, most breakfast favorites can be made higher on the EMI with just a little adaptation. For example, you can use fruit preserves instead of butter for your toast. You can also use it on pancakes or waffles without oil. You'll learn how as you begin to understand the underlying principles of the *Eat More, Weigh Less™ Diet*. For an example of how this works, see the following pancake and waffle recipes. The adaptations not only make them medium to high on the EMI, but many people say they actually improve the taste.

Blackstrap molasses can be another addition to your breakfast menu. Molasses is tasty, it satisfies your sweet tooth, and it's high in calcium *(see Eat More, Weigh Less™ Tip #54)*. Try putting molasses, honey, or maple syrup on the following whole grain pancakes for a hearty, country-style breakfast.

Pancakes and Waffles

Apple Raisin Pancakes

1-1/2 C	Whole wheat pastry flour
3/4 C	Bran
1/2 tsp.	Cinnamon
pinch	Nutmeg
3 Tbsp.	Applesauce
1 pkg.	Active dry yeast
3/4 C	Water, warm
2 tsp.	Egg replacer mixed with 4 Tbsp. water
1-1/2 C	Apple juice
2	Apples, peeled and grated
1/4 C	Raisins

Add yeast to warm water, stir until completely dissolved, and let stand while you prepare the other mixture.

Mix flour, bran, cinnamon, and nutmeg. Whisk applesauce, apple juice, grated apple, and yeast water into the flour mixture, stir well.

Mix the egg replacer with water, beat until frothy. Add to batter with raisins. Cover batter and let rest for 15 minutes while you heat a nonstick griddle.

Cook about 10 minutes on first side, about 5 to 8 minutes on other side. Smooth out the cakes on the griddle, make sure you don't turn them over until bubbles form on top. These thicker pancakes take a bit longer to cook, but the extra taste is well worth the extra bit of time you'll spend. Makes 4 portions. *(1 portion = 269.6 calories, 1.8 grams fat, 11% protein, 84% carbohydrates, 5% fat)*

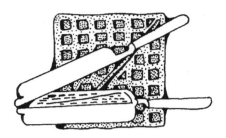

Waffles

3 C	Water
2 C	Rolled oats
1 C	Barley flour
1/2 C	Whole wheat pastry flour
2 tsp.	Double-acting baking powder
1 tsp.	Vanilla
2 Tbsp.	Egg replacer
1 Tbsp.	Blackstrap molasses or malt syrup

Combine ingredients and blend until smooth. Pre-heat waffle iron while batter rests *(15 minutes).* Ladle onto preheated iron and bake. *(1 cup of batter for a large 4-section hearty and filling waffle.)* Makes 4 portions. *(1 portion = 328.1 calories, 3.4 grams fat, 14% protein, 76% carbohydrates, 9% fat)*

Serve waffles with the following toppings: fruit puree, bean soups, gravy, vegetable sauce, or a little pure maple syrup.

▽ Lightly oil *(even nonstick)* waffle iron before heating, to prevent sticking. To keep warm before serving, place cooked waffles in a warm oven on the bare oven rack. ▽

Eat More, Weigh Less™ Tip

Zapf it!   16   *Save 430 mg.*
                                                   Cholesterol!

Cholesterol-Free Scramble

WOULD YOU BELIEVE: Two egg yolks contain more cholesterol than four 3-1/2-ounce beefsteaks.

SOME FACTS:
Two egg yolks
contain 430 mg.
of cholesterol, whereas four 3-1/2-ounce beefsteaks contain only 364 mg. of cholesterol. That's why I suggest that you find a substitute for eggs for breakfast.

Tofu provides us with a simple, no-cholesterol breakfast food that can resemble scrambled eggs. Tofu has 0 cholesterol, and a serving of this scramble is 2 grams of fat versus 5 grams for a large egg *(see Tip #55)*. If you use egg whites, there's no cholesterol and no fat. However, egg whites have the same potential problems associated with any animal protein.

WHAT YOU CAN DO: Try the scrambled egg substitute recipe below, then add your own variations.

Scrambled Tofu

1 block	Tofu, firm
1/4 C	Onions, minced
2 tsp.	Vegetarian chicken flavor seasoning
1/2 tsp.	Tumeric
1/4 tsp.	Sea salt
1/4 tsp.	Onion powder
1/4 tsp.	Garlic powder
	Canola oil cooking spray

Lightly spray a large nonstick skillet with spray canola oil. Sauté onions, adding a slight amount of water if they start to stick. As the onions cook, add seasonings and mix. Break up tofu into scrambled-egg consistency and add to the mixture. Cook until the mixture is thoroughly heated and resembles scrambled eggs. Serve with whole grain toast or pancakes. Makes 5 portions. *(1 portion = 47.4 calories, 2.0 grams fat, 40% protein, 25% carbohydrates, 35% fat)*

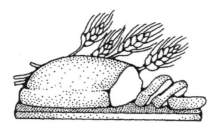

Whole Grain Breads

When was the last time you smelled the aroma of fresh baked bread? Can you imagine the sense of pride you would feel if you pulled a specially made loaf, just the right shade of golden brown, out of your own oven?

Bread making by hand is easier than ever before, with newly processed forms of yeast and the availability of a better quality of whole grain flours. Whole wheat flour is especially easy to bake with. The following recipes will give you a variety of choices, so you and your family can enjoy the delicious smell of fresh-baked bread. At the same time, I realize that bread baking is always a major endeavor when done by hand, so don't think you have to turn into a master baker to do the *Eat More, Weigh Less™ Diet*. Just bake these breads once in a while, when you're in the mood. Delicious whole grain breads can now be purchased at most supermarkets and health food stores, so make them a staple part of your diet. Once you start eating whole grain breads, you'll quickly lose your taste for any other kind.

Whole wheat breads are useful for snacking. They're also higher on the EMI if you stick to the low-fat version, and you can therefore eat a bit more bread. Other types of whole grain bread products are: whole wheat English muffins, whole wheat bagels, and whole wheat dinner rolls.

A word of caution, however. The Inverted Food Pyramid shows that whole grains can be eaten freely, on the *Eat More, Weigh Less™ Diet*. But breads are generally medium to low EMI and should therefore be eaten in moderation. This is because flour products tend to have little water in them, and they are not as bulky as they would be if cooked in their whole grain form.

Following are a few recipes. Try the one that looks easiest first, then when you find out what a snap they are to prepare, work your way up to the most difficult ones. And don't forget to stop and smell the fragrance, as your new taste treats are baking in your oven.

Simple Whole Wheat Bread

5 C	**Whole wheat flour**
2 C	**Warm water**
1 tsp.	**Sea salt**
1 Tbsp.	**Baker's yeast**

Mix ingredients together thoroughly, and let rise. If mixed well, kneading may be unnecessary. Place in floured bread pan and bake at 350° to 400° F. for 20 to 30 minutes. Makes 2 loaves or approximately 24 to 30 portions. *(1 portion = 76.7 calories, 0.4 grams fat, 16% protein, 80% carbohydrates, 5% fat)*

Golden Whole Wheat Rolls

1 C	Potatoes, mashed
3 C	Whole wheat flour
3 C	Unbleached bread flour
1-1/2 tsp.	Dry yeast
1 tsp.	Sea salt
1/4 C	Water, warm
2 C	Water
1/4 C	Honey
1 Tbsp.	Canola oil
	Canola oil cooking spray

Mix yeast with 1/4 cup warm water, let rest for 10 minutes.

Mix remaining water with honey, oil, and salt. Add yeast water.

Add half the flour, mixing well with wooden spoon. Slowly add remaining flour and mix until a ball of dough is formed. Add flour, if necessary, to keep the dough from sticking to the kneading surface. Knead until stiff yet elastic, about 8 to 10 minutes.

(continued next page)

Golden Whole Wheat Rolls (continued)

Oil a bowl with nonstick spray. Roll dough in it until fully coated. Cover the bowl with a damp cloth and set in a warm place until double in size *(about 1 to 1-1/2 hours)*.

Punch down dough and let rest 5 minutes. Pull apart and form into small balls. Place balls into a muffin tin and let rise again, for 45 minutes to an hour.

Bake at 350° F. for 25 to 30 minutes or until golden brown. Cover with cloth, and serve piping hot. Makes 30, 1 roll portions. *(1 roll = 111.4 calories, 1.0 grams fat, 12% protein, 80% carbohydrates, 8% fat)*

Eat More, Weigh Less™ Tip
Zip It!   ▽17▽   *Saves 1 hour!*

A Lazy Way
to Bake Bread

WOULD YOU BELIEVE: There is a way to make bread without having to knead it. *(We all need bread, but we don't have to knead it.)*

SOME FACTS: Making your own bread can be very easy, if you purchase a new invention, the bread machine. These machines cost between $125 and $300, but they're well worth the price. They make delicious whole-grain breads with little effort on your part. For most of these machines, all you do is put in the ingredients, press the button, and the machine does the mixing, the kneading, the rising and the baking, all on its own. You can customize your bread with your favorite ingredients such as raisins, cinnamon, apples, and whatever you might fancy. While your bread is baking, you can do something you'd rather be doing. The machine will let you know when the bread ready.

WHAT YOU CAN DO: Try making bread in an automatic bread maker.

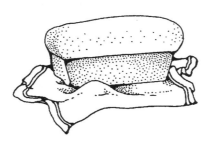

Automatic Whole Wheat Bread

3 C	Whole wheat flour
1-1/2 tsp.	Salt
1-1/2 Tbsp.	Blackstrap Molasses
3/8 C	Soy milk
1 C	Water
1-1/2 tsp.	Dry yeast

Your bread machine will have full instructions, which vary according to the brand. Follow them faithfully, and you'll have delicious golden-brown bread in about four hours. But during that time, your machine will be doing all the work! *(For another delicious recipe, see Whole Wheat Honey Bread, below).* To make your bread baking even easier, find and use various organic whole grain bread mixes. They offer rye, whole wheat, spelt, kamut, and whole grain. Each mix will cost about the same as a pre-made whole grain loaf, but the taste of fresh-baked bread is so much better that it's hard to make a comparison. Makes one, 1-1/2 lb. loaf or 18 portions. *(1 portion = 75.7 calories, 0.4 grams fat, 15% protein, 81% carbohydrates, 4% fat)*

Eat More, Weigh Less™ Tip

Zapf It!   \18/   *Save 12 gm. fat!*

Pastry Alternatives

WOULD YOU BELIEVE:

- An average 4-1/2" croissant is 235 calories and 12 grams of fat *(46% fat by calories)*.

- An average 4-1/2" Danish pastry is 235 calories and 13 grams of fat *(50% fat by calories)*.

- An average glazed donut is 210 calories and 12 grams of fat *(51% fat by calories)*.

SOME FACTS: Bagels and English muffins *(preferably whole wheat)* make very good morning foods, especially if they are substituted for oil-rich, sugary pastries, donuts, and croissants. Bagels and English muffins have about 1 gram of fat per serving *(about 7.5% fat by calories)*, whereas donuts and croissants are about 50% fat, or about 12 to 13 grams per serving. You can eat up to 10 bagels instead of one croissant and still get less fat! See how the *Eat More, Weigh Less™ Diet* works?

WHAT YOU CAN DO: Try whole grain English muffins or bagels, flavored with your favorite low-fat spread *(e.g., fruit preserves)* and leave the pastries alone.

Eat More, Weigh Less™ Tip

Zing It!   19   *Zip It!*

Two Convenient Exotic Breads

You can also use whole wheat and other whole grains in more exotic bread items such as pita bread *(from the Middle East)* and chapati *(from India)*. These breads, also known as flat breads, are easy to use, and commonly found in most mainstream grocery stores as well as health food stores. Pita and chapati breads can be used as sides for a full meal or as sandwich breads. Pita breads make especially good sandwiches. Slice them in half, and you can fill them with vegetables, bean spreads, or leftovers. You can even use them to make a form of "quick pizza." Whole wheat chapatis are similar to whole wheat tortillas and are excellent for "roll ups" or burritos for a quick meal or snack.

WHAT YOU CAN DO: Try the following recipes using pita bread and chapati, if you've never tried them before.

Quick Chapati Rolls

This is a simple way to dress up your vegetables or use leftovers in a creative way.

4	**Whole wheat chapatis** *(or whole wheat tortillas)*
2 C	**Your favorite stir-fried vegetables**
2 Tbsp.	**Your favorite sauce, or to taste** *(see page 242 for "9 Vegetable Sauces")*

Place large spoonfuls of vegetables in a line across the middle of the chapati. Add some of your favorite sauce. Roll the chapati together and hold with toothpicks. If you wish, you may toast it in a toaster oven. Serve as a side dish or as an entree with your favorite grain. Makes 4 portions.

Quick Pita Pockets

2	**Whole wheat pita bread pockets**
1 C	**Favorite beans or prepared bean dish**
4-8	**Romaine lettuce leaves**
4 slices	**Tomato**
1 Tbsp.	**Dijon mustard**

Slice the pita bread in half and place some of the beans into each pocket. Then add the vegetables. Condiments such as Dijon mustard or Dijon dressing can be added. Makes 2 portions.

Eat More, Weigh Less™ Tip
Zapf It! 20 *Save 8-13 gm. fat!*

When Baking, Use Oil Substitutes

WOULD YOU BELIEVE:

- A single muffin can contain up to 36 grams of fat and 640 calories!

- If made properly, a muffin can contain less than 1 gram of fat.

- Bran muffins can be 37% fat, with 5 to 10 grams of fat per muffin.

- Carrot cake with icing can be a surprising 53% fat, or about 15 fat grams per slice.

SOME FACTS: "640 calories, 36 grams fat," I was stunned when I read this on a label of a 6-ounce Hostess® Double Chocolate Hearty Muffin. It had more calories in fat than a McDonald's® Big Mac® *(see page 338)*. Even the Hostess® Apple & Spice Muffin contains 27 grams of fat and 580 calories.

Actually, muffins usually contain somewhere between 5 to 15 grams of fat, which is still a lot. The oil is the problem. This is what gives some baked products a moist consistency. Some recipes call for as much as a cup or more of oil. But the moist consistency can actually be attained without using oil. The trick is to modify a recipe by substituting a moist food such as applesauce, puréed prunes, mashed bananas, or a plum-based product called Wonderslim® for the oil.

WHAT YOU CAN DO:

- Use moist fruit purées *(mentioned above)* to replace some or all of the oil in baking recipes.

- Try some of the following examples of adapted recipes. All substitutes may have a slightly distinct flavor, but you can make this a part of the dish's charm.

Whole Wheat Honey Bread

4 C	Warm water
2 Tbsp.	Dry yeast
1/3 C	Honey
2 C	Whole wheat flour
1/4 C	Applesauce
1 Tbsp.	Salt
2 Tbsp.	Lecithin
7/7-1/2 C	Whole wheat flour

This is another excellent recipe for your bread machine, provided you divide the recipe into thirds. Just add the yeast to water, stir well to dissolve. Then add other wet ingredients, then the dry *(or the opposite if your machine requires, see instructions).*

If you don't have a bread machine, use some elbow grease. The delicious bread and your sense of satisfaction will amply repay you for your efforts.

Mix water, yeast, honey, and 2 cups of whole wheat flour. Let stand in warm place for 15 to 20 minutes.

Stir in lecithin and salt. Mix in most of remaining flour until it becomes stiff and hard to stir.

Place on a floured board, knead in remaining flour and continue to knead *(up to 10 minutes)* until dough is slightly sticky but springs back into shape when pressed lightly. Return to bowl, cover, and let rise in warm place until just about double in size.

Punch down and knead briefly in bowl. Cut into

(continued next page)

Whole Wheat Honey Bread (continued)

three equal pieces. Knead each piece on lightly-oiled board or counter. Shape into loaves and place in lecithin-oiled pans. Cover and let rise again in pans in warm place until not quite double in size. Bake at 350° F. for 40 to 45 minutes. Remove from pans and allow to cool standing on end or on cooling rack. Makes 3 loaves or 36 portions. *(1 portion = 119.6 calories, 1.4 grams fat, 14% protein, 77% carbohydrates, 9% fat)*

Corn Bread

2-1/2 C	Warm water
1 Tbsp.	Dry Yeast
1/4 C	Honey
2-1/2 C	Unrefined Cornmeal
1 C	Whole wheat flour
1 C	Oat flour, whole wheat pastry, or unbleached white flour
1-1/2 tsp.	Salt
1/4 C	Applesauce
1 Tbsp.	Oil
	Canola oil cooking spray or lecithin

In small bowl, stir together first three ingredients. Let bubble for 10 minutes. In another bowl, stir together remaining ingredients. Combine all ingredients and stir.

Put into lecithin-oiled or spray-oiled 8" x 11" baking dish and let rise in a warm place until just below top of dish *(about 15 minutes)*. Bake at 350° F. for about

(continued next page)

Corn Bread *(continued)*

40 minutes or until golden brown. Make 4-6 portions.
(1 portion = 393.4 calories, 5.0 grams fat, 10% protein, 79% carbohydrates, 11% fat)

Buckwheat Banana Muffins

1 C	Soy milk
1 Tbsp.	Lemon juice
1 C	Overripe bananas, mashed
1/2 C	Barley malt
1-1/2 tsp.	Vegetable oil
1-1/2 tsp.	Egg replacer plus 2 tablespoons water
1 tsp.	Vanilla extract
1 C	Buckwheat flour
1 C	Whole-wheat pastry flour
1 tsp.	Baking powder
1 tsp.	Baking soda
1/2 tsp.	Sea salt

Line 12 muffin tins with baking cups. Blend soy milk, lemon juice, bananas, barley malt, oil, reconstituted egg replacer, and vanilla until smooth.

In a separate bowl, blend flours, baking powder, baking soda, and sea salt. Fold in banana mixture just until the dry ingredients are moistened. **Do not over mix.**

Spoon batter into 12 muffin cups, 3/4 full. Bake 15 to 20 minutes at 420° F. or until done. Makes 12 portions. *(1 portion = 128.4 calories, 1.6 grams fat, 10% protein, 80% carbohydrates, 10% fat)*

Cinnamon Raisin Apple Muffins

2 cups	Whole wheat pastry flour or unbleached all purpose flour
1 tsp.	Cinnamon, ground
1 tsp.	Baking powder
1/2 tsp.	Baking soda
1/4 tsp.	Salt
1/2 cup	Raisins
1 cup	Apple juice
1/2 cup	Applesauce
1 Tbsp.	Canola oil

Whisk together first six *(dry)* ingredients.

Preheat oven to 350° F.

Mix together apple juice, applesauce, and oil *(wet ingredients)*. Add dry ingredients and raisins and stir until just combined. Spoon into lightly-oiled muffin tins and bake for 20 to 25 minutes, or until middle is done. Makes 12 portions. *(1 portion = 112.0 calories, 1.8 grams fat, 9% protein, 74% carbohydrates, 17% fat)*

Honey Oatmeal Cookies

1/2 C	Raisins, soaked for 10 minutes
3/4 C	Whole oats
1/2 C	Whole wheat flour
1/4 tsp.	Baking soda
1/4 tsp.	Salt *(optional)*
1/4 tsp.	Cinnamon
1/8 tsp.	Nutmeg
1/2 C	Honey
1 Tbsp.	Vanilla
2 Tbsp.	Prune purée
	Canola oil cooking spray

Preheat oven to 350° F., lightly spray cookie sheet with cooking spray.

Mix all dry ingredients together *(whole oats, flour, baking soda, salt, cinnamon and nutmeg)* in mixing bowl.

Mix wet ingredients *(honey, vanilla, prune purée)*, then blend into dry mix. Spoon onto cookie sheet and bake for about 12 minutes, until golden brown and crunchy. Makes 24 portions. *(1 portion = 60.9 calories, 0.4 grams fat, 8% protein, 86% carbohydrates, 6% fat)*

Apricot Cranberry Tea Bread

1 C	Unbleached flour
1/2 C	Whole wheat flour
1/2 C	Cornmeal
2 tsp.	Baking powder
1/2 tsp.	Salt
1 C	Cranberries, fresh or frozen
1/2 C	Dried apricots, chopped
1/2 C	Honey
3/4 C	Orange juice
1 tsp.	Egg replacer mixed with 2 tablespoons water
1 tsp.	Canola oil

In a large mixing bowl, combine dry ingredients. Add cranberries and apricots and toss. In a medium bowl, thoroughly mix honey, orange juice, egg replacer and oil. Make a well in center of dry ingredients and pour in wet ingredients. Mix just until blended. Pour into oil-sprayed loaf pan and bake at 350° F. for 50 minutes. Let cool for 5 minutes in baking pan, then turn onto rack to cool. Makes 12 portions. *(1 portion = 148.0 calories, 0.9 grams fat, 7% protein, 88% carbohydrates, 5% fat)*

Gingerbread

1 C	Unbleached flour
1 C	Whole wheat pastry flour
1-1/2 tsp.	Cinnamon
1 tsp.	Ginger
1/2 tsp.	Cloves
1/2 tsp.	Salt
1/2 C	Barley malt
1/2 C	Coffee, freshly brewed
1-1/2 tsp.	Baking soda
3/4 C	Blackstrap molasses
1 tsp.	Egg replacer mixed with 2 tablespoons water
1 tsp.	Canola oil

Thoroughly blend the first 6 dry ingredients in a large mixing bowl. Place baking soda into medium bowl and add coffee *(mixture will fizz)*. Add remaining ingredients and mix thoroughly. Make a well in dry ingredients and add wet ingredients, gently fold into dry. Do not over mix. Pour into a lined, sprayed 8-inch square pan. Bake at 350° F. for 35 to 40 minutes or until cake tests done. Let cool for 5 minutes in pan, then turn onto a cooling rack. Makes 9 portions. *(1 portion = 198.0 calories, 1.0 grams fat, 7% protein, 88% carbohydrates, 5% fat)*

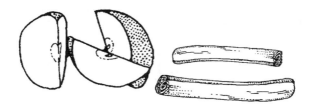

Cinnamon-Apple Bread

1-1/2 C	Whole wheat flour
1-1/2 C	Rolled oats
1 tsp.	Cinnamon
1/4 tsp.	Nutmeg
1/2 tsp.	Salt
1 tsp.	Baking powder
1 tsp.	Baking soda
1-1/3 C	Unsweetened applesauce
1/2 C	Soy milk
1/4 C	Honey
1 tsp.	Egg replacer mixed with 2 tablespoon water
1/2 C	Raisins
	Canola oil cooking spray

Thoroughly combine dry ingredients in a large mixing bowl. Combine wet ingredients in a separate bowl. Then add wet ingredients to dry, mix with a spoon until dry ingredients are moistened. Add raisins and stir to combine. Pour into an oil-sprayed loaf pan. Bake at 350° F. for 45 to 50 minutes or until done. Remove from oven and cool 5 minutes in pan, and remove from pan and cool. Makes 12 portions. *(1 portion = 146.5 calories, 1.3 grams fat, 11% protein, 82% carbohydrates, 7% fat)*

Eat More, Weigh Less™ Tip

Zapf It! $\triangledown{21}$ *Save 8 gm. fat!*

Try Delicious Bread Spreads

WOULD YOU BELIEVE: People add 8 grams of fat to their toast when they use two pats of butter.

SOME FACTS: One pat of butter contains about 4 grams of fat which comprises 100% of its 36 calories. A quick and delicious way to avoid using this much fat in a snack or a meal is to use simple spreads on your breads, muffins, toast, or other forms of baked grains. They are convenient, easy to make, and widely available in the stores.

Fruit Spreads

The first example, which is really quite obvious, is fruit spread. Look for fruit preserves. Try to find the kinds that have no sugar, probably in your health food store. Stay away from the simple jellies and jams that are high in fat and sugar.

Fruit Butter

Another delicious variation is fruit butter, such as apple butter. The so-called fruit butters are generally pure, puréed fruits which are much thicker than ordinary preserves. They have a "buttery" consistency and have a flavor closer to the natural taste of the whole fruit.

Bean Spreads

Bean spreads are another convenient way to have a quick snack or meal. These can be as simple as a bean dip for chips, or they can be a complete sandwich filling.

You can also make all types of bread spreads at home. Following are some quick and easy recipes. See bean spread recipes on pages 326-327.

Apple Butter

1 qt.	Apple juice
8 large	Tart applies
1 tsp.	Allspice, ground
1/2 tsp.	Cinnamon, ground

Boil apple juice to thicken *(2 cups)*.

Remove apple stems and cut apples into chunks.

Add allspice and cinnamon to thickened juice. Add apple chunks.

Boil, then reduce heat and simmer until soft *(about 20 minutes)*.

Blend apples into pulp and return to spice-juice mixture. Simmer and stir until thick *(about 2 hours)*. Let cool. Makes 30 portions *(about 2 cups)*. *(1 portion = 37.3 calories, 0.2 grams fat, 1% protein, 95% carbohydrates, 4% fat)*

All-Fruit Butter

1/2 C	Hot apple juice or water
1/2 C	Dried mixed fruit, packed into cup *(dates, apricots, etc.)*
1 C	Dried apples, packed into cup
1/8 tsp.	Salt
3/4 tsp.	Coriander
3/4 Tbsp.	Lemon juice

Soak apples in hot apple juice for 15 minutes, then blend. Add remaining ingredients. Blend again, on high pulsing contents *(that is, turn the blender off and on)* until smooth. Makes 48 portions *(about 3 cups)*. *(1 portion = 10.0 calories, 0.0 grams fat, 3% protein, 96% carbohydrates, 2% fat)*

Golden Raisin-Date Butter

1/2 C	Pitted dates
1/2 C	Golden raisins
3/4 C	Warm water

Soak dates and raisins in a saucepan of heated water for 15 minutes. Remove from heat, let stand for 5 minutes. Blend on high until smooth. Makes 24, 1 tablespoon portions. *(1 tablespoon = 20.6 calories, 0.0 grams fat, 3% protein, 95% carbohydrates, 1% fat)*

Eat More, Weigh Less™ Tip

Zapf It! ▽22▽ *Save 16 gm. fat!*

Fat-Free Garlic Bread

WOULD YOU BELIEVE: Garlic bread has 4 to 8 grams of fat per slice.

SOME FACTS: While garlic is a low-fat, healthy vegetable that can be used to enhance the flavor of many foods, when used on bread it is usually combined with butter or margarine. This dramatically increases the fat content of garlic bread. Many people eat two to four slices of bread with a pasta meal and can get up to 16 grams of fat by doing so.

Personally, I love garlic bread with Italian dishes, and sometimes just with salads. Fortunately, someone showed me how to keep the flavor but get rid of the fat in a garlic bread that is absolutely delicious.

WHAT YOU CAN DO: Try the following recipe for garlic bread and see if you don't agree with me.

Garlic Spread

1 head   Garlic cloves
1/2 tsp.   Olive oil *(optional)*

Remove all skin from garlic, leaving only bare cloves. Dash olive oil on top, and bake in oven at 425° F. for 30 minutes. Let cool, separate cloves, then slice open and scoop out the garlic, which should now have a pasty consistency, with a butter knife. Spread on crusty French bread, or use to spice up your sandwiches. Delicious!

It also stores well, so you don't have to cook it fresh every time. Simply bake several heads of garlic at once and store in the refrigerator. When needed, separate and slice open cloves. Then squeeze the roasted garlic out of its casing.

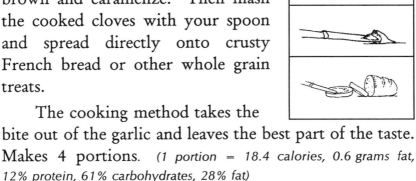

Another way to prepare this is to simply peel and smash garlic cloves, then sauté in a minimal amount of water or wine, in a very hot pan. Allow the bottom to brown and caramelize. Then mash the cooked cloves with your spoon and spread directly onto crusty French bread or other whole grain treats.

The cooking method takes the bite out of the garlic and leaves the best part of the taste. Makes 4 portions. *(1 portion = 18.4 calories, 0.6 grams fat, 12% protein, 61% carbohydrates, 28% fat)*

Pasta

Whole Grain Pastas

Whole grain pasta is another fast and simple way to keep your meals interesting. All you do is add some sauce, vegetables and pesto, and you have a delicious hot meal. There are so many varieties that you can experiment endlessly with the kinds of dishes you prepare. While spaghetti-type pasta is excellent, you might also try a small noodle such as vermicelli, or other common pastas such as macaroni, tortellini, corkscrew pasta — the list is endless. You can also present your dishes in colorful variety, by using green spinach pasta and orange-colored pasta, reddish pastas colored by beet juice, and so forth. Check your health food store for some possibilities.

Whole wheat pasta tastes excellent, and is also healthy. So is most Oriental pasta — for instance, buckwheat noodles. By using a variety of different pastas, you can make your dishes interesting in appearance and texture and keep your meals interesting.

Another type of pasta that is gaining popularity is couscous, which is excellent as a quick hot cereal, a dressed-up entree, or in a cold salad. Try some of the recipes you'll find on the side of the box, but remember to cut out at least most of the fat if it calls even for olive oil. Most dishes adapt well to a no-oil variation.

Couscous is a Mediterranean grain dish that most people think is a whole grain. Actually, it is a processed grain, as is pasta. Both are moderate on the EMI. But they're acceptable as entrees, and will enhance your *Eat More, Weigh Less*™  *Diet* so long as you remember to balance your diet with foods that are high on the EMI.

A word of caution. Most pastas are made from refined white flours, so I recommend that you use them moderately, depending on your health, because, ideally, the best grain to use is one that is not ground into flour in the first place. *(See page 43, regarding grains.)*

Most whole grain pastas have their own instructions for preparation on the package. One simple technique is to boil the water in a pot, place the pasta in the boiling water, turn off the heat and cover pot. About 10 to 15 minutes later, depending on the thickness of the pasta, it's ready. For Asian noodles, see special instructions on the package, and also check out the *Eat More, Weigh Less*™ Tip 26, Asian Soup Noodles, page 135.

Tomato Vermicelli

1 tsp.	Olive oil
3 cloves	Garlic, medium-size, peeled, and minced
1 med.	Onion, chopped
1 can	Tomatoes *(28 oz.)*, peeled, diced, undrained
1 can	Mushroom stems and pieces *(4 oz.)*
1-1/3 C	Vegetable broth, or water
1/3 C	Dry red wine
1 tsp.	Maple syrup or honey
1/4 tsp.	Cayenne pepper
1/2 C	Fresh basil *(1 tsp. dried)*
1/2 C	Fresh oregano *(1/2 tsp. dried)*
6 oz.	Vermicelli pasta, broken in halves
	Black pepper, freshly ground, to taste
dash	Sea salt

Sauté garlic and onion in olive oil, in large skillet. Add tomatoes, mushrooms, broth, wine, honey, cayenne, basil, and oregano. Bring to a boil and add the pasta. Cover and cook about 8 to 10 minutes, stirring often, until the pasta has softened. Add salt and black pepper to taste. Makes 3 portions. *(3 portions = 294.8 calories, 3.5 grams fat, 17% protein, 73% carbohydrates, 10% fat)*

Vegetarian Ravioli

1 bunch	Fresh spinach, chopped
1 box	Fresh mushrooms, diced 1/4"
1 med.	Onion, chopped
3 cloves	Garlic, minced
1 block	Firm tofu, diced into 1/4" cubes
2 pkg.	Mun doo wrappers *(20+)*

Sauté garlic and onions in 1/4 cup water until transparent. Add mushrooms, cook approximately 3 minutes, then add spinach and continue cooking on high for 5 minutes. Add tofu and cook 3 minutes on low. Set aside and cool.

To make raviolis, spoon tablespoonful of filling into mon doo wrapper. Moisten edge with water or liquid from filling and cover with another wrapper and press hard on edges to seal. Cook raviolis in large pot of boiling water for 3 minutes. Drain and serve with marinara sauce. Makes 8 portions. *(4 portions = 135.0 calories, 1.4 grams fat, 22% protein, 68% carbohydrates, 9% fat)*

Marinara Sauce

1 round	Onion, chopped
5 cloves	Garlic, crushed
2 cans	Tomatoes *(24 oz.)*, chopped
1/2 C	Water
pinch	Salt or to taste
dash	White pepper
3	Fresh basil leaves or 1 tsp. dried
1/2 C	Cilantro, chopped

Water-sauté garlic. Add onions and cook until transparent. Add tomatoes, cilantro, basil, salt, and pepper. Add 1/2 can water and simmer 30 to 60 minutes. Makes 12 portions. *(1 portion = 19.2 calories, 0.2 grams fat, 16% protein, 76% carbohydrates, 8% fat)*

Pasta With Eggplant Sauce

This is a great main dish for any gathering. Leftover sauce can be used over brown rice for lunch the next day.

1/2 tsp.	Olive oil
1-1/2 lb.	Eggplant, unpeeled and in 1/2" chunks
1 large	Red onion, chopped
3 large	Garlic cloves, minced
1 C	Mushrooms, coarsely chopped
1 C	Green peppers, coarsely chopped
2-3 cans	Plum tomatoes *(1 lb.)*
2 tsp.	Dry basil
1 tsp.	Dry oregano
1 tsp.	Sugar
2/3 C	Cilantro
	Salt, to taste
	Pepper, to taste
1 lb.	Pasta

Heat oil, add eggplant, onions, and sauté over medium heat until soft and lightly browned, stirring frequently. Add garlic, mushrooms, and bell pepper, and continue to sauté. Add tomatoes, basil, oregano, and sugar. Cook covered for 10 minutes. Add cilantro. Season with salt and pepper. Cover and simmer 15 to 20 minutes.

Cook pasta. Pour hot pasta sauce over pasta and serve. Makes 6 to 8 portions. *(1 portion = 265.5 calories, 2.0 grams fat, 19% protein, 75% carbohydrates, 7% fat)*

Pasta with Roasted Vegetables

12	Plum tomatoes, quartered lengthwise
1 lb.	Asparagus, trimmed
1	Zucchini, quartered
2	Yellow crooked-neck squash, quartered
1 head	Broccoli, cut in bite-size pieces
2	Long eggplant or 1 round eggplant, peeled
1 basket	Mushrooms, cut in halves
1 small	Garlic head
2 tsp.	Fresh lemon juice
1 Tbsp.	Fresh basil
1 Tbsp.	Fresh cilantro
	Salt to taste
	Pepper to taste
1 lb.	Pasta of choice

Seat oven rack in lower third of oven. Preheat oven to 450° F.

Cut asparagus, zucchini, yellow crooked-neck squash and eggplant in 2" lengths.

In large roasting pan, toss vegetables with olive oil and garlic. Roast 20 minutes until vegetables are tender.

In large pot of boiling water, cook pasta until tender but firm, about 8 minutes. Drain and transfer to roasting pan and toss gently to combine with vegetables. Serve immediately. Makes 8 to 10 portions. *(1 portion = 233.7 calories, 2.1 grams fat, 18% protein, 74% carbohydrates, 8% fat)*

Bow Tie Pasta With Miso Sauce

1 lb.	Bow tie *(Farfalle)* pasta, cooked and drained
1	Red bell pepper, julienned
1	Green bell pepper, julienned
1 small	Red onion, diced
1 sm. head	Broccoli, cut in florets and blanched
1 small	Zucchini, diced and blanched
2 Tbsp.	Olive oil
4	Green onions, sliced
2 cloves	Garlic, minced
1/4 C	Light miso
1-1-1/2 C	Veggie broth, warm
1/4 C	Parsley, chopped
1/4 tsp.	Pepper flakes *(or more to taste)*

Put cooked pasta in a large mixing bowl. Add bell peppers, onion, broccoli, and zucchini. In a medium skillet over medium heat, saute green onions and garlic in oil for 1 to 2 minutes. Add miso, stir. Stir in veggie broth. Add parsley and pepper flakes. Pour over pasta and toss. Makes 12 to 14 portions. *(1 portion = 93.2 calories, 2.9 grams fat, 15% protein, 58% carbohydrates, 27% fat)*

Eat More, Weigh Less™ Tip
Zapf It!   ▽23▽   *Save 12 gm. fat!*

"Elipidate™" Your Pasta Sauce

Would you believe: Some pasta sauces are as much as 53% fat and 12 grams of fat per cup, while other pasta sauces are only 1% fat with less than half a gram per cup.

Some Facts: When some pasta sauces are prepared, a substantial amount of oil can be added, either in the form of vegetables oils or oily meats. Pasta sauces can be made nonfat, if you prepare them from scratch and simply eliminate the oil from the recipe. You'll find that if the sauce is reasonably well seasoned with herbs and spices, you won't miss the taste of the oil at all. If you are buying a prepared marinara sauce, make sure it's one that is very low in fat *(i.e., 1 gram of fat or less per serving)*.

What You Can Do: Eliminate or minimize oil in marinara recipe — in other words "Elipidate™ it!" *(* See page 22 for "Elipidate™" explanation.)*

Eat More, Weigh Less™ Tip
Zing It!   \24/

Pizazz Your Pasta

Now that you've cut out the fats and oils, try some variations on your basic pasta sauce. You can do this by adding mushrooms and a variety of your favorite vegetables. Some of my favorite additions are mushrooms, onions, garlic, zucchini, bell peppers, and broccoli. Mushrooms are a special treat in pasta sauces. Their rich, earthy flavor is a delicious compliment to the tomato sauce and different types of whole grain pastas.

WHAT YOU CAN DO: Try the mushroom pasta sauce that follows. Use it over your favorite type of pasta, serve with a side of leafy green salad and some oil-free garlic bread (see *Eat More, Weigh Less™* Tip #22), and you'll have a quick, mouth-watering meal.

Mushroom Marinara Sauce

1/4 C	Red wine
2 oz.	Dried mushrooms *(any type)*
2 cloves	Garlic, peeled and pressed
1 large	Onion, sliced thinly
2 Tbsp.	Fresh basil
1 Tbsp.	Fresh rosemary
5 Tbsp.	Fresh parsley
2 tsp.	Fresh oregano
3 C	Plum tomatoes, canned with juices
	Salt and black pepper, freshly ground, to taste

Break the herbs apart. Twist the leaves or stems into 1/8" pieces or slightly smaller. This is the best way to release the full flavor of herbs. Put aside.

Soak dried mushrooms in 1 cup hot water for 15 to 20 minutes. Drain, reserving soaking liquid. Strain the soaking liquid through and set aside. Rinse and chop the mushrooms.

Heat a large nonstick skillet. Water-sauté garlic cloves, onion, then quickly add parsley, oregano, rosemary, and basil. When the herbs begin to wilt, add tomatoes with juice and mushroom soaking water. Bring to a boil, turn down heat, add salt and pepper to taste and let simmer for about 10 minutes. Makes 6 portions. *(1 portion = 69.5 calories, 0.6 grams fat, 16% protein, 76% carbohydrates, 7% fat)*

Eat More, Weigh Less™ Tip
Zing It!   ⟍25⟋

Use Asian Sauce on Pasta and Other Whole Grain Dishes

Most people think pasta is an Italian invention. In truth, it came from China and was brought back to Italy by Marco Polo. The Asian people have eaten pasta noodles for centuries, and they've invented thousands of delicious sauces to use on them. Try an occasional Oriental sauce on your pasta. The trick to making Oriental sauce is in using arrowroot or corn starch, or if you can find it at a health food store, kuzu *(also known as kudzu)* which is a Japanese form of arrowroot. All are excellent thickening agents, and your Oriental sauce will ideally be smooth and slightly thick. This consistency is very pleasant to the palate. Another trick is to use vegetarian oyster sauce as a base, available at your Asian or health food market.

When your sauce is properly thickened, you can add soy sauce, garlic, onions, ginger, and a dash of sesame oil — maybe even some sweetener such as brown rice syrup, barley malt, or other unusual taste treats. This will result in a tasty, gourmet sauce for all types of other dishes.

Oriental sauce is especially tasty when mixed into mushrooms, especially shiitake *(a form of Japanese mushroom)*. Other mushrooms are also enhanced, including straw mushrooms, oyster mushrooms, and button mushrooms. Then add other vegetables to the mixture, using your own taste buds as a guideline. But if you really feel like some exotic cooking and you've never tried oriental, you're in for a special treat.

WHAT YOU CAN DO: Try the following recipe and then tailor it to your taste.

Seitan Ginger Stir-Fry

1 Tbsp.	Vegetable broth
1 med.	Onion, finely sliced
2 cloves	Garlic, pressed or minced
1 med.	Carrot, cut in 1/2" segments
1 C	Bamboo shoots
1 C	Mushrooms, sliced
1 can	Water chestnuts *(8 oz., 5 oz. drained)*
1 tsp.	Ginger root, finely grated to taste
6 oz.	Seitan, cut in small chunks or thin strips
1 C	Bok choy or Chinese cabbage, finely sliced
2 C	Broccoli, florets and thinly-sliced stems
3/4 C	Vegetable broth
1 tsp.	Corn starch *(or kudzu, if you can find it)* mixed in 2 teaspoons water Low-sodium soy sauce, to taste
8 oz.	Soba noodles, precooked *(see package)*

Boil water for soba noodles. Dissolve corn starch/ kudzu and 2 tablespoons of cold broth or water. Set aside to dissolve.

Heat vegetable broth in a large skillet over moderate heat. *(Add water, if food begins to stick.)*

(continued next page)

Seitan Ginger Stir-Fry (continued)

Add onion and garlic, sauté until translucent. Then add carrots, mushrooms, bamboo shoots, water chestnuts, ginger and seitan. Continue to sauté until vegetables are tender *(about 4 to 5 minutes)*.

Add bok choy, broccoli, and 3/4 cup of stock. Cover and steam until broccoli is slightly tender *(about 3 minutes)*. Add more stock if necessary. Thicken with corn starch and water. Serve over warm soba noodles. Garnish with parsley and sliced ginger root. Makes 6 portions. *(1 portion = 290.6 calories, 1.3 grams fat, 27% protein, 69% carbohydrates, 4% fat)*

Eat More, Weigh Less™ Tip

Zing It! $\overline{\underline{26}}\!\!\diagdown$ *Save 13 gm. fat!*

Asian Soup Noodles

WOULD YOU BELIEVE: Some Asian soup noodles or "ramen" noodles are as much as 14 grams of fat per serving and others are as low as 1/2 grams of fat.

SOME FACTS: Noodles are Asia's fast food. Long before the fast food franchise restaurants opened in the United States, Asian people were stopping in small, neighborhood noodle shops to sate their hunger with a variety of savory noodle dishes. Now, Americans have finally discovered the rewards of eating Asian-style noodles, and small storefront shops are popping up all over the place. There is an endless variety of types and dishes, and they're healthier by far than any American fast food.

For the most part, Asian noodles are prepared as soups: that is, they're cooked in broth, with combinations of fresh ginger, garlic, onions, and various vegetables. Many Asian dishes also use light meat condiments, which I do not advise. Prepared without oil, such dishes can be very low in fat, and very tasty.

Also, be very careful of prepared dry noodles in a cup. Some of them are as high as 14 grams of fat per serving. Others are fat free *(e.g., Soken Brand)*. Read the labels.

Noodles may also be prepared in stir-fries, in salads, or plain with various combinations of accompaniments, such as miso or pickled cabbage. Whatever you choose, be assured that Asian noodles will delight your taste buds with a combination of delicate yet satisfying flavors.

Saimin (Asian Soup Noodles)

4 qts.	Water
1 Tbsp.	Vegetarian "chicken" or "beef" powder *(or to taste)*
1/3 C	Miso *(or 1/4 C low-sodium soy sauce)*
6	Shiitake mushrooms *(soaked and sliced)*
2 C	Cabbage *(preferably won bok or napa)* or other leafy green, sliced
1/2 med.	Carrot, julienned
1 pkg.	Buckwheat noodles *(8 to 10 oz. soba)*

Optional Vegetables

1 med.	Japanese turnips, julienned
1 oz.	Wakame, dried
	Other vegetables that you enjoy

Bring 2 quarts of water to a boil in each of two pots. Soak 6 shiitake mushrooms in a small amount of water and slice into thin strips. Blanche the cabbage, carrots, and other vegetables in water and keep separate.

When the water begins to boil in the first pot, bring it down to low heat, and add the vegetarian powder. In about a half a cup of water, mash the miso until it is a liquified thick soup and then add to the water. *(This is to avoid lumps of miso in the soup.)* If you are using Japanese turnips, add it to the mixture and simmer for 5 minutes.

To prepare the noodles, use the second pot of boiling water and prepare buckwheat noodles as described in the "Asian Cold Noodles" tip recipe.

(continued next page)

Saimin (Asian Soup Noodles) *(continued)*

Portion out the noodles in large bowls and pour soup over it. Then add the vegetables on top of the noodles. Garnish with chopped scallions if you wish. Makes 4 to 6 portions. *(1 portion = 244.1 calories, 1.9 grams fat, 17% protein, 77% carbohydrates, 6% fat)*

∇ Store the noodles and soup separately in the refrigerator if you want to use it the next day *(otherwise the noodles get soggy).* ∇

Eat More, Weigh Less™ Tip

Zing It! $\boxed{27}$ *Save 23 gm. fat!*

Asian Cold Noodles

WOULD YOU BELIEVE: A 1-cup serving of cold pasta salad can be as high as 24 grams fat and 51% of 420 calories? *(Kraft® Herb and Garlic Pasta Salad).*[25]

SOME FACTS: The reason cold pasta dishes, such as pasta salads, can be high in fat is the oil used in the dressing. Oil of all kinds is the most concentrated source of calories at 9 calories per gram. One solution is to use nonfat dressings or an Asian dipping sauce. They can be delicious this way and can be used as an entrée, a side dish, or they may form the base of a salad. The cooking process may be a bit different from the pastas you're used to cooking, so read the instructions carefully.

To make cold noodle dishes, drain the noodles when they're cooked. Immerse them in ice cold water quickly *(don't soak)*, drain, then prepare the rest of your dish.

Asian cold noodles are often eaten by dipping them into a delicious sauce. Seasoned rice vinegar, soy sauces, and other novel taste treats can be used. Prepared dipping sauces can also be found wherever Asian foods are sold.

To further enhance these dishes, you can also add cold vegetables of your own choosing. Asian vegetables will give you a nice break from routine. Sliced vegetables are especially good with cold noodle dishes. Choose your own combinations, and you'll soon be learning the secrets that it took Asian chefs centuries to perfect.

Two excellent suggestions are cold soba *(cooked according to directions on package, then cooled in refrigerator)* with soy sauce; and cold somen, also cooked according to package, dressed up with shredded cabbage, cold azuki beans, and thinly sliced cucumber, with a tablespoon of rice wine vinegar drizzled over the combination. Delicious.

WHAT YOU CAN DO: Try cold soba or cold somen noodles with a dip sauce as a side dish.

Basic Buckwheat Noodles

Buckwheat noodles are one of my favorite pasta dishes. This is one whole grain pasta that is commonly served even in restaurants. At Japanese restaurants, it is served hot or cold. It's also an excellent basic cereal grain product around which to plan a meal.

1 pkg.	Buckwheat *(soba)* noodle
1 Tbsp.	Green onion, chopped
1	Japanese soba sauce *(can or bottle)* or prepare dip sauce below
	Nori flakes *(optional)*

Boil enough water to immerse the noodles in a pot, and place the noodles in the boiling water. As it boils, it will foam so before it overflows, pour a small amount of cool water into the saucepan and the foaming will stop for a short while and will build up again. You'll have to do this about three times before it is cooked. If noodles already contain salt, do not salt cooking water. If they do not contain salt, a pinch of sea salt can be added to the cooking water.

After the noodles are cooked, drain and rinse in cool water and drain again.

Garnish with green onion and nori flakes. Serve cold. Use the following sauce for flavor as a dipping sauce. Makes 3 portions. *(1 portion = 281.3 calories, 1.0 grams fat, 19% protein, 78% carbohydrates, 3% fat)*

Asian Dipping Sauce

1/4 C   Low-sodium soy sauce *(for the simplest sauce you can just use soy sauce)*
2 C   Water
1 piece   Konbu *(about 3" x 2")*
1 tsp.   Ginger, grated

Boil the konbu in water for 5 minutes; remove the konbu *(it can be sliced and eaten with other vegetables)* and add the other ingredients. You can vary the taste of the sauce by adding the ingredients below.

1 tsp.   Wasabi *(Japanese horseradish, the kind used on sushi)*
1-2 tsp.   Lemon juice for a tangy taste
1 clove   Garlic, crushed

Serve in separate bowls for each person to dip their noodles. You can make several servings of this recipe, and keep some on hand in the refrigerator to use on quick-cooked Asian noodles when you're in the mood. Makes 8 portions *(2 cups)*. *(1 portion = 5.0 calories, 0.0 grams fat, 35% protein, 64% carbohydrates, 2% fat)*

Buckwheat Noodle Medley

1 pkg.   Buckwheat *(8-10 oz. soba)* noodles

1 Tbsp.   Fresh ginger, grated

Water to cover noodles

Water to cool noodles while cooking

Low-sodium soy sauce, to taste

Any leftover vegetables or beans, especially broccoli, peas, beans, cabbage, collards, kale, mustard greens, spinach, turnip greens

Prepare noodles as above, then cool.

In large bowl or pan, combine noodles, grated fresh ginger, and small amount of low-sodium soy sauce or tamari. Then cut lightly-cooked vegetables *(anything you choose to use)* into bite-size pieces.

Toss together with cold soba, and serve. Makes 3 portions. *(1 portion = 279.6 calories, 1.0 grams fat, 17% protein, 80% carbohydrates, 3% fat)*

Asian Pasta Salad

1/2 lb.	Buckwheat noodles
1 C	Yellow zucchini, julienne
1	Carrot, shredded
1 C	Celery, diced
1 C	Daikon *(Japanese turnip)*, diced
2 Tbsp.	Lemon juice
1 Tbsp.	Umeboshi plum paste
3	Scallions, minced *(green part only)*
1/2 can	Olives, sliced

Cook buckwheat noodles according to directions. Cool. Cook, cool, and julienne zucchini and set aside. Shred carrot, set aside. Blend lemon juice, umeboshi, and scallions into a dressing. Toss pasta with the vegetables and dressing. Garnish with parsley. Makes 5 portions. *(1 portion = 196.9 calories, 2.5 grams fat, 14% protein, 75% carbohydrates, 10 % fat)*

Potatoes

Potatoes are root vegetables, but I put them in this category because, like grains, they're a good source of complex carbohydrates. They are also a good weight-loss food, and they're higher on the EMI scale when compared to grains. The EMI value of potatoes is 9.6, which means it takes 9.6 pounds to provide an average daily intake of 2,500 calories. About 24 small potatoes are equivalent to 9.6 pounds. So you can see that it's okay to eat as many potatoes as you like. The days are long gone when potatoes were off-limits to people watching their weight.

Potatoes contain only 1% fat, which is about 0.17 grams per potato. This means that after eating 6 potatoes, you'd still have eaten only 1 gram of fat. They also contain 11% protein and 88% carbohydrate. They are a source of vitamins B and C, and they're high in fiber.

They're also easy on the pocketbook. You can eat them morning, noon or night, make them into soups, casseroles, salads and other dishes to serve at home, or carry the dishes to picnics or parties. They're delicious as potato slices or hash browns. You can even buy the frozen kind in your supermarket. Their succulent, yet neutral flavor, is complimentary to a whole variety of other foods, which is why they're often used as a side dish. But as you'll see in some of the following recipes, they can also and easily be the star of the meal, with just a little dressing up.

Eat More, Weigh Less™ Tip

28

Eat 9 Pounds of Potatoes?

WOULD YOU BELIEVE: It takes 9.6 pounds of potatoes to provide one day's calories for an average man or average active woman *(2,500 calories).*

SOME FACTS: Baked potatoes are an excellent *Eat More, Weigh Less™* food. It is a filling, 1% fat food and is so bulky that it takes 9.6 pounds to provide one day's calories *(which makes its EMI value 9.6).*

A favorite dish of mine is to use "new" potatoes — the smallest ones with the reddish skin. They bake or steam quickly, and you can take them to work the way people used to take boiled eggs.

WHAT YOU CAN DO:

- Try baked potato with one of the 9 toppings in Tip #29 *(instead of butter)* for your main staple at home or the next time you eat out.

- Try taking baked "new" potatoes for lunch or a snack and sprinkle with Old Bay® Seasoning.

Baked Potatoes and
Garlic Baked Potatoes

To bake: Scrub your potatoes and puncture with a fork several times. Then place on a cooking sheet in a preheated 375° F. oven and bake for approximately one hour. They'll be done when your fork easily penetrates through to the center.

To microwave: Follow the cooking instructions that came with your machine. Each microwave is different, and what yields you a fluffy perfect potato in one may deliver a burnt chunk of starch in another.

For Garlic Potatoes: To make simple "Garlic Baked Potatoes," make one or more slits in a potato, add slices of a garlic clove to the slits, and bake as indicated above. Then flavor to your taste.

See *Eat More, Weigh Less*™Tip #29 for potato toppers.

Baked Potatoes With Salsa

Potatoes:

6	Russet potatoes, cut in half lengthwise
4-5 cloves	Garlic, minced
1/4 tsp.	Olive oil

Score cut surface of each potato half. Season with salt and pepper. Combine minced garlic and olive oil. Brush mixture over surface of potatoes. Bake 400° F. approximately 40 minutes or until lightly browned and tender. Makes 5 portions. *(1 portion = 149.4 calories, 0.4 grams fat, 8% protein, 89% carbohydrates, 2% fat)*

Salsa:

2	Tomatoes, diced
1	Green bell pepper, diced
1 med.	Round onion, diced
2-3	Jalapeno or Serrano peppers, minced
2 Tbsp.	Fresh cilantro, minced
2 tsp.	Lime juice
1 tsp.	Ground cumin, or to taste
1 tsp.	Dried oregano
1/4 tsp.	Black pepper
1/4 tsp.	Salt
1/4 tsp.	Cayenne pepper
2 C	Tomatoes, canned, crushed

Mix all ingredients together, cover, and let set 1 hour. Serve salsa over baked potatoes. Makes 5 portions *(1 portion = 216.3 calories, 1.0 grams fat, 10% protein, 86% carbohydrates, 4% fat)*

Optional: Add one cup corn to the salsa.

Eat More, Weigh Less™ Tip

Zing/Zapf It! ▽29▽ *Save 22 gm. fat!*

Nine Potato Toppers

WOULD YOU BELIEVE: A large whole potato is about 200 calories and contains about 0.2 grams of fat. Adding 2 tablespoons of butter to a baked potato adds 22 grams of fat and doubles its calories from 200 calories to 400 calories.

SOME FACTS: Many fast food restaurants now feature baked potatoes with various toppings. These are intended to be used as alternative entrées to their fatty, meat-centered sandwiches and quick meals. This would in fact be an excellent idea, except that they dress the potato with globs of sour cream, butter, cheese, or other foods that sabotage and scuttle the entire concept. When I mention that I do not recommend butter or sour cream on potatoes, I usually hear groans and complaints. My answer to those complaints is that I'm simply taking two condiments away, but I'll give you back nine.

WHAT YOU CAN DO: Instead of using butter *(11 grams of fat in 1 tablespoon of butter or about*

100 calories), try one of the nine potato toppers I have listed below. They can all provide a lot of zing to the flavor of your potato, and contain from zero to less than a half of gram of fat per tablespoon.

These toppers are also good atop the small red potato known as new potatoes. When you're in the mood for a quick meal or treat, slice them thin and toast some of these potatoes, add one of the following toppings, and your appetite will be in for a treat.

These nine potato toppers are easy to use, and you'll be surprised at how good they are. You're also welcome to adapt your own favorite low-fat foods as potato toppers. It's a whole new field of culinary adventure that you can do quickly and cheaply. Have fun in your experiments.

Nine Potato Toppers

- A-1® Steak Sauce
- Barbecue Sauce
- Marinara Sauce
- Salsa
- Old Bay® Seasoning
- Creamed corn
- Chili
- Horseradish
- Low-fat Gravy *(See Tip #47.)*

Eat More, Weigh Less™ Tip
Zapf It!　　　　　 30　　　*Save 15 gm. fat!*

Fat-Free "Fries"

WOULD YOU BELIEVE: Turning a peeled baked potato into French fries adds 15.3 grams of fat per serving, increases the fat content from 1% to 49%, and raises the calorie content from 145 calories to 284 calories.

SOME FACTS: Most Americans are crazy about French fried potatoes. Unfortunately, the worst possible way to prepare potatoes is to deep fry them. Turning potatoes into French fries increases the fat content from 0.2 grams to 15.5 grams. To make it even worse, its mass falls from 156 grams to 86 grams, and its EMI value falls from 9.6 to 1.9.

WHAT YOU CAN DO: If you like "fried" potatoes, try the following recipes for American "fries," Home "fries," or Texas "fries." They're tasty, simple to prepare, and they're very low in fat *(around 1% by calories)*.

American Fries

4 med.	Potatoes
1 small	Sweet yellow onion
	Water or vegetarian broth, as needed
	Salt and spices, to taste

Partly cook potatoes in the oven. The potatoes should be almost done, but still firm.

Heat a medium-sized, nonstick skillet to very hot.

While the skillet is heating, slice the potatoes and onions into thin slices.

Put enough water or vegetable broth into the skillet to lightly cover the bottom, add onions and caramelize them — that is, let them turn golden brown and aromatic.

Add thinly sliced potatoes and small amounts of water as needed. Watch the skillet carefully. Add salt and spice to your taste such as pepper, garlic powder, curry powder, paprika, and Spike® seasoning. There's a fine line between the wonderful flavor of well-browned potatoes and onions, and the moment you let them burn. Makes 4 portions. *(1 portion = 230.2 calories, 0.3 grams fat, 8% protein, 91% carbohydrates, 1% fat)*

Variations:

Home Fries

Precook potatoes until almost done and prepare as described in "Tofu Nuggets" on page 344.

Texas Fries

Quarter a potato lengthwise and bake in an oven *(in a microwave its about 5 minutes on high)*. Then add spices as in "American Fries" or dip in a barbecue sauce, catsup, or balsamic vinegar.

More Potato Recipes

If you prefer to make your own hash browns, here's a recipe you'll like.

Hash Browns

1/3 C	**Onion, shredded and diced fine**
1/3 C	**Water**
3 C	**Leftover potatoes, grated** *(or cook new ones, according to recipe above)*
	Salt and pepper to taste
1-2 Tbsp.	**Soy sauce**

Water-sauté onion until translucent. Add remaining ingredients and cook, adding water as needed. Serve for breakfast, as a snack, or with ketchup, salad, and a green vegetable for a well-rounded meal. Makes 4 to 6 portions. *(1 portion = 161.2 calories, 0.2 grams fat, 9% protein, 90% carbohydrates, 1% fat)*

Potatoes With Horseradish Sauce

2 lbs.   Potatoes, cut in chunks

Sauce:

16 oz.   Soft tofu, smoothly blended
1 Tbsp.   White horseradish, bottled, grated
1/4 C   Onion, minced
1 tsp.   Soy sauce
3 Tbsp.   Lemon juice
3 Tbsp.   Red wine vinegar
1 Tbsp.   Fresh dill or 1 tsp. dried dill
1 Tbsp.   Fresh chives or 1 tsp. dried chives
1/2 tsp. Garlic powder
1/8 tsp. Maple syrup or honey
1/8 tsp. Pepper
1/2 tsp. Salt

Steam potatoes gently until they pierce easily. Remove from heat and drain. Combine sauce ingredients in blender *(or use hand blender)* until smooth and pour over the potatoes. Let sit for a few minutes for the flavors to merge. Makes 4 to 6 portions. *(1 portion = 227.0 calories, 3.1 grams fat, 17% protein, 71% carbohydrates, 12% fat)*

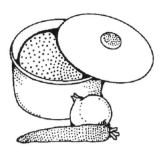

Potato Zucchini Stew

1-1/4 C	Onion, chopped
1 stalk	Celery, chopped
2 C	Potatoes, cubed
1/4 C	Carrots, sliced
1/2 C	Broccoli
1/2 C	Zucchini, sliced
1/2 C	Kale, chopped
3/4 C	Vegetable broth
1 clove	Garlic, minced
1/2 tsp.	Salt, or to taste
1/2 tsp.	Paprika
1/2 tsp.	Dill
1/4 C	Red wine
1-1/2 Tbsp.	Tomato paste
	Olive oil cooking spray

Spray nonstick skillet with olive oil cooking spray and heat. Sauté onions for 5 minutes in 3 tablespoons of vegetable broth. Add remaining ingredients and cook for 10 more minutes or until done to taste. Makes 2 portions. *(1 portion = 338.9 calories, 1.4 grams fat, 12% protein, 79% carbohydrates, 4% fat)*

Eat More, Weigh Less™ Tip
Zapf It! $\boxed{31}$ *Save 7 gm. fat!*

An Ideal Sweet Snack or Side Dish

WOULD YOU BELIEVE: The total fat content of 7 whole sweet potatoes combined is less than 1 gram of fat *(0.91)*.

SOME FACTS: Another excellent potato that you can use for the purpose of snacking or a side dish is the sweet potato. If you eat 3 slices of sweet potato instead of 3 average cookies *(7.8 grams of fat for 3 medium cookies)*, you'll save over 7 grams of fat.

WHAT YOU CAN DO: When you have some time, try steaming up a bunch of sweet potatoes and keep some in the refrigerator for snacking on later. When you have a sweet tooth or crave something like a cookie, instead use sweet potato slices to satisfy your desire for something sweet to snack on. You will find that they are very filling and quite satisfying. The best part about it is that sweet potatoes are not only moderate to high in EMI, they contain only about 1% fat by calories.

Steamed Sweet Potatoes or Yams

6 med. **Sweet potatoes or yams**
Water

Place whole sweet potatoes in steamer with 1" of water and steam for approximately 15 minutes or until fork tender. Slice and serve. Or create glazed sweet potatoes by covering with the following sauce and baking for 5 more minutes. Makes 6 portions. *(1 sweet potato portion = 117.0 calories, 0.125 grams fat, 7% protein, 93% carbohydrates, 1% fat) (1 yam portion = 127.8 calories, 0.1 grams fat, 5% protein, 94% carbohydrates, 1% fat)*

▽ Sweet potatoes and yams are simple and simply delicious by themselves. They don't have to be eaten only at Thanksgiving. They are great at any meal or as snacks. ▽

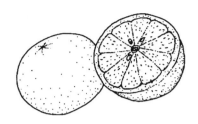

Orange-Date Glaze

3 C   Unsweetened orange juice
1 C   Dates, pitted and blended to a mush
1/4 tsp.   Vanilla
1/2 tsp.   Salt
1/2 tsp.   Corn starch
1/4 tsp.   Cloves *(optional)*

Cook over a low flame, adding ingredients in the above order. Add corn starch last, stirring constantly as it begins to thicken. You want it to be the consistency of a thick syrup. Remove from flame and spoon over steamed yams or sweet potatoes.

You can either serve directly, or place in a very hot oven and bake the flavors together for 5 minutes. Makes 6 portions. *(1 portion = 138.6 calories, 0.384 grams fat, 4% protein, 94% carbohydrates, 2% fat)   (1 sweet potato portion with 1 portion orange-date glaze = 256.0 calories, 0.5 grams fat, 5% protein, 93% carbohydrates, 2% fat)*

Sweet Potato Salad

1 lb.	Purple sweet potatoes, cooked and cubed
1 lb.	Sweet potatoes or yams, cooked and cubed
1 small	Maui onion, sliced
1/2	Green pepper, slivered
1/2	Red pepper, slivered
1/2	Yellow pepper, slivered
2 slices	Onion

Dressing:

1 tsp.	Salad oil
2 Tbsp.	Honey
1/4 C	Vinegar
3/4 tsp.	Salt
1/4 tsp.	Mustard
dash	Black pepper
dash	Worcestershire
1/2	Bay leaf

In a salad bowl, combine all cooked potatoes, onions, and peppers. Chill. In a small bowl, combine the remaining ingredients and chill. Before serving, remove garlic and bay leaf from dressing and pour over salad. Chill for another hour. Makes 8 portions. *(1 portion = 161.4 calories, 0.9 grams fat, 6% protein, 89% carbohydrates, 5% fat)*

Steamed Taro

2-4 med.   **Taro roots**

Place in steamer and steam for 2 to 3 hours *(depending on the size of the taro)* until fork tender. Then scrape the skin off, slice and serve. Pressure cooking for 1-1/2 to 2 hours is another way to prepare taro. Makes 4 to 8 portions. *(1 portion = 142.3 calories, 0.110 grams fat, 1% protein, 98% carbohydrates, 1% fat)*

▽ Taro is a root vegetable which was the primary staple of ancient Hawai'i and most of the rest of Polynesia. It is found on all continents including Asia, Africa, and the Americas. It must be cooked well or the oxalate crystals will make your mouth itch. It can be eaten alone or with stews. ▽

Some Final Thoughts On Grains

By now, I hope, you've added some delicious whole grain, pasta, and potato dishes to your *Eat More, Weigh Less™ Diet*. I hope you now center your diet on these staple foods and have found some selections that you like well enough to make them part of your life.

Now we'll talk about some delicious vegetables that will round out your whole grain entrées — or stand as entrées in their own right. Vegetables tend to be very high on the EMI. You can eat as much of them as you want — even more than the processed whole grains. Pick out several recipes, and start eating right today!

VEGETABLE DELIGHTS

Vegetables are especially important on the *Eat More, Weigh Less™ Diet*, which is why you'll find many delicious vegetable recipes in this cookbook. They're the highest food on the EMI, and I suggest you try to eat at least 3 to 5 full servings of vegetables each day *(see page 30 for definition of serving size.)* Fresh vegetables are by far and away the best, because most of their natural nutrition is retained *(if they are truly fresh and haven't sat in the refrigerator for too long)*. Fresh vegetables are followed by frozen vegetables, and canned vegetables are the lowest on the nutrition list.

Vegetables

In many of the grains dishes above, you've already been cooking with vegetables. Vegetables are the perfect compliment for grains. Eat your 3 to 5 vegetable servings in addition to the vegetables you'll use in sauces and other additions to your grain recipes. Use common sense, and you'll stay on track. Eat as many vegetables as you want.

They'll fill up your stomach, satisfy your hunger drive, and they'll also fill your body with wonderful nutrients to give you the extra lift that makes life a delight.

Vegetables are a key source of vitamins, minerals, and micronutrients. They're a source of fiber, they provide variety, and they allow you to present your foods as a palette of colors. Some of the pigments which give vegetables their color are proving to be part of their health benefits. *Remember that weight loss, while important, is never more important than maintaining good health.* In fact, it should be considered a part of maintaining the best possible health.

Basic Soups

Soup making is an art. Fortunately, it's an art that's easy to learn. With the quick and easy recipes you're about to try, you'll be making delicious soups. Soups are wonderfully versatile. There's one for every season, and for every occasion.

There are cold soups, noodle soups, chowders, stews, purees, grain soups, vegetable soups — even clear soups, or consommes. Soups can be featured at a gourmet dinner, they can make up the entrée at an old-fashioned family gathering, or they can become a quick and easy snack for a solitary diner. Soup can be as delicious as the love and care you put into it, but loving care doesn't have to mean a wealth of time.

Soups are a blend of wonderful aromas, textures, and imagination.   Try some of the following, familiarize yourself with the basics, then learn the EMI and start creating your own.   You'll soon make soup a feature of your *Eat More, Weigh Less ™ Diet*. These recipes will serve you well for the rest of your life.   Why not get off to a fast start right now, by preparing one of the simplest, tastiest soups you'll find?

Onion Soup

2 med.	**Onions, cut thin crescents**
1/2 tsp.	**Sesame oil**
1/4 tsp.	**Sea salt**
2 C	**Vegetable broth**
3 C	**Water**
1 Tbsp.	**Soy sauce**

Sauté the onions in sesame oil until they are transparent.   Add the vegetable broth and the boiling water. Cover and simmer for 5 minutes.   Add the salt, cover, and simmer for 30 minutes on a low flame *(still boiling)*. Add the soy sauce.   Serve immediately.   Makes 6 portions.   *(1 portion = 36.6 calories, 0.5 grams fat, 21% protein, 67% carbohydrates, 13% fat)*

Eat More, Weigh Less™ Tip
Zapf It! 32

The Lowest-Fat Soup

WOULD YOU BELIEVE: While chicken broth is 1.35 grams of fat per cup, vegetarian broth in only 0.19 grams per cup.

SOME FACTS: For most people, soup means using beef, chicken, or fish broth as a base. While this is much better than a cream base soup, you can do even better with a vegetarian broth. You can then add some "zing" by using onions or garlic or pepper, or your favorite herbs and spices. Try it with the soup recipes you'll find here. Make sure they taste exactly the way you want them, so you can enjoy eating more in order to weigh less.

If you can't find the "chicken" powder, use a brand of canned vegetarian broth. These convenient, low-fat products are found in health food stores or the soup section of almost any supermarket.

You can also use a seaweed, such as konbu, as a base for your soup. Simply soak the seaweed, boil it in water, and use the water as soup stock.

Another option is to save the broth from the steamer when you steam vegetables. Freeze it in ice trays or other small containers so you can defrost only as much as you want for any given soup base.

Making soups vegetarian and low fat can be easy, if you learn the simple secrets I'm sharing with you here.

WHAT YOU CAN DO:

- Use vegetarian chicken powder for soups.

- Try seaweed broth.

- Use canned vegetarian broth.

- Make your own vegetarian broth with the following recipe.

Chickenless Bouillon

1-1/2 C	Nutritional yeast flakes
3 Tbsp.	Onion powder
2-1/2 tsp.	Garlic powder
1 Tbsp.	Salt
1 tsp.	Celery seed
2-1/2 Tbsp.	Italian seasoning
2 Tbsp.	Dried parsley

Put all the ingredients, except parsley in a blender and make a fine powder. Stir in parsley. Store in an airtight container. Use about one tablespoon per cup of water. Makes 32 portions. *(1 portion = 20.08 calories, 0.085 grams fat, 43% protein, 53% carbohydrates, 3% fat)*

▽ Nutritional yeast is not the same as yeast used for baking bread. It can be purchased at the health food store. This is a good veggie broth that can be used as a soup stock, or to flavor rice. It has a lot less salt than commercially made veggie broth. ▽

Mushroom-Broccoli Noodle Soup

1 med.	Onion, cut into thin crescents
2 oz.	Dried mushrooms, soaked and sliced
1 med.	Broccoli bunch, stem cut in quarter rounds and florets cut into 2" pieces
1 can	Water chestnuts *(8 oz., 5 oz. drained)*, sliced
6 C	Water, boiling
2 C	Vegetable broth
1/4 tsp.	Sea salt
2 C	Soba noodles
2 Tbsp.	Sesame seeds, lightly toasted
2-3 Tbsp.	Low-sodium soy sauce or tamari

In a skillet, water sauté onions until transparent. If they begin to stick, add more water, as necessary.

Add broccoli stems, sauté briefly, then add mushrooms, water chestnuts, boiling water, vegetable broth, and sea salt. Cover and bring to a boil, then lower heat and simmer for 10 minutes.

Add noodles and simmer for a few minutes, until tender. Add broccoli florets, cook until bright green *(about 1 minute)*. Sprinkle sesame seeds onto soup broth. Add soy sauce. Stir and heat, without boiling, until done to taste. Makes 10 portions. *(1 portion = 78.3 calories, 1.1 grams fat, 20% protein, 68% carbohydrates, 12% fat)*

Eat More, Weigh Less™ Tip
Zapf It! \33/ *Save 12 gm. fat!*

Make Creamy Soup Without Cream

WOULD YOU BELIEVE: Cream of mushroom soup has 13 grams of fat per cup which makes up 59% of its calories. Cream of chicken soup can be as high a 194 calories and 13.6 grams of fat per cup and 63% fat from calories. *(Chicken noodle soup is 66 calories and 2.2 grams per cup.)*

SOME FACTS: Cream soups are deceptively high in fat content. The problem comes with the cream in the soup base. The good news is, there's a way to get that same creamy texture by using high EMI substitutes for the cream.

First, use potatoes, corn, frozen peas, lima beans, or puréed rice to make the soup stock creamier. To make it even creamier, take a portion of the soup and put it through a blender. Another way is to add miso. Just add and blend it in. You can also thicken the broth by using corn starch or arrowroot. Flour can also be added to make it a little heavier in texture.

WHAT YOU CAN DO: Try the following cream-less recipes for some delicious low-fat, high EMI soups, then experiment with your own ideas.

Potato and Corn Chowder

2 tsp.	Dry cooking sherry
1-1/4 C	Sweet yellow onion, finely chopped
2 cloves	Garlic, crushed
2 C	Red potatoes, cubed
1 can	Vegetable stock *(14-1/4 oz.)*
1 C	Soy milk
1 C	Corn kernels, fresh or frozen
1	Bay leaf
1/4 tsp.	Paprika
1/4 tsp.	Thyme
1 tsp.	Basil
	Salt, to taste
	Pepper, to taste
	Olive oil cooking spray

Add wine to a large oil-sprayed skillet and heat. Add onions and garlic and sauté for 5 minutes, stirring frequently to prevent browning. Add water as needed.

Add potatoes, bay leaf, herbs, and stock to sautéed onions and garlic. Cover pan, bring to a boil, and cook over medium heat for 10 to 15 minutes.

When the potatoes are tender, add the corn and milk. Simmer until the corn is tender, about 3 minutes. Discard the bay leaf.

Use your hand blender to partially puree the mixture, or remove a cup of soup and puree in blender or food processor, then return it to the pot. This will give

(continued next page)

Potato and Corn Chowder (continued)

your soup a creamy texture. Season with salt and/or pepper to taste. Makes 6 to 8 portions. *(1 portion = 113.4 calories, 1.0 grams fat, 15% protein, 78% carbohydrates, 7% fat)*

This and other cream soups are a snap to make if you have a hand blender. With this, you can partially blend the soup right in the pot. Just wait until it's almost done then do your blending, leaving enough chunky ingredients to give the soup texture. Watch out for spattering though, if it's really hot. Try the three following simple recipes to see how this is done.

Cream of Broccoli Soup

5 C	Vegetable broth
1-1/2 C	Broccoli, both tops and stems, but separated, chopped
1 small	Yellow onion, diced
1-1/2 C	Brown rice, cooked or leftover oatmeal
1 Tbsp.	White or barley miso

Boil broth or water, add broccoli stems and onion. Cover and simmer for 10 minutes.

Put 2 cups of the soup liquid in the blender with rice or oatmeal, blend until smooth, then return to the pot.

Add broccoli tops and simmer briefly, until they're tender. Flavor with miso to taste and serve. Makes 6 to 8 portions. *(1 portion = 86.9 calories, 0.8 grams fat, 21% protein, 71% carbohydrates, 7% fat)*

Creamy Zucchini Soup

2 med.	Onions, sliced
2	Crook-neck squash
2	Zucchini, sliced *(about 3 cups not peeled)*
6 C	Vegetable stock or "chicken" stock
1/4 C	Green onion, chopped
2 C	Lima beans *(one 10 oz. package, frozen)*
1/4 C	Corn, frozen
1 C	Peas *(1/2 of 10 oz. package, frozen)*
1 Tbsp.	Low-sodium soy sauce, or to taste
	Pepper, to taste

Place onions and zucchini in a 4-quart saucepan. Add the stock and bring to a boil. Add the other vegetables.

Bring the mixture to a boil again, reduce heat and simmer for about 1/2 hour, or until the vegetables are soft. Add soy sauce and pepper.

Purée mixture, reheat, then serve. Makes 10 to 12 portions. *(1 portion = 91.1 calories, 0.5 grams fat, 25% protein, 70% carbohydrates, 5% fat)*

Cream of Potato

4 med.	**Potatoes, peeled and cut into large chunks**
6 C	**Water**
	Sea salt, to taste
5	**Green onions, with stalks, chopped fine**
1/4 C	**Onion, chopped**
1/8 C	**Whole wheat flour** *(optional)*

Boil the potatoes with onion and salt, until they're cooked through and getting very soft.

Use your hand blender *(carefully, don't let it spatter)* to blend the soup into a creamy texture. Leave enough lumps to give the soup good texture.

Add chopped green onion to the top and cook briefly, then serve, garnished with more chopped green onion tops. Makes 6 to 8 portions. *(1 portion = 80.8 calories, 0.1 grams fat, 9% protein, 90% carbohydrates, 1% fat)*

▽ For a thicker variation, add a few tablespoons of whole wheat flour near the end of the cooking process, but remember to use just a little or you'll have a gravy instead of a soup. ▽

Eat More, Weigh Less™ Tip
Zing/Zip It! △34▽

Zip Delicious Soup

WOULD YOU BELIEVE: One of the best tasting soups is almost an "instant" soup.

SOME FACTS: If basmati is the King of Rice, miso is the Queen of Soups. In fact, the two can make a perfect match in a variety of menus.

Miso is made from fermented soybean paste. It is a traditional Japanese soup base that has served Asian chefs well for centuries. Deliciously robust, highly nutritious, this soup stock is simple and easy to prepare. The trick is to find a good source of miso. Today, miso is quite common in health food stores. You can even find various types of miso in Oriental food stores. It may be a little more difficult to get miso in a supermarket, unless it has an Oriental food section, but if you ask the manager, often he'll get it for you. More and more people are becoming enchanted with Asian foods.

QUICK, BUT NOT INSTANT: To make basic miso soup *(Zip Miso Soup)*, boil water and just before serving dissolve some miso in it, as described below. Make sure it is blended smoothly to get the lumps out. Garnish it with some chopped green onions or seaweed, and it's ready to serve.

For one variety of miso soup, simply prepare some of your favorite vegetables in water. Just before you serve them, dissolve the miso into the hot water, and you've created a delicious miso-based soup. Miso is very high in protein and is a great substitute for any animal product-based soup. It is also quite high in sodium. However, this can be controlled by the amount of miso you use, per cup of hot water.

WHAT YOU CAN DO:

- Try "Zip Miso Soup" with bread or rice as a quick snack.

- Try miso soup for breakfast or with dinner.

- Try the following miso recipes for a variation that will satisfy your appetite for something special.

Breakfast Miso Soup

2-1/2 C	Water
1	Wakame seaweed *(3" strip)*
1/8 C	Firm tofu, chopped to 1/2" chunks
1	Green onion, with stems, chopped fine
1 Tbsp.	Barley miso

Bring water to a boil, add wakame and one-half of green onion, simmer 5 minutes.

Turn off heat, add miso to taste by diluting 1 to 2 tablespoons of miso in a ladle full of the soup water, mashing and smoothing out the miso and adding it back to the pot.

Pour into a large bowl, over small chunks of tofu. Garnish with chopped green onions, serve steaming hot. Makes 4 to 6 portions. *(1 portion = 18.1 calories, 0.8 grams fat, 30% protein, 34% carbohydrates, 35% fat)*

Wakame Onion Mushroom Soup

1 handful	Wakame
1	Onion, diced
4 C	Water from soaking the wakame
1-2 Tbsp.	Miso
2	Shiitake mushrooms, dried

Soak wakame and mushrooms in 1 cup of water until soft, cut into 1" pieces.

Sauté onions in 1/4 cup of water. Add water from soaked wakame and mushrooms and the rest of the water. Bring to a boil, add the wakame and mushrooms, and cook over low flame until it is tender.

Add miso to taste by diluting 1 to 2 tablespoons of miso in a ladle full of the soup water, mashing and smoothing out the miso and adding it back to the pot. Leftover grain or noodles may be added if desired. Makes 6 portions. *(1 portion = 23 calories, 0.3 grams fat, 16% protein, 73% carbohydrates, 12% fat)*

Variations:

Other variations on this soup would include adding onions, cauliflower, shiitake mushrooms, celery, tofu chunks, etc., to wakame broth. You can also add medium grain brown rice, or barley, or use miso soup as a broth to pour over your whole grains.

▽ One delicious breakfast treat is cream of buckwheat cereal with a tablespoon of miso mixed in. It's wholesome, hot, and delicious. ▽

More Special Soup Recipes

Portuguese Bean Soup

6 cloves	Garlic, crushed
1-1/2	Round onions, chopped
2 stalks	Celery, chopped
4	Carrots, diced
1 can	Vegetable broth *(14-1/2 oz.)*
2 cans	Whole tomatoes plus juice *(large)*, cut in chunks
3	Potatoes, cubed
3 C	Beans, cooked
1/2 head	Cabbage, chopped
1 C	Cooked macaroni

Sauté garlic and onions in 2 cups water until transparent. Add celery and carrots. Continue cooking 5 minutes. Add tomatoes and vegetable broth. Add 2 cups more water to mixture. Cook 15 minutes, then add remainder of ingredients, except beans and macaroni. Continue to cook 30 minutes on warm, after bringing to a boil. Add beans and simmer on warm for 30 minutes, until done to taste. Add cooked macaroni a few minutes before serving. Makes 8 portions. *(1 portion = 215.7 calories, 1.0 grams fat, 19% protein, 77% carbohydrates, 4% fat)*

Vegetable Barley Soup

3 C	Vegetable broth
2 cans	Tomato sauce
2 large	Carrots, sliced
1 med.	Onion chopped
2 stalks	Celery
1-2	Bay leaves
1 clove	Garlic, chopped
1/2 C	Barley

Combine all ingredients in a large pot. Bring to a boil, cover, reduce heat and simmer 1 hour. Remove bay leaves and serve. Makes 6 portions. *(1 portion = 118.0 calories, 0.7 grams fat, 18% protein, 77% carbohydrates, 5% fat)*

Potato Bean Barley Soup

1/2 C	Celery, sliced
2 med.	Carrots, thinly sliced
1 clove	Garlic
1 med.	Onion, chopped
5 C	Vegetable broth
3 med.	Potatoes, peeled and cut up
2 Tbsp.	Fresh dill
1	Bay leaf
1 can	Great northern beans *(15 oz.)*, drained
	Sea salt, to taste
	Pepper, to taste
1 C	Barley, cooked

Sauté first four ingredients in large saucepan with part of the broth *(about 4 minutes)*. Stir in broth, potatoes, dill, bay leaf. Bring to a boil, reduce heat. Simmer covered until potatoes are tender. Add drained beans and cooked barley. Heat and serve. If too thick, add water or more broth. Makes 8 to 10 portions. *(1 portion = 148.7 calories, 0.5 grams fat, 20% protein, 77% carbohydrates, 3% fat)*

Lentil Leek Soup

2 C	Lentils
2 qts.	Vegetable broth
1 small	Sweet yellow onion, chopped fine
2	Carrots, chopped fine
2 C	Mushrooms, sliced
2 med.	Potatoes, diced
3	Leeks, washed and chopped fine
3	Tomatoes, diced
1 C	Kale, chopped
2 cloves	Garlic, minced
1 tsp.	Dried basil
1/8 C	Sherry

Wash lentils, soak in cold water for 1 hour, then drain. Cook the lentils in vegetable broth in a soup pot, about 45 minutes.

During that time, simmer the onions, carrots, mushrooms, potatoes, and leeks in 1/4 cup of water.

Add remaining ingredients except tomatoes to the onion, carrot mixture in soup pot. Cook for 20 more minutes.

Add the tomatoes and drained lentils and simmer for 20 more minutes, or until lentils are tender.

Purée with your hand blender or leave chunky. Garnish with parsley. Serve hot. Makes 8 portions.

(1 portion = 289.2 calories, 0.8 grams fat, 22% protein, 74% carbohydrates, 2% fat)

Mulligatawny Soup

1/2 C	Brown rice, cooked
1/2 C	Red lentils, cooked
1 med.	Carrot, diced
1 med.	Onion, finely chopped
1 stalk	Celery, diced
1	Potato, diced
3 C	Vegetable broth
2 Tbsp.	Lemon juice
2 cloves	Garlic, minced
1/2 C	Water
1/2 tsp.	Dry mustard
1/2 tsp.	Fenugreek seed, ground
1 tsp.	Turmeric, ground
1 tsp.	Cumin, ground
1/2 tsp.	Coriander seed, ground
1/2 tsp.	Black pepper
	Sea salt, to taste *(optional)*

Sauté garlic and onion in small amount of water, until soft. Add spices and continue to cook for 3 to 5 minutes more. In a large pot, heat the broth, combine the remaining ingredients and simmer for 15 minutes. Salt to taste. Makes 6 portions. *(1 portion = 98.3 calories, 0.6 grams fat, 20% protein, 75% carbohydrates, 6% fat)*

Peking Hot and Sour Soup

2 tsp.	Corn starch
2 Tbsp.	Cider vinegar
1 can	Vegetable broth with 1-1/2 cup water
1 Tbsp.	Low-sodium soy sauce
1/2 C	Water
1/2 tsp.	Sea salt
1/4 C	Dried wood ears *(black fungus)*
1/4 C	Dried golden needles *(dried lily flowers)*
1/4 C	Tofu, cubed *(about 1/2 small cake)*
1/4 tsp.	White ground pepper
1 Tbsp.	Scallions, minced *(for garnishing)*

Boil water and soak wood ears and golden needles separately for about 15 minutes.

Break off hard pieces from wood ears and hard stems from golden needles, if any. Cut golden needles in halves and snap the large pieces of wood ears into smaller pieces. Wash and drain.

Mix the corn starch with 1/2 cup cold water. Stir until smooth.

Mix vinegar and pepper.

Mix vegetable broth and water. Add salt and soy sauce. Bring to a boil and add wood ears and golden needles. Boil 1 minute. Add tofu.

As soup boils, stir in the well-stirred corn starch mixture until it thickens.

(continued next page)

Peking Hot and Sour Soup (continued)

Serve in bowl with vinegar and pepper. Garnish with scallions. Serve Hot. Makes 4 to 6 portions. *(1 portion = 46.9 calories, 1.2 grams fat, 30% protein, 48% carbohydrates, 21% fat)*

Special Salads

Salads and Dressings

Salads are super high on the EMI scale. They're one of the easiest and tastiest ways to eat your high-EMI foods. However, there is one key problem. Most people ruin their salads before they take their first bite by dousing them with oily, high-fat salad dressings. Oily salad dressings are the lowest in EMI of all foods. They'll instantly ruin the weight-loss value of a salad. The trick is to use salad dressings that are medium to high in EMI and contain little or no oil. You'll learn how in the section below on salad dressings.

You can also try different types of salads that don't rely quite so heavily on the dressing. There are any number of varieties: corn salads, beet salads, three-bean salads and others that will delight your taste buds without tempting you to resort to high-fat dressings. Some of the cold noodle dishes also adapt well to salad recipes. Or you can modify the following to create your own.

Fennel Bulgur Salad (Tabouleh)

1 C	Bulgur wheat
2 C	Water, boiling
1 C	Parsley, coarsely chopped
1/4	Fennel bulb, minced
2	Green onions, chopped
1	Tomato, diced
1	Celery stalk, chopped fine
1/4 C	Olives, green or black, sliced
1/4 C	Mint leaves, minced
1/4 C	Lemon juice
1/2 tsp.	Salt
1/2 tsp.	Pepper, freshly ground
	Lettuce leaves, crisp

Place bulgur in a bowl, add boiling water to cover. Let stand 30 to 60 minutes, until wheat is soft, then drain through a sieve, pressing out any excess water.

Mix all remaining ingredients together, then fold into the bulgur, mixing thoroughly.

Whisk together lemon juice, olive oil, salt, and pepper. Use to dress the salad, then toss well.

Line a platter with lettuce leaves, mound salad mixture in center. Garnish with several sprigs of fresh mint and lemon wedges. Makes 6 portions. *(1 portion = 107.7 calories, 1.7 grams fat, 13% protein, 73% carbohydrates, 13% fat)*

Garden Salad

1 head	Romaine lettuce
4	Cherry tomatoes
2 sprigs	Parsley
1	Cucumber, halved and thinly sliced
2 stalks	Celery, cubed small
1/2 C	Purple cabbage, shredded
1/2 C	Alfalfa sprouts

Wash ingredients and place on cutting board to pat dry, or add to salad spinner that draws off moisture. Toss or spin salad, then arrange on a platter or in a bowl, keeping each ingredient separate. Toss in a bowl or arrange ingredients separately on a platter. Serve with your favorite dressing. Makes 4 to 6 portions. *(1 portion = 29.8 calories, 0.4 grams fat, 24% protein, 67% carbohydrates, 9% fat)*

Eat More, Weigh Less™ Tip

Zapf It! \35/ *Save 21 gm. fat!*

Use No-Oil Salad Dressings

WOULD YOU BELIEVE: Most salad dressings are somewhere between 85% to 99% fat and contain up to 21 grams of fat per 3-tablespoon portion.

SOME FACTS: We often find ourselves eating salads in order to avoid fat, yet defeating ourselves by pouring a helping of fat onto the salad in the form of dressing. The solution is to lose the fat but keep the flavor by switching to fat-free dressings. Fortunately, there are many varieties to choose from. Choose wisely.

Here are some dressing comparisons:

1 Tbsp. Regular French	1 Tbsp. Fat-Free French
60 Calories 6 Grams Fat 87% Fat	20 Calories 0 Grams Fat 0% Fat

1 Tbsp. Regular Italian	1 Tbsp. Fat-Free Italian
63 Calories 7 Grams Fat 94% Fat	6 Calories 0 Grams Fat 0% Fat

1 Tbsp. Regular Thousand Island	1 Tbsp. Fat-Free Thousand Island
59 Calories 5.6 Grams Fat 86% Fat	20 Calories 0 Grams Fat 0% Fat

1 Tbsp. Regular Ranch	1 Tbsp. Fat-Free Ranch
54 Calories 5.7 Grams Fat 93% Fat	16 Calories 0 Grams Fat 0% Fat

You can see from this that switching to the fat-free dressing will save you approximately 40 calories and 6 grams of fat per tablespoon, and the dressing should be just as tasty. Most people use between 3 to 5 tablespoons of dressing per salad, so those fat grams and calories really add up. On the average, with just one salad, you will cut down on fat by as much as 18 to 30 grams simply by switching to a fat-free dressing. Don't be shy about taking it with you when you eat out. The trick is to have it available whenever you're ready to eat.

WHAT YOU CAN DO:

- Buy fat-free dressings and take them with you to restaurants.

- Remove the oil from your dressings and rely on other flavors such as vinegar, herbs, spices, lemon juice, mustard, and even fruit to add "zing" to your salads.

- Try the following dressings.

Pineapple-Ginger Dressing

1 C	Rice vinegar
1/4	Pineapple, finely chopped
1/8 C	Soy sauce or tamari
1 clove	Garlic *(medium)*, crushed
2 Tbsp.	Maple syrup or barley malt
1 med.	Tomato, diced
1/2	Yellow bell pepper, diced
1/2	Red onion, finely diced
	White pepper, to taste
1 Tbsp.	Fresh tarragon, finely chopped
1 Tbsp.	Ginger, grated

Combine all ingredients together and chill overnight, if possible. Makes 25 portions *(about 4+ cups)*. *(1 portion = 14.5 calories, 0.1 grams fat, 8% protein, 88% carbohydrates, 4% fat)*

Thousand Island Dressing

1/4 C	Water
1/8 tsp.	Salt
1/8 tsp.	Pepper
1 tsp.	Seasoned salt
2 Tbsp.	Tomato ketchup
1 C	Soft tofu, crumbled
4 sprigs	Fresh parsley *(optional)*
1 Tbsp.	Cucumber, chopped fine
1 Tbsp.	Celery, chopped fine

Whiz all ingredients except cucumber and celery in blender. Add cucumber and celery. Chill and serve. Makes 12 portions *(about 1-1/2 cups)*. *(1 portion = 14.1 calories, 0.6 grams fat, 28% protein, 35% carbohydrates, 37% fat)*

Oriental Salad Dressing

1/3 C	Water
1/3 C	Shoyu
1/3 C	Rice wine vinegar
1/2 tsp.	Sesame oil
1/4	Lemon, juice only
1/4 tsp.	Ginger, minced
1/4 tsp.	Round onion, minced
2 tsp.	Honey
1 clove	Garlic, minced

Combine ingredients and refrigerate. Makes 12 portions *(about 1+ cups)*. *(1 portion = 14.9 calories, 0.3 grams fat, 14% protein, 72% carbohydrates, 14% fat)*

Optional: A pinch of crushed red chili flakes. A little of this fiery spice goes a long way, so use very sparingly.

Eat More, Weigh Less™ Tip
Zing/Zapf It! 　　　36

A Nonfat Salad Enhancer

One of the best ways to add some zing to your salad dressings and other foods without adding fat is to use a vinegar or vinegar-based salad dressing or vegetable marinade. There are many kinds of vinegars, but my favorite for salads is a brownish, full-bodied vinegar known as balsamic.

Balsamic vinegar is made from white Trebbiano grapes, found in northern Italy. It costs a little more than most vinegars, but it's worth the price. It has a mild flavor, with a hint of sweetness yet a touch of tartness. Most of all, it doesn't have that "fermented" taste and aroma that makes some vinegars unpleasant. You can usually find it in your gourmet markets, supermarkets, or your local health food store. You can dress it up a little by mixing several tablespoons with a crushed clove of garlic and a couple of tablespoons of lemon juice. Drizzle this or the plain vinegar over your salads or use it in a dressing recipe, and get ready for an aromatic treat.

Dijon Vinaigrette

1/2 cup	Balsamic vinegar
2 Tbsp.	Dijon mustard
2 Tbsp.	Soy sauce
2 Tbsp.	Maple syrup

Blend on high in a blender until smooth or place ingredients in a small bowl and whisk together. Let sit for at least 15 minutes to allow flavors to meld. Toss with your favorite green salad or pasta salad. Makes 7 portions. *(1 portion = 38.9 calories, 0.3 grams fat, 6% protein, 88% carbohydrates, 7% fat)*

White Wine 'n Spice Dressing

2/3 C	Water
4-1/2 Tbsp.	White wine vinegar
1 tsp.	Canola oil
2-3 cloves	Garlic, minced
1 tsp.	Round onion, minced
4 tsp.	Dijon mustard
1/4 tsp.	Thyme
1/2 tsp.	Salt
1/4 tsp.	Pepper
2 tsp.	Honey

Combine all ingredients and store in container. Refrigerate. Makes 8 portions *(about 1 cup)*. *(1 portion = 15 calories, 0.7 grams fat, 6% protein, 52% carbohydrates, 42% fat)*

Papaya Seed Dressing

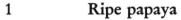

1	Ripe papaya
1/3	Papaya seeds of 1 papaya
1 Tbsp.	Dijon mustard
2-3 Tbsp.	Balsamic or red wine vinegar
1 Tbsp.	Soy sauce

Slice one ripe papaya, discarding all but 1/3 of the seeds. Scoop out flesh of the papaya and put into blender. Add in the rest of the ingredients and blend on high until smooth. Makes 10 portions *(about 1+ cups)*.
(1 portion = 24.9 calories, 0.2 grams fat, 7% protein, 87% carbohydrates, 6% fat)

California Sunshine Dressing

2	Oranges, juice only *(12 oz.)*
2 cloves	Garlic
4 Tbsp.	Soy sauce

Combine all of the ingredients in a blender and blend on high until smooth. Makes 8 portions *(about 1 cup)*.
(1 portion = 24.7 calories, 0.1 grams fat, 13% protein, 84% carbohydrates, 3% fat)

Other Delicious Salads

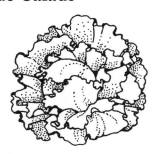

Sunset Salad

1 can	Red kidney beans *(medium)*, drained
1 can	Green beans *(medium)*, drained
1/4 C	Yellow bell peppers, chunked
1/4 C	Red bell pepper, chunked
6 oz.	Red cabbage, shredded
6 oz.	Green cabbage, shredded
1 can	Crushed pineapple *(small)*, with juice
	Salt, to taste
	Black pepper, freshly ground
1 small	Radicchio or other red-leaf lettuce
1 small	Red onion, sliced

Combine both red and green beans, all peppers, shredded cabbage and pineapple in a bowl.

Dress to taste, using the low-fat salad dressings. Salt and pepper to taste. Toss well and serve on bed of radicchio or red-leaf lettuce, rinsed and prepared just before serving. Top with red onion slices. Makes 6 portions. *(1 portion = 113.2 calories, 0.3 grams fat, 20% protein, 78% carbohydrates, 3% fat)*

Three-Bean Carrot Salad

1 C	Red beans
1 C	Black beans
1 C	Fresh green beans, lightly steamed
1 C	Carrots, cut into thin strips
1 small	Onion, finely chopped
1 clove	Garlic, crushed
1 Tbsp.	Cider vinegar
1 tsp.	Honey
	Salt, to taste
	Black pepper, finely ground

Mix the vegetables and canned beans together in a large bowl. Mix the onion, garlic, vinegar and honey, salt and pepper to taste. Pour dressing onto the beans and vegetables and mix thoroughly. Makes 4 to 6 portions. *(1 portion = 125.1 calories, 0.5 grams fat, 21% protein, 76% carbohydrates, 4% fat)*

Exciting Entrées and Side Dishes

Now that we have the soups and salads taken care of, let's take a look at some wonderful vegetable entrées and side dishes, and the *Eat More, Weigh Less™* Tips that make them fast, easy and tasty.

Eat More, Weigh Less™ Tip
Zapf It! $\overline{\underline{37}}$ *Save 8 gm. fat!*

Sauté Without Oil

WOULD YOU BELIEVE: A one-cup serving of vegetables sautéed in oil can be as high as 8.4 grams of fat per cup or 42% fat by calories.

SOME FACTS: Usually, people sauté their vegetables in oil. *(This is also called frying.)* Unfortunately, sautéing with oil causes the fat to seep into the vegetables, and your High EMI dish slides all the way down to the low end of the EMI scale.

Frying in oil is never necessary. It always adds calories to any meal. A better solution is to learn how to cook without oil. One way is to use a nonstick skillet and simply sauté your foods in water. The small amount of water keeps the vegetables from sticking to the pan and will cook the vegetables nicely.

If you want to add some flavor, simply sauté in vegetable broth. You can use a vegetarian powder to mix with water, or simply use a low-fat canned vegetable broth, which can be found in any supermarket.

Another flavorful sauté sauce is wine or sherry. Cooking wines are delicious and you can experiment with other wines as well.

One way to make foods especially tasty is to sauté onions and/or garlic in vegetable broth first until they are slightly translucent and then add other vegetables to complete the sautéing process. In this way, you can get a delicious vegetable stir-fry without adding oil. You've already been using this method in some of the preceding recipes.

WHAT YOU CAN DO: Now try the following to see how delicious a vegetable stir-fry can be.

Vegetable Stir Fry

1 can	Mushrooms or 1/4 cup dry shiitake mushrooms, soaked and sliced
1 med.	Carrot, sliced diagonally
2 stalks	Broccoli, sliced diagonally
2 stalks	Celery, sliced diagonally
1-1/2	Round onion, sliced into thin crescents
1 piece	Ginger, crushed
1 clove	Garlic, crushed
1-1/2 Tbsp.	Corn starch
1/4 C	Water

Seasoning:

1 Tbsp.	Oyster sauce *(vegetarian)*
1 tsp.	Soy sauce
1 C	Stock

Heat pan. Sauté ginger, garlic, and onion in water, remove from pan. Add seasonings and cook 2 minutes. Add stock, mushrooms, carrot, broccoli, and celery and cook until vegetables are crisp and tender. Make a paste with corn starch and water to thicken the gravy. Makes 4 to 6 portions. *(1 portion = 59.4 calories, 0.3 grams fat, 19% protein, 77% carbohydrates, 5% fat)*

Eat More, Weigh Less™ Tip
Zapf It! $\triangledown$38   *Save 11 gm. fat!*

"Elipidate™" Your Stew

WOULD YOU BELIEVE: Beef stew can be up to 12 grams of fat per cup or 49% fat *(by calories)*. *(Armour® Star brand)*

SOME FACTS: Beef stews *(with vegetables)* are high in fat because beef is in general high in fat. An average cut of beef is 65% to 75% fat *(by calories)* and in the stewing process, much of the fat melts and permeates the sauce and vegetables with fat. The result is a high fat dish. The same holds true for beef curry with vegetables. By sharp contrast, a vegetable stew such as a French dish called ratatouille is about 5% fat *(by calories)*. If you like the taste of stew, you don't really need the beef.

WHAT YOU CAN DO:
- Elipidate™ your stew primarily by removing the beef.
- Try the Ratatouille recipe in the original *Eat More Weigh Less™ Diet* Book.
- Try the following beefless stew recipe and curry recipe.

Hawaiian Savory Stew

3 Tbsp.	Water
1 large	Onion, chopped
2 cloves	Garlic, minced
1 piece	Ginger *(1")*, mashed
1 box	Seitan *(wheat gluten)*, cut in 1" pieces or 1 C mushrooms
1 Tbsp.	Soy sauce
2 large	Carrots, cut in 1" chunks
2 stalks	Celery, cut in 1" chunks
3	Red potatoes, quartered
1 can	Tomatoes, whole packed
3	Bay leaves
2 C	Vegetable broth
	Water, to cover
	Salt, to taste
	Pepper, to taste
2 Tbsp.	Whole wheat flour dissolved in 4 Tbsp. water

Sauté onion and garlic in 3 tablespoons of water in a large pot. Add seitan, ginger, soy sauce, carrots, celery, potatoes, tomatoes, vegetable broth, water to cover, salt, pepper, and bay leaves. Cook until vegetables are tender. Thicken with whole wheat flour dissolved in 4 tablespoons of water. Serve hot. Zing it with a few drops of Tabasco sauce. Makes 6 to 8 portions. *(1 portion = 256.1 calories, 1.2 grams fat, 32% protein, 64% carbohydrates, 4% fat)*

Local Style Curry Stew

3 Tbsp.	Water
1 lg.	Onion, chopped
2 cloves	Garlic, minced
1 piece	Ginger *(1")*, mashed
1-2 tsp.	Soy sauce
1 tsp.	Honey
1-3 Tbsp.	Curry powder
2 lg.	Carrots, cut in 1" chunks
2 stalks	Celery, cut in 1" chunks
3	Red potatoes, quartered
3 C	Cauliflower florets
1/2 C	Lima beans, frozen
2 C	Vegetable broth
	Water, to cover
	Salt, to taste
1 Tbsp.	Corn starch or arrowroot dissolved in 1 tablespoon water

Sauté onion and garlic in 3 tablespoons of water in stainless steel saucepan. Add ginger, soy sauce, honey, curry powder, carrots, celery, potatoes, cauliflower, lima beans, vegetable broth, water to cover, and salt to taste. Cook for 20 minutes or until carrots become tender. Then thicken with corn starch or arrowroot mixture. Makes 6 portions. *(1 portion = 118.5 calories, 0.6 grams fat, 15% protein, 81% carbohydrates, 4% fat)*

Cajun Jambalaya

Jambalaya is a Cajun stew. Cajun cuisine is noted for its hot and spicy bayou flavors. This is a quick, vegetarian version of a favorite bayou dish. If you prefer your foods less spicy, remember that you are always encouraged to adjust these recipes for your own, personal taste.

1 large	Red onion, chopped
1 med.	Yam, peeled and cubed
1	Green bell pepper, chopped
1	Red bell pepper, chopped
1 C	Frozen corn
1/2 C	Celery, chopped
1	Bay leaf
3 cloves	Garlic, minced
2 cans	Tomatoes, chopped *(with peppers)*, including liquid *(14-1/2 oz.)*
1 C	Brown rice, precooked
1 tsp.	Dried basil, crushed
1 tsp.	Black pepper
1/4 tsp.	Salt
1/4 tsp.	Ground red pepper
1 Tbsp.	Tabasco sauce
	Canola oil cooking spray

(continued next page)

Cajun Jambalaya (continued)

Sauté all vegetables in a large nonstick skillet, beginning with the onions and garlic, then adding others. Cook until tender, adding oil as needed to keep the vegetables from sticking. The cooking time will vary, depending on how small you cut your vegetables. To speed up the cooking time, dice vegetables; then it will take about 10 minutes. Next, stir in tomatoes with liquid, add rice, and all spices. Bring to a boil then reduce heat, cover, and simmer until foods are well blended. Serve as you would a stew. Makes 9 portions. *(1 portion = 116.9 calories, 0.6 grams fat, 10% protein, 86% carbohydrates, 4% fat)*

Eat More, Weigh Less™ Tip
Zapf It!　　　　⬛39⬛　*Saves 58 grms. fat!*

Turn the Worst Salad Entrée Into One of the Best

WOULD YOU BELIEVE: One of the highest fat fast foods has the word "salad" in it?

SOME FACTS: Of all the items on the regular menu of the best known fast food restaurants, one of the worst item in terms of fat content is surprisingly the Taco Salad from Taco Bell®. It contains a stunning 905 calories and 61 grams of fat![25] Where does all that fat come from? To start with, any taco usually has a fried "shell." In this example, the giant shell has 30 grams of fat *(most regular sized taco shells are much smaller and have about 3 to 5 grams of fat)*. Here are the fat contents of other items that make up taco salads.

Item	% Fat *(by calories)*	Gram Fat/ Ounce
Ground Beef	68%	6.40
Cheese *(chedder)*	74%	9.30
Sour Cream	86%	5.90
Guacamole	69%	3.80
Refried Beans	44%	1.10
Salsa	8%	0.05
Lettuce	12%	0.05
Alternates		
No-fat Refried Beans	4%	0.10
Baked Tostito® Chips	4%	1.00

As you can see, you can make a very low fat taco salad by using Baked Tostito® chips, no-fat refried beans, greens, and some zesty salsa. One trick to making zesty Mexican food is in using fresh salsa with cilantro. Then you can turn one of the highest fat dishes into one of the lowest.

What You Can Do:

- Try the taco salad recipe that follows.

- Add some zing by adding fresh chopped cilantro and using fresh chopped tomatoes, onions, and chili peppers.

Zip Taco Salad

1 can	No-fat refried beans *(16 oz.)*
3-4 C	Lettuce, chopped
1-2	Tomato, chopped
2 Tbsp.	Cilantro, chopped
2 Tbsp.	Onion, chopped
1/2 C	Salsa *(recipe on page 332)*
4 oz.	Baked Tostito® chips

Warm refried beans in small saucepan. Lay Baked Tostito® chips on plates, add beans and other ingredients, and top with fresh salsa. Put a few chips on the side and serve. Makes 4 portions. *(1 portion = 335 calories, 2.7 grams fat, 7.2% fat)*

A Garden of Vegetable Recipes

Crispy Onion Rings

2 large	Sweet onions
1 pkg.	Corn flakes cereal *(7 oz)*, crushed
2 tsp.	Honey
1 tsp.	Paprika
1 tsp.	Seasoned salt *(or a pinch of seasonings, garlic powder, and 3/4 teaspoon salt)*
1 C	Powdered egg substitute *(in 2 cups of water)* Vegetable oil cooking spray

Cut each onion into 4 thick slices; separate into rings, reserving small rings for other uses. Set aside.

Combine cereal, honey, paprika, and salt; divide in half, and set aside.

Beat egg substitute at high speed with an electric or hand mixer until soft peaks form. Divide onion, egg whip, and cereal into two portions. Dip one portion of the onion rings in egg substitute foam, then dredge in crumb mixture. Place in a single layer on nonstick baking sheets or lightly coat regular baking sheets with cooking spray.

Repeat procedure with other portion of onion rings, egg foam, and crumb mixture. Bake at 375° F. for 15 minutes, or until crisp; serve warm. These do not save well; eat 'em now or forget 'em. Makes 4 portions.

(1 portion = 254.0 calories, 0.5 grams fat, 50.6 grams carbohydrates, 10.8 grams protein) [2% fat by calories]

Spicy Tofu With Cabbage

16 oz.	Firm tofu
2 lbs.	Won bok, bok choy, or choy sum

Sauce:

1 med.	Onion, minced
2 cloves	Garlic, minced
1 C	Vegetable broth
2 tsp.	Red peppers, crushed
2 Tbsp.	Tamari or low-sodium soy sauce
1 tsp.	Sesame oil
1 tsp.	Maple syrup
1 Tbsp.	Corn starch mixed with 2 Tbsp. water
	Sesame seeds, toasted, to garnish

Drain tofu and cut into squares. Cut cabbage leaves into quarters, then across into 3 sections. Wash, drain, and dry.

Combine sauce ingredients in a large pot and simmer. Thicken with corn starch and water, if desired. Add tofu and keep warm.

Parboil cabbage *(adding tougher bottom parts of cabbage first)* until crisp-tender. Place cabbage on platter and pour tofu and sauce mixture over. Garnish with sesame seeds and serve. Makes 6 portions. *(1 portion = 170.7 calories, 7.8 grams fat, 35% protein, 26% carbohydrates, 38% fat)*

Confetti Rice Stir-Fry

1	Tomato, diced
1	Bell pepper, diced
1 med.	Sweet yellow onion, diced
2	Celery stalks, diced
1 C	Snow peas
3 large	Mushrooms, sliced
1 Tbsp.	Vegetable broth powder
	Tamari sauce
2 C	Brown rice, cooked
1/2 C	Peas and carrots, frozen
	Canola oil cooking spray

Heat wok to sizzling. Spray lightly with canola oil spray, scald with tamari sauce, toss in vegetables. When cooked to the desired tenderness, toss with hot brown rice and sunflower seeds. Add a small amount of tamari, to taste. Makes 2 portions. *(1 portion = 340.6 calories, 3.2 grams fat, 14% protein, 78% carbohydrates, 8% fat)*

Herbed Asparagus

1 lb.	Fresh asparagus
4 Tbsp.	Water, for steamer
1 Tbsp.	Vegetable broth
3-4	Green onions, thinly sliced
1 Tbsp.	Fresh tarragon, chopped
1 Tbsp.	Fresh dill or 1 tsp. dried
	Sea salt, to taste

Steam asparagus until tender *(about 5 minutes, do not overcook)*. Rinse, drain, and serve to plate.

In a small skillet, sauté scallions for 1 to 2 minutes in vegetable broth. Add the tarragon, dill, and salt to skillet. Add water if it begins to dry out.

Cook for 1 to 2 minutes till liquid reduces slightly. Use as sauce over asparagus. Serve warm or cool. Makes 4 portions *(1 portion = 34.3 calories, 0.7 grams fat, 38% protein, 43% carbohydrates, 19% fat)*

Quinoa Pumpkin Casserole

1 med.	Sweet yellow onion, chopped
8-10	Mushrooms, sliced
1	Green bell pepper, diced
1 small	Zucchini, diced
2 cloves	Garlic, minced
3 C	Water
1-1/2 C	Quinoa
4 C	Pumpkin or butternut squash, peeled and diced
4 C	Swiss chard, chopped
1/4 C	Fresh parsley
1-1/2 tsp.	Fresh Basil
1 tsp.	Salt
1/2 tsp.	Pepper
	Canola oil cooking spray

Preheat oven to 400° F.

Sauté onion, mushrooms, peppers, zucchini, and garlic together in skillet, about 3 to 5 minutes. Stir in remaining ingredients and bring to a boil.

Move all ingredients to casserole dish and cover. Bake about 30 to 35 minutes, until liquid is absorbed into quinoa and dish is fluffy and fully cooked. Makes 6 portions. *(1 portion = 210.5 calories, 3.0 grams fat, 15% protein, 73% carbohydrates, 12% fat)*

Baked Eggplant Marinara

1-1/2 lbs. Eggplant, unpeeled,
cut into 12 slices
14 oz. Low-fat spaghetti sauce
Olive oil cooking spray

Coat baking sheet with olive oil cooking spray. Add sliced eggplant, put about 1 tablespoon of spaghetti sauce on each slice, spread to cover.

Bake at 350° F. oven for about 30 to 35 minutes. Eggplant slices are done when they are tender enough to be easily pierced with a fork. Serve in sandwiches, as a side dish, or in other creative ways. Makes 4 portions.

Sukiyaki

4 C	Watercress
4 C	Won bok cabbage
2-3	Carrots, sliced into matchsticks
2-3 C	Mung bean sprouts
1-1/2 C	Bamboo Shoots
6-8	Shiitake mushrooms *(half dollar size)*
1 med.	Round onions or green onions, slivered
1 pkg.	Cellophane noodles, soaked in 2 cups boiling water *(3 oz. – available in Oriental sections of markets)*

(continued next page)

Sukiyaki *(continued)*

1 tsp.	Sesame oil
1/4 C	Low-sodium soy sauce
2-4 Tbsp.	Maple syrup
pinch	Sea salt
1 C	Water
1/2 block	Tofu *(about 6 oz.)*

Rinse the shiitake mushrooms and soak in 1 cup of water. Save the water for sukiyaki stock.

Sauté slivered onions and slivered mushrooms in water and a dash to a teaspoon of sesame oil. Sprinkle some sea salt to prevent sticking. Add mushroom water and season to taste with low-sodium soy sauce and maple syrup. Add bamboo shoots to mixture, bring to a boil, and simmer at a low boil. Add soaked and drained cellophane noodles to mixture. Sprinkle julienned carrots. Layer watercress, bean sprouts, and won bok.

Cover and allow layers of vegetables to be steamed. Makes 6 to 8 portions. *(1 portion = 173.2 calories, 3.1 grams fat, 18% protein, 67% carbohydrates, 15% fat)*

Garden Dumplings

1/2	Round onion, finely chopped
1/2 bunch	Chinese parsley *(cilantro)*, chopped
1	Zucchini, finely diced
6	Won bok leaves, finely chopped
1 basket	Mushrooms, diced
2	Carrots, finely diced
1 block	Firm tofu, drained and finely diced
6	Bok choy leaves, finely diced
4 stalks	Green onion, finely chopped
2 small bundles	Long rice, soaked, chopped into 1/2" lengths
3 Tbsp.	Shoyu
1 tsp.	Sesame oil
32	Won ton wrappers

Heat sesame oil in skillet. Add all ingredients, except long rice, tofu, and green onions. Cook quickly on high heat for 3 to 4 minutes. Add long rice and shoyu. Mix well and remove from heat. Add tofu and green onions to the cooled mixture.

To Make Won Tons:

Place 1 heaping teaspoon filling in middle of won ton wrapper, dampen edges with water and fold over into triangle. Drop into boiling water and cook 1 to 2 minutes. Serve in hot konbu broth and garnish with chopped green onions and Chinese parsley. *Optional:* Serve boiled dumplings tossed with shoyu, sesame oil, touch of chili sauce, chopped green onions, and Chinese parsley.

(continued next page)

Garden Dumplings (continued)

This mixture will make 2 to 3 packages of won ton wrappers. Makes 6 to 8 portions. *(1 portion = 223.8 calories, 2.7 grams fat, 17% protein, 72% carbohydrates, 11% fat)*

Spicy Szechuan Eggplant

1-1/2 lbs.	Eggplant, peeled and cut into 3" strips
1 C	Chinese wood ear fungus *(or shiitake straw, or other mushrooms)*, soaked and sliced into strips
	Canola oil cooking spray

Garlic Sauce:

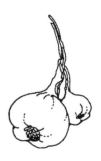

1/4 C	Soy sauce
1 Tbsp.	Honey
1 Tbsp.	Distilled white vinegar
1 Tbsp.	Corn starch
2 red	Chili peppers, minced
2 slices	Ginger, minced
2 cloves	Garlic, minced

Mix all sauce ingredients and set aside.

Spray pan with oil. Sauté eggplant over medium flame until golden brown, about 5 minutes.

Combine sauce for 1 minute with eggplant and fungus. Makes 4 portions. *(1 portion = 148 calories, 1.0 grams fat, 15% protein, 79% carbohydrates, 5% fat)*

Eat More, Weigh Less™ Tip

Zapf/Zing It!   ▽40▽   *Save 16 gm. fat!*

Pizazz Your Pizza

WOULD YOU BELIEVE: A 4-ounce slice of sausage and pepperoni pizza has about 18 grams of fat.

SOME FACTS: A lot of dieters have given up on pizza because pizza usually means a lot of high-fat cheeses and meat and oil in the sauce.

The good news is that you can start eating pizza again. Lots of it. Just adapt your favorite recipes by "elipidating them," and you can once again indulge in this delicious Italian treat. The trick is to avoid the cheese *(usually around 74% fat)* and meats *(usually around 70% fat)* and use mushrooms and a variety of your favorite vegetables, for example tomatoes, peppers, onions, garlic, zucchini, and broccoli. If you must have cheese, choose a nonfat cheese. Add your favorite herbs and spices and special ingredients such as sun dried tomatoes, fresh basil, and even chopped pineapple for a tiny bit of zing.

WHAT YOU CAN DO:

- Elipidate™ your pizza by removing oil, meats, and cheese.

- Add your favorite vegetables.

- Try the following recipe.

- If in a hurry, try the next tip — "Quick Pizza."

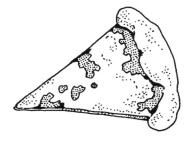

Garden Pizza

Now is the time to break out your bread machine, if you have one. With it, making pizza dough is reduced to a 5-minute job. If you don't have a bread machine, follow the kneading directions below.

Crust:

3/4 C	Whole wheat flour
3/4 C	Unbleached all purpose flour
2 tsp.	Honey
1 tsp.	Salt
2 tsp.	Olive oil
2 tsp.	Active dry yeast
1/2 C + 2 Tbsp.	Warm water

Combine flour, honey, salt, and olive oil in a medium bowl.

In custard cup, dissolve yeast in warm water.

Add yeast mixture to dry ingredients. Mix until dough is formed. Knead dough until smooth *(about 150 times)*. Shape dough into a ball and set aside for about 20 minutes.

Roll dough on floured board to fit 12" pizza pan. Prebake in 400° F. oven until barely brown, about 12 minutes.

(continued next page)

Garden Pizza *(continued)*

Toppings:

The beauty of pizza is its adaptability. Use the following recipe as a suggestion. Add your own vegetables, in your own proportions and to suit your own taste.

> **Zucchini, sliced**
> **Mushrooms** *(any kind)*, **sliced**
> **Tomatoes, sliced**
> **Peas, fresh or frozen**
> **Corn kernels, fresh or frozen**
> **Broccoli florets**
> **Broccoli stalks, finely chopped**
> **Sweet red or yellow onions, etc.**
> **Small amount of soy or almond cheese,**
>   **shredded and sprinkled lightly over**
>   **top** *(optional)*

Pizza Sauce:

1 clove	Garlic, minced
1/2 can	Whole tomatoes *(14 oz.)*, drained
1/2 can	Tomato paste *(6 oz.)*
1/2 tsp.	Oregano
1/8 tsp.	Salt, to taste
dash	Pepper, to taste

Chop drained tomatoes. Combine all sauce ingredients in a saucepan and simmer on medium-high flame for 15 minutes. Sauce for one 12" pizza.

(continued next page)

Garden Pizza (continued)

Final Preparation:

When the pizza dough is baked into a crust and the toppings are ready, open the oven, remove crust *(carefully, it will be hot)* dough, and spread with pizza sauce. *(You can also buy several tasty low-fat varieties at your health food store.)* Pile on the vegetables, then thinly slice or shred about 1/2 cup soy or almond cheese, scatter across the top.

Replace in oven until the vegetables are cooked through. Cooking time will vary according to how thickly you sliced the vegetables and how much you heaped on.

When the vegetables are lightly browned but still slightly crunchy, and when the cheese is bubbling, your pizza is done. Slice with a wheel and enjoy. Makes 12 portions. *(1 portion = 99.7 calories, 1.3 grams fat, 13% protein, 75% carbohydrates, 12% fat – not including soy/almond cheese)*

> ▽ You can make the crusts several at a time and store them, so you'll have one when you're in the mood for pizza. Be careful not to store them in the refrigerator for very long, though, or the moisture will ruin it. ▽

Eat More, Weigh Less™ Tip
Zip It! \\41/

Zip Pizza

WOULD YOU BELIEVE: You can make pizza from scratch in less than 9 minutes?

SOME FACTS: Most people don't think of pizza as an easy-to-prepare food unless they buy it frozen. But if you think of it as toast and spread, you can imagine how fast it can be. Simply start with a whole wheat English muffin or pita bread. Then find a nonfat, prepared pizza sauce or marinara sauce. Add pizza spices, then add mushrooms and your favorite veggies *(see suggestions below)*.

WHAT YOU CAN DO: Quick pizza is another delicious snack food that can be prepared as fast as peanut butter and jelly on toast. Just keep the basic ingredients available, such as whole wheat English muffins or whole wheat pita bread, nonfat bottled tomato sauce, and some spices and toppings.

Simply take the English muffin, spread the tomato sauce on it as if you were "buttering" the muffin. Sprinkle on some pizza spice *(some stores sell a mixture of spices called "Pizza Spice")*, then add whatever toppings you enjoy. Personally, I like zucchini, mushrooms, and broccoli. If you have fresh basil, it also makes a wonderful addition to a quick pizza. Cut the basil in thin strips and sprinkle onto the surface of the pizza.

Then place the English muffin pizza in the toaster oven and it should be done in about the time it would take to make a slice of toast.

Eat More, Weigh Less™ Tip

Eat More of It!   \42/

A Forgotten Weight Loss Food

WOULD YOU BELIEVE: It takes 28.7 pounds of summer squash to provide one day's worth of calories? *(2,500 calories)*

SOME FACTS: Squash is a simple, delicious food that we often forget to include in our menu. It is also one of the healthiest side-dishes. There are two basic types of squash, summer and winter. Winter squashes generally have a mildly sweeter taste. Winter squash can even be eaten without any seasoning. It is one of the easiest of all foods to prepare. Squash is high in EMI, ranging between 28.7 for summer squash and 16.6 for winter squash *(i.e., it takes 28.7 pounds of summer squash and 16.6 pounds of winter squash to provide 2,500 calories).* In all, it provides a surprisingly tasty and versatile food.

Summer squashes are generally lighter, softer, and have pale-colored flesh. They are generally high on the EMI, high in vitamin C, and very low in calories, averaging 18 calories and 0.3 gram fat per one-half cup *(15% fat by calories)*. The best known types are spaghetti, zucchini, and yellow crook-neck.

Winter squashes are generally hard-skinned, and tend to have yellow or orange flesh. These varieties are high in beta carotene, which is likely to provide protection against certain cancers. They are also high on the EMI and low in calories, averaging 39 calories and 0.6 gram fat per one-half cup *(18% fat by calories)*. Some examples are acorn, butternut, delicata, and kabocha squash. Pumpkins may also be considered a form of squash. With some varieties such as acorn and kabocha, you can pressure cook, bake, or steam them, and they are delicious even with no further seasoning.

WHAT YOU CAN DO:

- Try simple kabocha squash as described below.
- Don't forget squash as an excellent high EMI dish.

Melt-In-Your-Mouth
Kabocha Squash

1   **Kabocha or acorn squash**

Cut the kabocha squash into 4" squares or cleaned acorn squash in quarters. Place on a baking pan with a tiny bit of water and bake at 350° F. until tender *(about an hour)*. Makes 2 portions.   *(1 portion = 115.0 calories, 0.290 grams fat, 7% protein, 91% carbohydrates, 2% fat)*

For a little zing, try adding a tablespoon of miso and a teaspoon of sweetener such as barley malt. *(See Squash Deluxe in the Eat More, Weigh Less™ Diet Book, page 215.)*

▽ Remember, you can eat the skin and all, so wash it all before you prepare it. For a more elaborate squash dish, try the following recipe. ▽

Butternut Squash with
Whole Wheat, Wild Rice,
and Onion Stuffing

This satisfying dish makes an especially handsome centerpiece for a holiday meal such as Thanksgiving.

4	**Butternut squashes** *(medium-small, about 1 lb. each)*
2 C	**Water** **Canola oil cooking spray**
1 C	**Red onion** *(heaping)*, **chopped**
1 clove	**Garlic, minced**

(continued next page)

Butternut Squash . . . (continued)

1 C	Fresh orange juice
2-1/2 C	Whole wheat bread, torn and firmly packed
3/4 C	Wild rice, raw, rinsed
1/2 tsp.	Dried sage
1/2 tsp.	Dried thyme

Preheat the oven to 375° F. Halve the squashes and scoop out seeds and fibers. Place them cut side up in shallow baking dishes and cover tightly with covers or more foil. Bake for 40 to 50 minutes, or until easily pierced with a knife but still firm.

In the meantime, bring the water to a boil in a saucepan. Stir in the wild rice, reduce to a simmer, then cover and cook until the water is absorbed, about 40 minutes.

Spray heating skillet with canola oil cooking spray. Add the onion and garlic and sauté until the onion is limp and golden.

In a mixing bowl, combine the cooked wild rice with the sautéed onion and the remaining ingredients. When the squashes are cool enough to handle, scoop out the pulp, leaving firm shells about 1/2" thick. Chop the pulp and stir it into the rice mixture. Stuff the squashes, place in foil-lined baking dishes, and cover.

Before serving, place the squashes in a preheated 350° F. Bake for 20 minutes, or until well heated through. Makes 8 portions. *(1 portion = 259.9 calories, 2.2 grams fat, 12% protein, 81% carbohydrates, 7% fat)*

Zucchini Caliente

Caliente means "fiery." The key to this dish is to make it just hot enough, without being too hot. If you like mild dishes, you'll want to cut down on the spices here. If you like your food hot, leave as is and serve with a side dish of jalapeños.

2 tsp.	Olive oil
1 C	Onions, chopped
1 C	Sweet red pepper, chopped
2 cloves	Garlic, finely chopped
2-1/2 C	Zucchini, unpeeled, cut into 1/4" slices
1 lb.	Tomatoes, chopped
1/4 C	Tomato juice
1/4 tsp.	Coriander, ground
1/2 tsp.	Cumin, ground
1/2 tsp.	Chili powder
	Salt to taste

Sauté onions, pepper, and garlic in a large nonstick skillet, until tender, about 10 minutes. Add zucchini, tomatoes, and tomato juice. Sprinkle spices evenly over vegetables. Mix well. Cover and cook 5 minutes, until zucchini is tender-crisp. Makes 4 portions. *(1 portion = 91.4 calories, 3.0 grams fat, 13% protein, 62% carbohydrates, 26% fat)*

Eat More, Weigh Less™ Tip
Zing It!   ▽43▽

Mushroom Magic

WOULD YOU BELIEVE: It takes 19.5 pounds of mushrooms to provide one day's calories (EMI = 19.5).

SOME FACTS: Mushrooms are a delicious way to add some zing to your foods without adding much fat or calories. They are even delicious by themselves or sautéed with onions *(see following recipe)*. They are convenient and are available fresh, canned, or dried. Some of the delicious varieties include the familiar button mushrooms, canned straw mushrooms, dark brown Japanese shiitake mushrooms, or the delicate long-stemmed enoki mushrooms. There are trumpet-shaped French chanterelles, Italian porcinis, or giant portobellos.

What I like best about mushrooms is that they add texture and bulk to food, such as in side dishes, soups, stews, stir frys, pizzas and pasta sauces but provide only 0.5 grams of fat per quarter pound. One of the most convenient to have around is the Japanese Shiitake mushroom because it keeps without refrigeration and you can add them as a last minute flavor enhancer.

What You Can Do:

- Try some mushrooms as a side dish or as an added ingredient to soups, salads, stews, rice, beans, pastas, or pizzas.

- Use mushroom magic in any soup by adding dried shiitake mushroom.

- Try the following recipes.

Oil-Free Sautéed Mushrooms

2 C	Mushrooms, sliced stem to cap
1 clove	Garlic, crushed
2 tsp.	Garlic salt, or to taste
2 Tbsp.	Water

Heat nonstick skillet to very hot, add water *(careful, it will steam almost instantly)*, then add crushed garlic clove and sliced mushrooms. Water sauté, stirring constantly, until heated throughout. Sprinkle with garlic salt, to taste, toss in pan for another 1 to 2 minutes, and serve as a side dish. Makes 2 portions. *(1 portion = 25.7 calories, 0.3 grams fat, 21% protein, 70% carbohydrates, 9% fat)*

▽ To make this a more elaborate side dish, add the following vegetables, using several tablespoons of red or white wine along with the water for an extra special taste. ▽

Additional Options:

1 med.	Tomato, sliced thin or chunked
1 med.	Zucchini, sliced into thin rounds
1 small	Sweet yellow onion, sliced thin

Cook as above, but add the zucchini and onion at the same time as the mushrooms, sauté until the zucchini is completely heated through and beginning to soften *(about 5 to 10 minutes)*, add the tomatoes and cook till they are warmed through but still slightly crisp. You may cook longer, if you prefer well-done vegetables.

Mushroom Vegetable Stew

1 med.	Onion, chopped
1/2 cup	Water
2	Tomatoes, chopped
1 clove	Garlic, minced
3	Carrots, cut into 1/2" slices
1/2 lb.	Fresh mushrooms, small
1 small	Bell pepper, seeded and diced
3 med.	Red potatoes, unpeeled, cut into 1/2" cubes
1	Bay leaf
1/2 tsp.	Basil, dried
1/2 tsp.	Oregano, diced
1/2 tsp.	Fine herbs, dried *(mixed Italian herbs)*
	Salt, to taste
1/2-1 cup	Green peas, fresh or frozen
1 Tbsp.	Corn starch mixed in 2 Tbsp. water

Sauté onions in water until soft. Add other ingredients, holding the salt and peas. Cover and simmer for 30 minutes until vegetables are just tender. Season to taste. Add peas and heat through. Remove bay leaf and thicken with corn starch. Makes 4 portions. *(1 portion = 206.4 calories, 0.9 grams fat, 13% protein, 84% carbohydrates, 4% fat)*

Eat More, Weigh Less™ Tip
Zing It! \\44/

Zing Kebobs

WOULD YOU BELIEVE: Kebobs taste better without meat.

SOME FACTS: If you don't believe me, try taking a piece of meat and chew it about 100 times. You will for the first time learn the true taste of meat. It tastes like cardboard or worse. Kebobs taste good because of the sauce. So you don't need the meat.

The trick is to get the right sauce. In my original *Eat More, Weigh Less™Diet* book, you can find four delicious marinades for kebobs. One was so good that one of my patients took vegetable kebobs to a party, used the Dijon marinade and found that even the meat eaters enjoyed them. In fact, they liked the dish so much, they were taking the meat off their kebobs, using my friend's sauce, and enjoying a better tasting kebob.

Five of the nine sauces described in the "Nine Zesty Sauce" section of this book on page

242 are excellent marinades.   They are Dijon Sauce, Asian Sauce, Miso Sauce, BBQ Sauce, and Curry Sauce.

WHAT YOU CAN DO:

- Try vegetable kebobs with vegetables of your choice.

- Use one of the sauces from the "Nine Zesty Sauces" in the following section or from the Kebob Section in the original *Eat More, Weigh Less™ Diet* Book *(page 194)*. Personally, my favorite is the Dijon Sauce.

Kebob Salad

2 C	Firm tofu cubes or Tofu Nuggets *(see page 344)*
1 large	Red bell pepper
1 large	Green bell pepper
1 large	Yellow bell pepper
16	Cherry tomatoes
16	Fresh pineapple chunks
16	Button mushrooms
1 med.	Zucchini
2-3 Tbsp.	Any of this cookbook's dressings Shredded lettuce for bed

Wash all vegetables well. Cut all the bell peppers into small, equal-sized chunks.

Skewer the tofu cubes or nuggets, peppers, tomatoes, pineapple chunks, and mushrooms onto wooden kebab sticks, alternating the colors and textures, starting and ending with a cherry tomato.

Arrange on shredded bed of lettuce on platter, drizzle favorite dressing over bed of kebabs, to taste. Makes 4 portions. *(1 portion = 296.5 calories, 12.3 grams fat, 30% protein, 37% carbohydrates, 33% fat – dressing not included)*

Sauces and Gravies

Sauces and gravies enhance the flavor of your meals. Unfortunately, most of the sauces and gravies we grew up eating were made from a base of animal grease and/or cream, both high in fat. With the following recipes, the *Eat More, Weigh Less™ Diet* once again proves that low fat doesn't have to mean low taste. You can eat gravy again. Just learn the *Eat More, Weigh Less™* Tips and stick to the low-fat recipes below. Use these gravies and sauces to dress up vegetables, beans, noodles or grains. Mix and match, use your creativity. You'll soon be turning simple dishes into something special.

Sauces For Steamed Vegetables

Steamed vegetables should be a staple part of your *Eat More, Weigh Less™ Diet*. There are several techniques for steaming, including a bamboo basket over boiling water, a metal steamer over boiling water, or a modern electric steamer that is compact, low cost *(between $20-$30)*, has a timer, and makes your steaming foolproof. If at all possible, invest in an electric steamer. A good one is a Black and Decker®, at about $30. It will make your steaming so simple that you'll do a whole lot more of it, and steaming is one of the healthiest ways to prepare your food.

A good combination of steamed vegetables, for use with dipping sauces, is cauliflower, broccoli, julienned carrots, zucchini squash, and so on. These same vegetables may be sliced and used raw, too. Use the sauces above to dip them in, experiment with a variety of them. You'll find that turning your vegetable dishes into wholesome easy snacks — whether raw or steamed — is one of the easiest ways for you to get your 3 to 5 servings of vegetables per day. Try sauces to give your vegetables variety.

Eat More, Weigh Less™ Tip
Zing It!   45

Nine Zesty Vegetable Sauces

When using vegetables as a main or side dish, the challenge is to make them interesting. You also want to make them tasty, and the dishes should have enough variety to satisfy those who eat with you. Sauces can be your answer. Some are made from scratch, some are as simple as opening a bottle you buy at the market. The following nine ideas are examples of sauces you can either buy or prepare from scratch. Use them to dress up your vegetables, while keeping them high on the EMI.

WHAT YOU CAN DO: Try these sauces to add some zing to your vegetables.

1. *Marinara Sauce*

Marinara sauce can be used on vegetables, as well as on pastas and potatoes. This was described previously. Marinara sauces can be bought bottled or you can make your own. In selecting bottled marinara sauces, pick one of the no-fat varieties. If you make your own, keep it low or no fat. See recipes on pages 124 and 130.

2. *Dijon Mustard Sauce*

One of my favorite sauces is what I call "3221" sauce. This is a lip-smacking mustard sauce that can be used to make vegetables absolutely delicious. It's also simple to prepare.

It's called "3221" because you use:

3 Tbsp. Soy sauce
2 Tbsp. Dijon mustard
2 Tbsp. Lemon juice
1 clove   Garlic, crushed

Mix them all together, and you have a delicious dipping sauce that is out of this world. It's incredibly easy. Try it and see. Makes 3 portions. *(1 portion = 25.6 calories, 0.6 grams fat, 26% protein, 52% carbohydrates, 22% fat)*

3. Asian Sauce

Oriental sauce is delicious on vegetables. You can make a variety of these sauces from scratch, or buy them bottled. Also, for your convenience, you can use a vegetarian oyster sauce, a miso sauce, or a ginger sauce. Ginger is a superb condiment and can be used as an ingredient in any number of different sauces. Ginger has a little bit of zip, similar to horseradish or chili sauce. For additional delicious sauce recipes, see pages 273-274.

Oriental Ginger Sauce

1 C	Water
4 Tbsp.	Low-sodium soy sauce
1 Tbsp.	Arrowroot or corn starch
1 Tbsp.	Ginger, grated

Mix arrowroot or corn starch in 1/4 cup of cool water. Add to a saucepan with the water, soy sauce, and ginger. Heat at medium until thickened and stir. Serve with steamed vegetables. Makes 10 portions. *(1 portion = 6.9 calories, 0.0 grams fat, 21% protein, 78% carbohydrates, 1% fat)*

4. Plum Sauce

Oriental plum sauce is a delicious treat that can be used for dishes such as "Mu-shu" vegetable. One variation of plum sauce is known as "Hoisin." You can buy this bottled, and use it as is. You'll find it in Oriental or health food stores.

5. *Miso-Based Sauce*

Miso-based sauces are also savory on vegetables. All you have to do is dilute some miso with a little bit of flour, water and other spices, then use this as a delicious dipping sauce for raw or steamed vegetables. You can also use this sauce as a variation when you're making a stir-fry.

Ginger Miso Sauce

4 Tbsp.	Sweet white miso
1 Tbsp.	Fresh ginger juice
1 Tbsp.	Ginger, grated
1 clove	Garlic *(large)*, minced
	Juice of one lemon
1/2 tsp.	Corn starch *(for thicker sauce)*
1 C	Water

Blend ingredients until well mixed, then heat gently. Add corn starch for a thicker sauce. Serve over vegetables, use as dipping sauce, or use as base in stir-frys. Keeps well. Makes 8 portions. *(1 portion = 22.7 calories, 0.6 grams fat, 19% protein, 59% carbohydrates, 21% fat)*

6. *Barbecue Sauce*

Barbecue sauces are great for dressing up vegetables. They also make good sauces for sandwich fillings and protein-based foods such as the meat substitutes you'll find in a following *Eat More, Weigh Less*™ Tip.

You can make your own sauce, or barbecue sauce can be bought in the store. Most of these sauces are low in fat. Nevertheless, make sure that you read the bottle or you might be surprised.

The brands of bottled barbecue sauces I recommend include the following: Robbie's Barbecue Sauce®, Hickory Flavor; Bull's Eye Original Barbecue Sauce®; and Hunt's All Natural Thick & Rich Barbecue Sauce®, to name a few.

BBQ Sauce

1/2 C	Water
1 tsp.	Soy sauce
1 large	Onion, minced
3 cloves	Garlic, minced
1 can	Tomato sauce *(8 oz.)*
1 C	Tomato ketchup
1 C	Water
1 Tbsp.	Honey
1 tsp.	Chili powder
2 Tbsp.	Cider vinegar
1 tsp.	Dry mustard
2 Tbsp.	Tamari
1/2 Tbsp.	Corn starch, whole wheat flour, dissolved in 2 tablespoons water

In a large pan, heat water and soy sauce. Add chopped onion and the garlic. Cook until the onion is soft. Add other ingredients and cook over medium heat for 10 minutes. Stir often.

To thicken, add corn starch, whole wheat flour, or kuzu, dissolved in water. Makes 36 portions. *(1 portion = 22.8 calories, 0.1 grams fat, 10% protein, 85% carbohydrates, 5% fat)*

7. Curry Sauce

Curry sauce is an exotic dipping sauce you can use to impress your friends — or to treat yourself. Because the ingredient list is long, most people think it will be difficult to prepare. However, once you have the ingredients together, the sauce can be deceptively simple to make. Try the following recipe on vegetables, seitan, tempeh, and other meat substitutes; in corn dishes or over whole grains.

Simple Curry Sauce

4 tsp.	**Whole wheat flour**
2 tsp.	**Curry powder** *(choose mild, medium or hot, to taste)*
1 C	**Vegetable broth**
1 C	**Water**
2 tsp.	**Ginger, finely chopped**
1 med.	**Onion, chopped**
1	**Bay leaf**
1 clove	**Garlic, crushed**

Blend all ingredients, then cook over medium heat until thickened. Simmer 10 minutes. Remove bay leaf. Makes 24 portions. *(1 portion = 6.2 calories, 0.1 grams fat, 19% protein, 74% carbohydrates, 7% fat)*

8. *Tofu Sauce*

Some people like creamy sauces. Tofu provides a creamy texture for vegetables dips and other dishes, and is somewhat similar in texture to mayonnaise, a dish that most of us grew up with. A lot of people like mayonnaise but don't want the high-fat content. *(Mayonnaise is almost totally fat, at about 12 grams of fat per tablespoon, and with about 98% of its calories coming from fat.)*

Tofu-based sauces are far better than that. But don't forget, tofu still has a fair amount of fat. It's 51% fat by calories, with about 5 grams of fat per quarter pound. It has about 0.8 grams of fat per tablespoon. This means it's not all that good for you when you're watching your weight. But it's still a lot better than the 12 grams of fat per tablespoon in regular mayonnaise.

Using tofu as a sauce base saves you about 11 grams of fat per tablespoon. That's not bad. In addition, tofu is moderate on the EMI scale, whereas mayonnaise is at rock bottom. To use tofu as a sauce base, put it in a blender with a couple of other ingredients and blend till smooth. Try the following recipe for tofu mayonnaise, use it on sandwiches, vegetables, and other places where you might ordinarily use mayonnaise.

Tofu Dip Sauce

1 blk.	**Soft tofu** *(16 oz.)*
1 Tbsp.	**Onion, minced**
1/2 C	**Vegetarian broth** *(e.g., vegetarian chicken, konbu, etc.)*
2 Tbsp.	**Low-sodium soy sauce** *(or to taste)*
1 tsp.	**Lemon juice**

Mash tofu and mix in other ingredients. Place in a blender and puree. Use this as a vegetable topping or a dip for steamed vegetables. Makes 20 portions. *(1 portion = 14.2 calories, 0.6 grams fat, 34% protein, 26% carbohydrates, 40% fat)*

9.   *Mediterranean Herb Sauce*

Mediterranean dishes are characterized by the creative use of herbs, spices, vinegar, olive oil, and even wine. The trick to making use of these flavors in the *Eat More, Weigh Less™Diet* is to eliminate or minimize the olive oil. As good as olive oil may be in other respects, in terms of weight loss, it has the same number of calories *(9 calories per gram)*, the same low EMI value, and the same potential for making weight loss difficult as do other fats and oils. So concentrate on the delicious other flavors such as basil, garlic, oregano, etc., and be creative with Mediterranean sauces for pastas and vegetables.

Mediterranean Herb Sauce

1 clove	Garlic, minced
2 Tbsp.	Dijon mustard
1/2 C	Red wine vinegar
1 tsp.	Black pepper
1/2 C	Basil leaves, sliced
1/2 tsp.	Onion powder
1 Tbsp.	Honey

Combine all ingredients and serve over steamed vegetables. Could be used as a marinade or over vegetable kebobs. Makes 7 portions. *(1 portion = 17.1 calories, 0.3 grams fat, 8% protein, 80% carbohydrates, 12% fat)*

Eat More, Weigh Less™ Tip
Zing It!   \46/

Seven Secrets to Delicious Low-Fat Asian Sauces

WOULD YOU BELIEVE: Many of those delicious Asian sauces contain virtually no fat *(soy sauce 0 gram fat, teriyaki sauce 0 gram fat, and sushi sauce 0 gram fat per tablespoon).*

SOME FACTS: Asian foods have always been known for their delicious exotic taste; and yet, the diets of the people of Asia are uniformly low in fat and associated with low rates of chronic diseases. The secret to the good taste is in their low-fat sauces.

WHAT YOU CAN DO: Let me help you unravel these seven secrets of low-fat Asian sauces so you can use them in your kitchen.

1.   Start With a Basic Stock

This generally provides the basic salty taste to the sauce. The simplest Asian sauce is soy sauce, which can be used alone. Here are some others:

Soy Sauce   Miso
Vegetable Broth   Plum Paste
Mushroom Broth   Konbu Stock

Try this: Simple soy sauce on tofu with optional garnish of chopped green onions.

2.   Sweet

The secret to teriyaki sauce and some other Asian sauces is the addition of sweetener such as:

Rice Syrup   Maple Syrup
Barley Malt
Mirin *(a sweet Japanese cooking wine)*

Try this: 3 tablespoons soy sauce and 1 teaspoon sweetener for a delicious, simple teriyaki sauce

3.   Sour

To give the sauce a little zing, adding vinegar or lemon juice adds a zesty tang to the sauce. In some sauces, the vinegar provides the base such as in the "Clear Dip" on page 281. Some examples:

Rice Vinegar   Lemon Juice
Umeboshi Plum Vinegar

Try this: 4 tablespoons low-sodium soy sauce with 1 tablespoon lemon juice for a delicious steamed vegetable dipping sauce.

4. *Spicy*

To liven up the sauce even more you can use the following. Dry mustard gives a Chinese flavor. Garlic and chili pepper gives a Korean flavor. Ginger and wasabi adds a Japanese flavor.

Dry Mustard	Garlic
Dijon Mustard	Ginger
Chili Pepper	
Wasabi *(a Japanese green horseradish usually used on sushi)*	

Try this: My famous and simple "3221 Sauce" is 3 tablespoons low-sodium soy sauce, 2 tablespoons lemon juice, 2 tablespoons Dijon mustard, and 1 crushed clove of garlic. Use as a dip sauce or marinade. Or add a little chili pepper, garlic, and a dash of sesame oil to the Asian Sauce on page 244 to make Korean Sauce.

5. *Thickener*

Thickeners are optional and give the sauce a full texture. To use arrowroot, you should dissolve it first in a little warm water before use.

Arrowroot	Miso	Corn Starch
Chinese black, white or yellow bean sauce		

Try this: Try the "Asian Sauce" on page 244 or the "Amber Dip" on page 281.

6. Nuts, Seeds, Oil

While I discourage the use of oil in general, when you are willing to compromise a little for an added flavor, a hint of dark sesame oil can give a sauce a distinctive Asian flavor for parties. Toasted sesame seeds also give a similar character to the sauce; and if you want a Southeast Asian flavor, add a small amount of crushed peanuts. Just remember that these are all high in fat and can ruin the healthfulness of a sauce so use them sparingly if at all.

Sesame Oil   Peanuts
Sesame Seeds

7. Prepared Sauces

When all else fails, use a prepared sauce such as bottled "Hoisin" sauce or vegetarian oyster sauce. These can be found in Asian markets or the Oriental section of some supermarkets.

Gravies

We've talked about several delicious, easy-to-prepare sauces. Now let's get back to the basics. Gravy is another way to make vegetables and entrées taste great, and when you're hungry for good, hearty fare, gravy always dresses up your meal. In order to make vegetarian gravies, there are three simple elements to attend to. These are the **aroma**, the **texture**, and the **body of the gravy**. The following three *Eat More, Weigh Less*™ Tips address each of these elements, so you'll make gravy like an expert.

Eat More, Weigh Less™ Tip
Zing It!

47

Three Secrets to Robust Gravies

Most gravies use animal fat drippings to flavor the gravy. This adds unnecessary fat and cholesterol. Here are three secrets to create delicious gravies without fat or cholesterol.

Secret #1: Flavor

Start with a nonfat flavor base. Try vegetarian broth and flavor it with seasonings such as pepper, onion powder, or garlic powder. You can even sauté onions, garlic, and/or mushrooms in the broth for more flavor.

Secret #2: Texture

Add texture by using arrowroot or corn starch. This will give the gravy a smooth thicker consistency. Another option is to add miso to the gravy. If you want a slightly coarser texture, add some whole wheat flour.

Secret #3: *Aroma*

Roast the flour *(dextrinize)* before adding it to the gravy and you'll get a nice rich aroma to the gravy.

WHAT YOU CAN DO:

- Try the following recipes.

- Experiment with them using your own combination of flavors, spices, and textures.

Savory Gravy

2 C	Vegetable broth
1 C	Water
1 Tbsp.	Old Bay™ seasoning *(found in your health food store)*
1/2 C	Whole wheat flour, pan toasted
1/4 tsp.	Black pepper
1/4 tsp.	Garlic powder

Place flour in dry pan in oven at 300° F. for about 10 to 15 minutes to lightly brown. Blend, then cook in a saucepan, stirring until thickened. Cover and simmer for about 10 minutes. Makes 9 portions. *(1 portion = 30.6 calories, 0.2 grams fat, 22% protein, 74% carbohydrates, 5% fat)*

Seasoned Gravy

2 C	Water
1 tsp.	Onion powder
1/4 C	Whole wheat or other whole grain flour, pan toasted
1/2 tsp.	Salt, to taste
1/4 tsp.	Black lemon pepper
1 tsp.	Corn starch, dissolved in a little water

Lightly brown flour in a skillet over medium heat. Dissolve 1 teaspoon of corn starch or arrowroot in a little water.

Blend all ingredients until thoroughly mixed and cook until mixture boils. Makes 6 portions. *(1 portion = 18.3 calories, 0.1 grams fat, 15% protein, 81% carbohydrates, 5% fat)*

▽ Serve with baked potatoes, seitan dishes, or vegetables. This also makes a good base in certain stews and vegetable pot pies. ▽

Brown Rice Miso Gravy

1/4 C	**Whole grain flour**
2 C	**Water**
1-2 Tbsp.	**Brown rice miso, according to taste** *(Erewhon™ brand is an especially high quality, and is generally available.)*

Preheat nonstick skillet. In the meantime, in a separate bowl add miso to water and mix gently, until the miso is dissolved. Set aside. When skillet is sizzling hot, pour in whole grain flour. Brown the flour. As it browns, you'll enjoy the nutty, toasty aroma.

When flour is totally browned, slowly pour in liquid, stirring all the while to avoid lumping. Take off heat as it begins to thicken, to keep it smooth and creamy. Makes 4, 1/2 cup portions *(2 cups).* (1/2 cup = 38.7 calories, 0.5 grams fat, 17% protein, 71% carbohydrates, 12% fat)

▽ This is an especially fast recipe. Use it over brown rice, baked potatoes, potato-bean burgers, or in other creative ways. You can easily double this recipe, if you prefer larger servings. Delicious! ▽

HIGH CALCIUM

VEGETABLES

You're probably wondering why I suggest you eat two to three servings per day of "High Calcium Vegetables" instead of using dairy foods. If you're like most of us, you grew up believing that whole milk and other dairy products were the best sources of calcium, and without them, we would all be malnourished. This simply isn't true.

Non-Dairy Calcium Foods

A New Way of Looking at Calcium

The way we look at calcium is beginning to evolve because of our changing understanding of osteoporosis and calcium absorption. We have long known that calcium balance, that is, how much is kept in the body, is what is important and not simply the total calcium in a food. Unfortunately, most calcium tables only display total calcium values and dairy seems to be best.

In reality, the absorbability of calcium from milk *(32%)* is much less than that of calcium from greens *(52% to 67%)*.[23]   When this is factored in, the quantity of absorbable calcium from a cup of milk is not as good as a cup of some greens and seaweed *(as shown in the table on the next page)*.

In addition, high protein intakes can cause loss of calcium in the urine and so some of the absorbed calcium should be deducted from high protein products such as milk and tofu. The resulting figure would be more realistic in terms of how much calcium is kept in the body. This would also make the real calcium value of many greens and seaweed even more superior to that of dairy in terms of calcium balance.

The following table is a more useful representation of calcium, in terms of calcium balance, than those that provide simply the total quantity. Unfortunately, we don't have exact numbers for calcium loss from protein in individual foods, but we know that it is a significant factor in high protein foods so I have indicated it below.

In addition, if weight loss is the concern, calories should be factored into the equation. This would add an additional advantage to greens in terms of calcium per calorie. *(See table in the original Eat More, Weigh Less™ Diet book, page 82.)*

The Evolving Calcium Table

Comparison of calcium from one cup of selected foods.[a]
Calcium tables should display absorption and calcium loss.

Food	Portion 1 cup (gm)	Calcium (mg)	Fraction Absorbed[b]	Estimated Absorption (mg)	Loss Due to Protein
Kelp *(konbu)*	144	242	0.59[c]	142.8	
Wakame *(seaweed)*	144	216	0.59[c]	127.4	
Watercress	144	169	0.67	113.2	
Kale *(from frozen)*	130	178	0.588	104.7	
Turnip Greens	144	198	0.516	102.2	
2% Milk	244	297	0.321	95.3[d]	Significant[d]
Broccoli	155	178	0.526	93.6	
Tofu	126	258	0.310	80.0[d]	Significant[d]
Mustard Greens	144	128	0.578	74.0	
Spinach	180	244	0.051	12.4[e]	

[a]   Greens are cooked and seaweed is raw in this table.

[b]   Absorption figures from Weaver and Plawecki.[23] Some of this comes from animal data.

[c]   Seaweed absorbability estimated from an average of figures for land greens.

[d]   Calcium balance is less than absorption figure due to calcium loss resulting from high protein content of this food.

[e]   This figure is low due to high oxalate content of the food.

So Why Is Dairy Not Necessary?

There are a number of reasons why the *Eat More, Weigh Less™ Diet* places dairy in the "not necessary for health" category. *(For a more complete explanation see the original Eat More Weigh Less™ Diet book.)*

The advice in this book is directed toward reasonably healthy adults. Individual needs do vary. As I said in the front of this book, for those with special conditions or needs, for children and pregnant women, modifications may be necessary and should be made under guidance of your medical doctor or registered dietitian.

Osteoporosis Is NOT a One Nutrient Disease

First of all, the main reason dairy is recommended by USDA is because of its calcium content, and the main reason calcium is recommended is to prevent osteoporosis. The fallacy in this approach is that osteoporosis is not a single nutrient disease. There are many factors that affect osteoporosis, such as a high intake of animal protein *(including dairy protein)*. Perhaps even more importantly the nations that consume the most dairy products appear to have the most osteoporosis.[24] *(For a full explanation, see the Eat More, Weigh Less™ Diet.)* Even more worrisome is the fact that in at least one clinical trial to improve calcium balance by adding skim milk, it was found that those drinking milk daily lost more bone than those not drinking milk.[26] The high protein content of milk was implicated in causing the calcium to be lost in the urine.

Most Humans Don't Eat Dairy

A second concern in connection with calcium intake is bone growth in children. However, most of the world has thrived very nicely for millennia without any dairy food in their diets, such as in Asia, Africa, and South America. Certainly, the ancient Hawaiians did not consume any dairy products and many of them grew to 6-1/2 to 7 feet tall! So much for the requirement of dairy for strong bones. Another indication that dairy is not a natural food for humanity is that 70% of the world's people are lactose *(milk sugar)* intolerant as adults. In addition, there are some other concerns about the association between dairy and a number of diseases.

Some Other Concerns About Dairy Products

Most dairy is high in fat *(8.1 grams per cup of whole milk)*, saturated fat *(63% of the fat is saturated)* and cholesterol. Clearly, these are risk factors for heart disease and certain cancers. Of course, you can skim the milk and practically eliminate *("Elipidate™")* these substances from the milk.

However, there are other concerns that skimming doesn't answer. Skimming still leaves the dairy protein which contributes to calcium loss through the urine. This may be why, in the study described above, skim milk failed to produce a positive calcium balance.[26] Dairy protein is also the leading cause of allergy in this country. Dairy protein is also implicated in a number of autoimmune diseases such as Type I Diabetes or juvenile diabetes[29] and arthritis.[30, 31]

A Better Source of Calcium

Fortunately, nature provides plenty of calcium from other healthier food sources. As we talk about greens and sea vegetables, you'll see that they are far more nourishing sources of calcium than milk. If you know you're not going to eat the greens, then it's reasonable to take a supplement and even nonfat dairy products for calcium provided you are aware that it is not ideal and that there are potential health consequences in doing so. For a more comprehensive explanation, read the information in the companion book, *Dr. Shintani's Eat More, Weigh Less™ Diet*.

We've talked about greens in the context of salads, vegetable dishes, and soups. The following *Eat More, Weigh Less™* Tips will give you more information on greens as high calcium foods, and will provide easy tips on how to dress up your greens so you'll want to eat plenty of them all the time. Start with the following salad, either as a meal in itself or as a side dish to other tasty foods. Watercress is especially high in calcium, and it also makes a wonderful base for a salad.

Watercress Sesame Salad

1 bunch	Watercress, cut into 1-1/2" lengths
2 C	Water, boiling
2 Tbsp.	Low-sodium soy sauce
1-1/2 Tbsp.	Sesame seed, toasted
2 Tbsp.	Rice wine vinegar
2 Tbsp.	Green onions including stems, chopped
1/4 tsp.	Cayenne
1 clove	Garlic, minced
1/4 tsp.	Honey

Place watercress in boiling water and cook for about 4 minutes, rinse and drain thoroughly. Add remaining ingredients and mix well. Chill before serving. Makes 4 portions. *(1 portion = 32.3 calories, 1.6 grams fat, 18% protein, 42% carbohydrates, 41% fat)*

Here's another excellent high-calcium dish.

Spicy Broccoli

1 bunch	Broccoli
2 tsp.	Dry mustard
1/2 C	Seasoned rice vinegar
2 cloves	Garlic, pressed or minced
1/4 C	Onion, minced
2 Tbsp.	Honey
2 Tbsp.	Low-sodium soy sauce

Break broccoli into bite-sized florets. Slice peeled stems into 1/4" thick rounds. Steam until tender *(about 3 minutes)*.

While broccoli is steaming, mix other ingredients in a serving bowl. Add broccoli and mix. Serve immediately. Makes 4 portions. *(1 portion = 68.1 calories, 0.6 grams fat, 16% protein, 77% carbohydrates, 7% fat)*

Ginger Mustard Cabbage with Konbu

2 lbs.	Mustard cabbage
1 Tbsp.	Sea salt
1/3 C	Dried konbu, cut in 1/2" strips
1/3 C	Barley malt
1/4 C	Low-sodium soy sauce or tamari
1/4 C	Rice vinegar
1 Tbsp.	Sesame seeds, toasted
1 Tbsp.	Ginger root, minced

Chop cabbage, add salt and soak for 30 minutes.

Wash konbu and soak, then cut into 1/2" lengths.

Mix barley malt and soy sauce, heat until sugar dissolves. Add vinegar then konbu while still hot.

Cool the sauce a little, then mix in the rest of ingredients. Let sit overnight to blend flavors. Makes 4 to 6 portions. *(1 portion = 92.1 calories, 1.5 grams fat, 15% protein, 71% carbohydrates, 14% fat)*

Eat More, Weigh Less™ Tip
Zapf It!   ▽48▽

The Most Natural
Source of Calcium

WOULD YOU BELIEVE: Cows get plenty of calcium without drinking milk.

SOME FACTS: Leafy greens include the many types of lettuce and other salad greens, but I also recommend steamed greens such as kale, broccoli, collard greens, watercress, and so on to make a delicious side dish for your entrées. Greens are not only the highest in EMI and will help induce weight loss, but the dark green leafy vegetables are among the best sources of calcium, iron, and beta carotene.

Cows have strong bones and put out a great deal of calcium in their milk. Ever wonder where they get their calcium? It isn't from drinking milk. They get it from greens. As I mentioned above, dark leafy greens are an excellent source of calcium.

WHAT YOU CAN DO:

- Have some steamed greens daily such as:

  Broccoli
  Chinese cabbage
  Collard greens
  Kale
  Mustard cabbage
  Nappa cabbage
  Savoy cabbage
  Turnip tops
  Watercress

- Use toasted sesame seeds sprinkles *(see page 272)*, add one of the vegetable sauces *(see Tips #44 and #45)*, try lemon zest, or balsamic vinegar to add some zing.

- Don't forget sea vegetables *(pages 282-294)*.

Cabbage-Wrapped Watercress

1 bunch   **Savoy cabbage** *(won bok)*
1 bunch   **Watercress**

Wash and boil large outer leaves of cabbage until stem area is pliable. Blanch watercress. Overlap several cabbage leaves. Place 5 to 6 stems of watercress to one long side of cabbage. Roll like jelly roll on cheesecloth or old clean dishtowel. Squeeze tightly to remove some excess water. Unwrap. Slice as for sushi. Serve with soy mustard sauce. Makes 6 to 8 portions. *(1 portion = 12.0 calories, 0.1 grams fat, 28% protein, 69% carbohydrates, 3% fat)*

Sesame Salt Sprinkles

5 Tbsp.   **Black sesame seeds**
2-1/2 Tbsp.   **White sesame seeds**
1/2 Tbsp.   **Sea salt**

Lightly toast sesame seeds in frying pan at medium heat. Use no oil. When almost toasted, add salt and toast till golden brown. Salt will look dried. Serve as is, or grind in a suribachi *(into powder)*. Makes 48, 1/2 teaspoon portions. *(1 portion = 8 calories, 0.7 grams fat, 11% protein, 17% carbohydrates, 72% fat)*

Zip Dip

2 tsp.	Sesame seeds, pan roasted and pulverized
2 Tbsp.	Rice vinegar
1 tsp.	Red peppers, crushed
4 Tbsp.	Low-sodium soy sauce
1 Tbsp.	Honey

Toast sesame seeds. Turn to powder in suribachi or Sees grinder. Mix with other ingredients, and use as dip for your high-calcium land and sea vegetables. Makes 8 portions. *(1 portion = 18.0 calories, 0.4 grams fat, 12% protein, 71% carbohydrates, 17% fat)*

Miso Dip

1/2 C	Miso
2 Tbsp.	Rice vinegar
1 Tbsp.	Soy sauce
1 tsp.	Ginger, finely grated

Blend ingredients, pulsing, or mix in a suribachi. This is great over raw shredded cabbage or other high-calcium vegetables, and it's also good over brown rice. Makes 4 portions. *(1 portion = 76.2 calories, 2.1 grams fat, 22% protein, 55% carbohydrates, 24% fat)*

Sweet and Sour Dip

1/4 C	Low-sodium soy sauce
2 Tbsp.	Lime juice
2 tsp.	Rice vinegar
2 Tbsp.	Honey
1 tsp.	Dashi *(Japanese soup stock)* or vegetable broth

Mix well. Keep in the refrigerator in a glass jar until ready to use. Makes 4 portions. *(1 portion = 22.0 calories, 0.0 grams fat, 8% protein, 91% carbohydrates, 0% fat)*

▽ Drizzle or sprinkle this over sea vegetables or high-calcium greens, or you can even use it as a regular salad dressing. Delicious! ▽

Eat More, Weigh Less™ Tip
Zing It!   \49/

Calcium and Weight Loss, Too

WOULD YOU BELIEVE: Broccoli is a better source of calcium than milk . . . and it helps you lose weight!

SOME FACTS: Among all the common sources of calcium, broccoli has one of the highest levels of absorbable calcium. Its estimated absorbability is 52.6% compared to 32.1% for milk.[23] And while one cup of milk has 297 mg. of calcium and one cup of broccoli has about 155 mg.,[25] when you factor in the absorbability, broccoli turns out to have about 93.6 mg. of absorbable calcium, while milk has about the same at 96.3 mg. When you factor in the fact that the protein in milk will cause some loss of the milk's calcium through the kidneys, broccoli turns out to be the better source of calcium.   To top it off, broccoli has many fewer calories than milk and a very high EMI value *(17.1)*, so it is a weight-loss food as well. And from the perspective of cancer prevention, broccoli is loaded with beta carotene and is a "cruciferous vegetable" known to have other nutrients that may prevent certain cancers.

WHAT YOU CAN DO:

- Try some steamed broccoli as a side dish with your next meal, seasoned with one of the sauces in this book *(pages 243 to 250, 273-274)*.

- Add sliced broccoli to marinara sauces or to your pizza for delicious variety.

Eat More, Weigh Less™ Tip
Zing It!   \50/

Kale for Kalcium?

WOULD YOU BELIEVE: The best green vegetable on a salad bar for calcium is often used as a decoration.

SOME FACTS: Another good source of calcium is kale. Its estimated absorbability is 58.8% compared to 32.1% for milk. A cooked 1-cup portion contains 94 mg. of calcium; and if made from frozen, it contains 178 mg. of calcium. When you factor in absorbability, it turns out to be a significant calcium source. [23, 25]

So, what is kale, you might ask? Many people are more familiar with kale as the crinkly green leaves that adorn many a salad bar and which hide the areas between the containers that contain the salad bar food. Kale is best served lightly parboiled or steamed. The thicker the leaves, the longer you have to cook them.

What You Can Do:

- Try some steamed kale as a side dish with your next meal. Season with one of the sauces in this book *(page 243)*.

- Try a kale sandwich *(see the Eat More, Weigh Less™ Diet, page 140)*.

- Add some steamed kale to any soup for a quick way to get calcium.

Eat More, Weigh Less™ Tip
Zing It! \51/

Sumptuous Summer Rolls

One very delicious way to prepare high calcium vegetables, or any vegetable, is to make summer rolls. This is a nice variation on the familiar Thai summer roll filling of noodles or bean thread. In summer rolls, if you want to maximize the calcium, use plenty of crisp leafy greens and some tofu.

Summer rolls are easy to make and can actually be a finger food, if you want them to be. The trick is the dipping sauce, which will enhance the dish and bring it to life.

WHAT YOU CAN DO: Try the following recipe for summer rolls.

Summer Rolls

1 pkg.	Rice paper *(10 or 20 sheets)*
1 C	Rice sticks, softened by cooking
1 head	Romaine lettuce
1/8 C	Fresh basil *(optional)*
1 C	Mint leaves
1/8 C	Fresh cilantro *(optional)*
1 C	Fresh bean sprouts
1 C	Carrots, shredded
1 C	Firm tofu, cut into strips

Cook rice sticks according to package instructions. Dip rice papers in water and place on paper towels to allow them to soften.

Place lettuce, rice sticks *(now soft as noodles)* along with other ingredients in a row across the middle of rice paper and roll like a burrito. Place seam side down on serving tray. Makes 20 portions. *(1 portion = 131.0 calories, 1.2 grams fat, 8% protein, 84% carbohydrates, 8% fat)*

Clear Dip

2 cloves Garlic, crushed
6 Tbsp.   Barley malt, rice syrup, or sugar
1 Tbsp.   Lemon juice
1 Tbsp.   Rice vinegar
4 Tbsp.   Water
          Fresh chili, to taste

Mix ingredients together and use as a dipping sauce. Makes 20 portions to be used with above 20 summer rolls. *(1 portion = 10.4 calories, 0.0 grams fat, 1% protein, 99% carbohydrates, 0% fat)*

Amber Dip

1 C   Chinese bean sauce
1/4 C   Barley malt, rice syrup, or sugar
2 cloves Garlic, minced
1/2 C   Water
          Corn starch, as needed for texture

On medium heat, cook bean sauce, sugar, and garlic together for 3 to 4 minutes, stirring constantly. Add water and stir. Thicken with corn starch mixed with water, if necessary. Makes 20 portions to be used with summer rolls. *(1 portion = 19.2 calories, 0.3 grams fat, 12% protein, 73% carbohydrates, 15% fat)*

▽ Ground peanuts can also be added as a garnish. Just remember that using a lot of peanuts will increase the fat content of this dish. ▽

Sea Vegetables

In the July 31, 1995 issue of Newsweek®, the National Fluid Milk Processor Promotion Board provided a special advertising section on milk. Its focus was calcium. In it, there was an attempt to laugh off the fact that there was indeed a better source of calcium than milk. I would like to place that statement into its proper perspective. They said:

> "What are the best sources of calcium?
>
> Well, if you like raw seaweed kelp, you're in luck! Just kidding! Actually, . . . it does contain a tremendous amount of calcium: a whopping 1,093 mg. per 3-1/2 ounces and only 10 calories for that amount . . . ."

They go on to list sources of calcium in a table without including seaweed which they acknowledged to be the best source. Are they afraid that the nation will learn how to use calcium from sources other than milk?

High In Calcium

Sea vegetables *(seaweed)* are among the best sources of calcium. Some varieties have more calcium than milk and more iron than beef. They're low in fat and have no cholesterol. The only drawback to cooking with sea vegetables is that they're quite salty if you don't rinse them well. Also, most people are unfamiliar with sea-weed as a food, though in many parts of the world it's considered a delicacy. This is one of the health secrets of the longest-lived people in the world, the Japanese. In the past, sea vegetables, or seaweeds as they're more commonly known, were eaten by numerous cultures around the world. In Ireland, they ate dulse centuries ago. The next few *Eat More, Weigh Less*™ Tips will teach you what you'll need to know to make sea vegetables a part of your life. Try some of the following recipes and you'll wonder why it's taken you so long to discover this delicious and nutritious food.

Eat More, Weigh Less™ Tip
Zip It!/Zing It! ▽52▽

Quick Greens

WOULD YOU BELIEVE: One of the most convenient ways to add greens to your menus is to use sea vegetables *(seaweed).*

SOME FACTS: Most sea vegetables *(seaweed)* are much like dark, leafy greens in that they are quite high in calcium *(see table on page 263)* and other nutrients and have practically no fat. Most people, however, don't know how to use them. Most of them are sold dried and thus keep well without refrigeration. Three of the most convenient are dulse, wakame, and nori.

Dulse, a dark, leafy seaweed used in Ireland and New England, is sold in dried leafy pieces. They can be used as snacks or in salads, stews, bean dishes, and others.

Wakame, another leafy seaweed is usually sold dried in long stringy lengths or flakes. All you have to do is add water and it turns into a full-bodied green in minutes. You can add it to stir-frys, salads, soups, or any other dishes. It can even be portable. Try taking some in a plastic bag to a restaurant and add it to a soup like a condiment.

Nori, commonly known for its use as the black wrapper for "sushi," is sold in paper-like sheets or as sprinkles known as "furikake" *(a Japanese word for "sprinkle over")*.

WHAT YOU CAN DO:

- Try dulse in salad as in the recipe below.

- Take some wakame flakes *(or cut-up pieces of stringy wakame)* and add them to any soup, salad, or cooked dish.

- Try nori as a snack or as sprinkles on rice.

Mediterranean Sea Dip

2 C	Hummus *(see recipe on page 327)*
1/4 C	Dried dulse
1 C	Green onion, stems included, minced
dash	Paprika, to garnish
sprigs	Parsley, to garnish

Stir dulse and onion into prepared hummus. Serve to bowl and garnish with paprika and sprigs of parsley. Serve as chip dip, or in the following sandwich recipe. Makes 20 portions. *(1 portion = 75.8 calories, 1.0 grams fat, 22% protein, 67% carbohydrates, 12% fat)*

Seafarer's Submarine

1/2 C	Mediterranean Sea Dip *(see recipe above)*
1 piece	Whole grain pita pocket bread
1/2 C	Lettuce, shredded
1/2 C	Tomato, cubed

Lightly heat your pita bread in either toaster oven or microwave. Spread Mediterranean Sea Dip inside pita pocket. Add lettuce and tomato to taste. Makes 2 portions. *(1 portion = 250.6 calories, 3.1 grams fat, 19% protein, 71% carbohydrates, 10% fat)*

Sea Vegetable Salad

1/4 C	Dulse, soaked and chopped fine
1 C	Mung bean sprouts *(or other bean sprouts)*
1/2 C	Button mushrooms
1 C	Lettuce, shredded
1/2 C	Tomato, diced
1/8 C	Onion, minced

Dressing:

2 tsp.	Ginger juice
1 tsp.	Lemon juice
1 tsp.	Lemon zest

Prepare the lettuce in a bed. Mix all other ingredients and spoon onto top. Dress with the above dressing *(adapt for your personal taste)*, or with your favorite other low-fat salad dressing. Makes 3 portions. *(1 portion = 36.8 calories, 0.4 grams fat, 24% protein, 68% carbohydrates, 8% fat)*

Wakame Ginger Soup

4 C	Water
1" piece	Ginger, crushed
2 cloves	Garlic, sliced
1 med.	Onion, chopped
1 med.	Carrot, chopped fine
1/2 C	Water chestnuts, sliced
1 oz.	Dried wakame, wash and chop into small pieces
1 piece	Konbu *(4" x 4")*, soaked and chopped into small pieces
3	Shiitake mushroom
1 Tbsp.	Low-sodium soy sauce

Make konbu broth by soaking konbu and mushrooms in 4 cups of water for 1 hour. The wakame will swell up to about 5 times its dry size and become leafy. Add ginger, garlic, onion, carrot, water chestnuts, and wakame to water and simmer until vegetables are tender. Add soy sauce to serve. Makes 4 portions. *(1 portion = 56.1 calories, 0.2 grams fat, 11% protein, 85% carbohydrates, 3% fat)*

Wakame with Onions

1 oz.	Wakame *(dry weight)*
1-2	Onions, medium-sized
	Water, as needed
1 Tbsp.	Low-sodium soy sauce

Rinse, and soak the wakame in water until tender, then slice into roughly 1" pieces.

Peel and slice onions vertically into crescents. Place onions in a pot, then cover with wakame.

Add water to nearly cover the wakame. Bring the mixture to a boil, and reduce the heat to low. Simmer for about 15 minutes. Season with low-sodium soy sauce to taste, and cook for 10 minutes longer. Makes 4 to 6 portions. *(1 portion = 16.5 calories, 0.1 grams fat, 16% protein, 79% carbohydrates, 4% fat)*

Wakame with Carrots
(or other vegetables)

1 oz.	Dried wakame
2 C	Carrots, cut in large chunks *(or other vegetables such as cauliflower, turnips, daikon, celery burdock, or lotus root)* **Water to cover vegetables**
3 tsp.	Low-sodium soy sauce Cilantro, scallions, chives or parsley for garnish *(optional)*

Rinse, and soak wakame. Slice into large pieces.

Put the carrots *(or other vegetables)* in a pot and add water to half cover the carrots. Bring to a boil, cover and reduce the heat to low.

Simmer until the carrots are nearly done *(about 20 to 30 minutes. Adjust cooking time for other vegetables)*. Then add the wakame and low-sodium soy sauce to taste and simmer until carrots are done. Garnish. Makes 4 to 6 portions. *(1 portion = 40.8 calories, 0.2 grams fat, 11% protein, 85% carbohydrates, 4% fat)*

Eat More, Weigh Less™ Tip
Zing It! $\boxed{53}$

What Are Hijiki and Arame?

Hijiki is a delicious string-like or thread-like sea vegetable that is very high in calcium and iron *(as are all sea vegetables)*. It is virtually interchangeable with arame *(described next)* although it takes longer to cook hijiki. It has a strong ocean aroma that disappears after it is cooked off, so don't let the initial fragrance prevent you from using it. It is delicious with other vegetables.

Arame *(pronounced "are-ah-meh")* appears to be another "stringy" sea vegetable like hijiki when you buy it, but it is actually a flat seaweed that is finely sliced to its stringy appearance. Because it is sliced, the cut edges are exposed and it therefore cooks slightly faster than hijiki. It is nonetheless interchangeable in hijiki recipes. However, it can be used in soups and pilafs more easily than hijiki.

Remember that hijiki and arame are interchangeable in the following recipes.

Arame With Corn
(or Carrots)

1 oz.	**Arame** *(dry weight)*
1/2 tsp.	**Sesame oil**
1 C	**Onions sliced vertically into thin crescents**
	Water, as needed
2-3 Tbsp.	**Low-sodium soy sauce**
1-2 C	**Fresh corn kernels or 1 C julienned carrots**

Wash and drain the arame. After washing, be sure to place in a separate bowl to eliminate any sand that may be present.

Lightly oil a frying pan, add a little water and heat it. Sauté the onions for 1 to 2 minutes, stirring gently. *(If using carrots, add julienned carrots at this time on the onions.)* Place the arame on top and enough water to cover the onions. Add a little low-sodium soy sauce.

Cover and bring to a boil, then turn flame to low and simmer for about 20 minutes. Place the corn on top and a little more soy sauce to taste. Simmer for another 10 or so minutes or until the water is nearly gone. Makes 4 portions. *(1 portion with corn = 256.3 calories, 3.6 grams fat, 11% protein, 77% carbohydrates, 12% fat)   (1 portion with carrots instead of corn = 51.8 calories, 0.8 grams fat, 13% protein, 75% carbohydrates, 13% fat)*

Hijiki With Onions
(or Other Vegetables)

1 oz.	Hijiki or arame *(dry weight)*
1/2 tsp.	Sesame oil
2	Onions or other vegetables such as carrots, burdock root, lotus root, or tofu
	Water, as needed
	Low-sodium soy sauce to taste *(about 2 to 3 Tbsp.)*
dash	Sweetener such as barley malt *(optional)*

Wash and rinse the hijiki in a strainer or colander. After washing, be sure to place in a separate bowl to drain to eliminate any sand that may be present. Then soak hijiki for about 10 minutes.

While soaking, slice onion vertically into thin crescents. Lightly oil a frying pan, and heat it. Add the onions and a little water and sauté for 2 to 3 minutes. Place the hijiki on top of the onions and add water to cover the onions.

Bring to a boil, turn the heat to low, then add a small amount of low-sodium soy sauce. Cover and simmer for about 40 minutes *(depending on the vegetable)*. Add soy sauce to taste. Simmer for another 15 minutes, or until the liquid is almost gone. Makes 4 to 6 portions.

(1 portion = 36.3 calories, 0.6 grams fat, 14% protein, 72% carbohydrates, 14% fat)

Hijiki With Mushrooms and Tofu

4	Shiitake mushrooms
4	Button mushrooms
2 C	Water
1 oz.	Hijiki or arame
4 oz.	Firm tofu, cubed
2 Tbsp.	Low-sodium shoyu *(natural soy sauce)* or to taste
1/4 tsp.	Honey
1/4 tsp.	Sesame oil

Cover mushrooms and hijiki with water and soak for 10 minutes.

Remove hijiki from the water, keep water.

Heat the slight bit of sesame oil *(just to flavor)* and sauté hijiki briefly. Slice mushrooms and add to the sauté. Strain out any gritty residue and add hijiki-soaking water to sauté.

Bring to a boil, reduce heat, cover, and simmer for 15 minutes. Add the tofu and shoyu and simmer for 15 minutes longer. Makes 4 portions. *(1 portion = 40.8 calories, 1.2 grams fat, 27% protein, 49% carbohydrates, 23% fat)*

Eat More, Weigh Less™ Tip
Zing It!   \54/

A High Calcium Beverage for Your "Coffee" Break

It surprised me when I first learned that blackstrap molasses is actually high in calcium. The molasses is a byproduct of sugar production, filtered out after sugar cane is cooked. A lot of the mineral residues from the sugar cane plant, such as calcium and iron, become concentrated in blackstrap molasses. It's a tasty, high-mineral food. It's also high in sugar, so it needs to be used sparingly. It also has a rather strong flavor. However, some people enjoy that and use it instead of coffee as a drink in the morning. You can use a teaspoon or more in hot water and it will look like coffee because of its dark brown color. Try it some morning when you want a sweet, dark drink that looks like coffee and has a little bit of the roasted flavor of coffee. Or you can use it as a sweetener in a delicious grain coffee substitute, which you can find at your health food store.

Eat More, Weigh Less™ Tip

55

Calcium Surprise

WOULD YOU BELIEVE: Tofu is a high calcium food!

SOME FACTS: Tofu, a product made from soybeans, is not only a good no-cholesterol substitute for meat, but it is also unusually high in calcium. It becomes a high-calcium food because in the manufacturing of tofu, calcium chloride is used. *(Tofu prepared without it doesn't have the same high calcium content.)* The result is that a 4-1/2-ounce portion of tofu contains approximately 258 mg. of calcium which is close to the 297 mg. of calcium in 8 ounces of milk. This means that ounce-for-ounce tofu has more calcium.

As good as this sounds, tofu does have some drawbacks. As indicated above, absorption is a factor, and it appears that the absorbability of calcium from tofu *(0.31)* is similar to that of milk *(0.32)*. In addition, like milk, it is high in protein, which can cause some urinary calcium loss, and it's also high in fat. Tofu ranges from 4.7 to

9.9 grams of fat for 4 ounces.* This is still less than the 15 to 21 grams of fat in a hamburger patty, and is comparable or less than the 8.1 grams in a glass of whole milk.

WHAT YOU CAN DO:

- Use tofu as a substitute for meat in any dish.

- Try the "tofu nugget" recipe on page 344 as a side dish or sandwich filler.

- For quick tofu, eat it chilled as is with a little soy sauce and a little chopped scallion for garnish.

---

* Nutrient values per weight or serving of tofu are only an approximation because the water content may vary greatly.

SWEETS THAT CAUSE

WEIGHT LOSS

The Inverted Food Pyramid suggests you eat two to four servings of whole fruit each day. Most fruits are high on the EMI. They also contain a wealth of vitamins such as beta-carotene and vitamin C. But there are different rules for fruits than for vegetables. Both are about the same on the EMI, but fruit has a very high sugar content. Fructose, the natural sugar in fruit, can be absorbed very quickly. It's

Fruits

not as bad as white sugar, but it's still not good for you in large amounts. As with sugars, it tends to cause a rise in triglycerides *(storage fats)* in our blood. High triglycerides are a co-risk factor with cholesterol for heart disease.

Have a piece of raw fruit, such as a banana, orange, apple or other treat, either as a snack or for breakfast. Use fruits as a dessert to satisfy your sweet tooth, but don't eat too much fruit. Two to four servings is fine for most people. And remember, eating the whole fruit is better than drinking fruit juice. Some people find that fruits are easier to digest if they are cooked. Others do better with raw fruit. Some people go on "fruit fasts" as an effective way to lose weight. I don't recommend this approach. It would cause weight loss, because fruits are high on the EMI. But I believe a more balanced diet is important for good health. If possible, try to eat fruit in season, and from your own locality.

Fruit and Other Desserts

Most cookbooks put desserts last, since they're usually eaten at the end of the meal. But Fruits are side-by-side with vegetables in the Inverted Food Pyramid, and therefore they are next in line of importance to your *Eat More, Weigh Less™ Diet*. Remember that your main food should be grain and vegetables. Fruits are for treats — and for desserts.

It's okay to eat dessert, so long as you stay away from most prepared desserts, which have a lot of simple sugar, butter, oil and shortening added, so that they become quite low on the EMI. For example, a whole apple is about 90 calories and less than half a gram of fat *(0.49 gram)*. A slice of apple pie can be 411 calories and 19 grams of fat. Use whole fruits in your desserts, and watch the other ingredients closely. In this section, you'll find examples of prepared dishes based on whole fruits that are high in EMI and also healthy. Enjoy your dessert.

Eat More, Weigh Less™ Tip
56

Try Natural "Gelatin"

WOULD YOU BELIEVE: Jello® is not vegetarian.

SOME FACTS: It surprises many people to learn that most gelatin is made from animals' collagen, which is a protein derived from boiling down the joints and tendons of animals such as cows. While this is a non-fat, non-cholesterol product, it is made of animal protein. Another problem with commercial gelatins is that they are usually artificially colored and contain a great deal of sugar. A far better alternative is agar *(also called agar-agar)*. This is a form of seaweed which provides a gelling effect. I use natural fruit and fruit juices for the sweetening. Agar gelatin is just as easy to prepare as commercial gelatins, and it has a better flavor because natural foods are used.

WHAT YOU CAN DO: Try the recipe below to sample a very tasty and additive-free gelatin dessert.

Apple-Strawberry Jel

8 Tbsp.	Agar flakes
6 C	Apple juice
1 pint	Strawberries
1/2 C	Apples, cut into very small chunks

Mix agar, juice, and water in a saucepan, bring to a boil then simmer 4 to 5 minutes until dissolved.

Wash, clean, and slice strawberries. Clean and cut apples.

Use a fancy gelatin mold in a fruit shape if you have one. Otherwise, line the bottom of a 9" shallow rectangular baking pan with two-thirds of the strawberries, setting the remainder aside. Add a small layer of apples.

Gently pour the hot agar mixture over the fruits in the first pan to a depth of about 1". Pour any remaining agar mixture over fruits in the second pan. Chill until firmly set.

To serve, slice into appropriate serving sizes. Blend the mixture that has set in the second dish until smooth. Serve as a sauce over the molded gelatin slices or squares. Makes 4 portions. *(1 portion = 218.4 calories, 0.3 grams fat, 1% protein, 97% carbohydrates, 1% fat)*

Eat More, Weigh Less™ Tip

Zing/Zapf It! ▽57▽ *Save 19 gm. fat!*

Baked Fruit

WOULD YOU BELIEVE: A slice of apple pie can be as much as 411 calories and 19 grams of fat.

SOME FACTS: The idea of baked fruit may seem strange, until you realize that apple pie is principally baked fruit.

The problem with apple pie is the pie crust, which contains a great deal of fat. Baked apples may contain as little as 1% fat by calories, and even canned apple pie filling is only .1 grams per serving, at 1% fat. However, when you add it to a regular apple pie, one slice can be as much as 411 calories with 19 grams of fat in it. Obviously, just about all the fat came from the crust. So if you want to try a baked fruit desert, consider baked apples or other fruit without the crust.

WHAT YOU CAN DO: Try the following baked apple and see how good baked fruit can be.

Baked Apple With Raisin Sauce

5	**Apples, any variety** *(Rome, Pippin, Granny Smith, or Jonathan are good baking apples)*
1 Tbsp.	**Arrowroot or corn starch**
1 C	**Apple juice**
1 tsp.	**Cinnamon**
1/4 C	**Raisins**
1/2 tsp.	**Vanilla**

Preheat oven to 375° F. Wash apples, cut off the top, and core into the apple about halfway down to get the seeds out but do not poke through the bottom.

Place into a baking pan with a small amount of water and bake for 15 to 20 minutes.

Place apple juice, raisins, cinnamon, vanilla and a pinch of salt into a saucepan and bring to a boil. Then simmer at low heat for 5 minutes. Dissolve the arrowroot in cool water and add to mixture and stir. Spoon sauce into the apples and enjoy. Makes 5 portions. *(1 portion = 126.7 calories, 0.449 grams fat, 1% protein, 96% carbohydrates, 3% fat)*

Eat More, Weigh Less™ Tip
Zapf it!   58   *Save 17 gm. fat!*

Low-fat Pies

You now know that pie crusts are high in fat. What do we do if we want to keep the EMI of pie as high as possible, keep the fat as low as possible, and still keep the crust? There are a couple of solutions. First, try a dish with a "crust" sprinkled on top of it. An example of this is apple crisp. This is baked apple pie filling with a whole grain-based topping sprinkled atop it. You can use a number of items for the sprinkles.

You can also use a very low-fat recipe for pie crust. The problem is that it's difficult to find one that holds together. Following are a couple of examples of pie with crusts that are low fat and still have the texture and consistency of a good, rich pie crust.

First, use Grape Nuts®, with apple juice to hold it together. Simply grind up or blend Grape Nuts® to a fine yet crunchy consistency, then add apple juice till it's just the right texture to line a pie pan. Once you've lined the pan, pour in the filling as you normally would.

Another idea for low-fat pie crust is to use mashed potatoes and soy milk to help hold the pie crust together. For a really special treat, add tofu topping, but don't eat too much topping or you'll slip off the EMI scale.

WHAT YOU CAN DO:

- Try the "crisped" pie recipe.
- Try the following low-fat crust pie recipes.

Peach Crisp

Filling:

4 C	Canned sliced peaches in juice
3 Tbsp.	Whole wheat flour
1/8 C	Fruit-juice-sweetened apricot preserves
4 Tbsp.	Honey
2 tsp.	Lemon juice
1/8 tsp.	Nutmeg

Topping:

1 Tbsp.	Maple syrup
1/2 tsp.	Vanilla
1/4 C	Whole oats
1 Tbsp.	Cornmeal
1/4 tsp.	Cinnamon

Fold peaches into flour and pour mixture into a 9"
pie pan. Mix preserves with honey, lemon juice, and
nutmeg. Spoon mixture over peaches and bake at 375° F.
for 30 minutes.

Take out of oven. Mix toppings. Crumble over
peach filling. Bake for 15 more minutes. Makes 8 portions. *(1 portion = 128.5 calories, 0.5 grams fat, 6% protein,
91% carbohydrates, 3% fat)*

Quick Apple Pie

1/2 C	Grape Nuts® cereal
4 C	Delicious apples *(large)*
2 tsp.	Cinnamon
2 tsp.	Corn starch
2 tsp.	Lemon juice
1/3 C	Frozen apple juice concentrate, thawed
1/2 tsp.	Ground coriander
1/4 C	Raisins

Preheat the oven to 400° F.

Core the apples, slice thin, and sprinkle with lemon juice.

Blend Grape Nuts®, pulsing until it's almost pulverized. Spread over the bottom of a covered casserole dish.

Dissolve corn starch in 1/3 cup of apple juice and cook until thick.

Mix apples, juice, and spices in a bowl. Spread the apple mixture over the cereal in the casserole dish. Sprinkle with additional cinnamon, if desired.

Cover and bake for 45 minutes, or until apples are tender. Remove cover and return to oven to allow pie to brown for 10 to 15 minutes longer. Makes 6 portions. *(1 portion = 127.5 calories, 0.4 grams fat, 5% protein, 93% carbohydrates, 3% fat)*

Green Apple Pastry Pie

▽ The yeasted pastry uses mashed potatoes and soy milk, not fat, to make it tender. It works well with any juicy fruit filling, or with soft savory filling. ▽

Yeasted Pastry:

1/2 C	Soy milk, warm
3 Tbsp.	Mashed potatoes
1 Tbsp.	Maple syrup
1 tsp.	Regular dry yeast
1/4 tsp.	Salt
1/4 C	Whole wheat flour
1 C	Unbleached flour
2 Tbsp.	Frozen apple juice concentrate, thawed, for brushing

Filling:

8 med.	Green apples, peeled, cored, and thinly sliced
1-1/2 tsp.	Lemon juice
1 tsp.	Grated lemon zest
3/4 tsp.	Cinnamon
1/8 tsp.	Cardamom
1/8 tsp.	Salt
1/8 tsp.	Nutmeg
1/2 C	Frozen apple juice concentrate, thawed
2 Tbsp.	Corn starch

Yeasted Pastry: Mix together soy milk, potatoes, syrup, and yeast in a medium bowl. Let stand 5 minutes.

(continued next page)

Green Apple Pastry Pie (continued)

Add salt and flours. Mix and knead mixture on a lightly floured surface 5 minutes.

Place dough in an oiled bowl, oil top lightly, cover, and let rise until doubled, about 1 hour. *(You can also let dough rise in refrigerator from 2 to 24 hours.)*

Filling: In a large bowl, toss apples, lemon juice, zest, cinnamon, salt, nutmeg, and cardamom.

Mix juice concentrate and corn starch in small saucepan and cook until smooth and thick, stirring constantly. Pour over apple mixture and mix well.

Pie Making: Preheat oven *(350° F.)*. Flour a bread board and roll pastry into a 16" circle. Transfer dough to a greased cookie sheet. Spoon apple filling into center of dough, then pinch edges around filling to make a 10" free-form pie. Pleat edges of dough. Leave a 5" hole in center, to display filling. Cover hole *(not pastry)* with foil.

Bake about 25 minutes. Brush pastry with 2 tablespoons of juice concentrate. Bake until golden brown *(about 5 minutes)*. Remove foil and serve hot. Makes 8 to 10 portions.   *(1 portion = 183.4 calories, 0.6 grams fat, 6% protein, 91% carbohydrates, 3% fat)*

Eat More, Weigh Less™ Tip
Zapf It!   59   *Save 14 gm. fat!*

Frozen Dessert

WOULD YOU BELIEVE: A cup of a typical ice cream has 14 grams of fat and a premium ice cream has 23 grams of fat.

SOME FACTS: Desserts can be festive and healthy if you use just a little bit of imagination. One of the best desserts I ever tasted was frozen bananas run through a Champion® juicer. This produces a consistency very much like soft-serve ice cream. If you add just a hint of vanilla you'll actually get a very tasty ice creamy product, though it's really not necessary. In fact, you can use frozen bananas as a base and then add frozen strawberries, or any other flavor by adding a frozen version of the fruit to the banana mixture.

WHAT YOU CAN DO: Try the following, slightly simpler recipe with your kids, they'll love it. Try it on your adult friends. They'll love it too.

Iced Fruit Cream

4 C	Bananas, frozen
1/4 C	**Water or juice**

Put 4" segments of frozen bananas pieces in the blender with 1/4 cup water or juice. Add more liquid if needed. Blend smooth. Serve immediately. Makes 8 portions. *(1 portion = 111.5 calories, 0.581 grams fat, 4% protein, 92% carbohydrates, 4% fat)*

Top with fresh banana slices, nuts, or cherries. Add other fruits as desired, or no-sugar-added extracts such as strawberries, blueberries, pears, vanilla, maple, and almond.

A Few More Sweet Delights

Strawberry-Banana Pudding

1-1/2 C	**Low-fat firm tofu** *(Mori Nu firm tofu is suggested)*
1-1/2 C	**Fresh strawberries, sliced**
1	**Banana**
1 tsp.	**Vanilla**
1 Tbsp.	**Lemon juice**
1/4 tsp.	**Salt**
2 Tbsp.	**Honey**

Blend all ingredients together in blender or food processor until creamy and smooth. Pour into individual serving dishes, or pour into individual-sized Grape Nuts® pie shells *(make by putting muffin cups in muffin pan then pouring in Grape Nuts®)*. Chill overnight. Makes 4 to 6 portions. *(1 portion = 109.4 calories, 1.886 grams fat, 23% protein, 62% carbohydrates, 15% fat)*

Honey Almond Fruit Cocktail

1 C	Watermelon
1 C	Honeydew melon
1 C	Apple
1/2 C	Cantaloupe or pineapple chunks
1	Peach or pear
6 Tbsp.	Agar
2 C	Water
1 C	Unsweetened soy milk
3 Tbsp.	Honey
	Almond extract, to taste

Dissolve agar in water, heat. When completely dissolved, add soy milk, honey, and almond extract, to taste. Cool and let set. Cut into small chunks.

Cut watermelon, honeydew melon, apple, cantaloupe, and peach or pear into 1/2" chunks.

Mix agar chunks together with chunks of various fruits for an unusual and colorful fruit cocktail. Makes 8 portions. *(1 portion = 84.72 calories, 0.588 grams fat, 7% protein, 87% carbohydrates, 6% fat)*

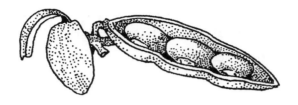

NON-CHOLESTEROL
PROTEIN/IRON GROUP

Meats/beans is one distinct category in the USDA's food pyramid, and you are advised to eat two to three servings per day from this group. Most people interpret this to mean that you should eat two to three servings per day of meat.

For years people have told us that we need animal products in order to get enough protein. Times have changed. Even the American Dietetic Association now considers this to be a myth.[21] Current nutritional analysis shows us there's

Non-Cholesterol Protein/Iron Foods

plenty of protein in grains, beans and vegetables, provided we eat them in their whole, unprocessed form.

Furthermore, recent studies have associated high intake of animal proteins with a number of health problems such as cancer and kidney disease. Studies even show that an excess intake of protein, especially animal protein, leads to loss of calcium. Even worse, all animal flesh contains cholesterol and nearly all animal flesh is high in fat. We now know that high-fat diets increase the risk of heart disease, cancer, and obesity.

Vegetable proteins were once thought to be adequate only if they were "combined." New information indicates that most vegetable proteins are complete in and of themselves. If you have any doubt about the adequacy of individual vegetable, grain or legume proteins, please refer to the table on page 86 of *Dr. Shintani's Eat More, Weigh Less™ Diet* book.

Today, rather than having a protein deficiency, most Americans have excessive protein in their diets. The health implications of having too much protein, especially too much animal protein, include increased risk of osteoporosis, certain cancers, heart disease, and kidney disease.[22]

The good news is — when I turned the food pyramid upside down, I moved all animal products into the small tip of the pyramid, and relegated them to the optional foods category. You'll see why, when you try all the delicious bean and legume recipes that follow. Why eat meat, when you can get the same or better nutritional benefits by eating these

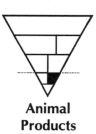

Animal Products

far less expensive, far more filling foods? Furthermore, once you've learned all the delicious ways to prepare meatless meals, you'll wonder why you ever bothered with such high-fat, potentially hazardous foods as meat, poultry and fish. Eat roughly two to three servings of noncholesterol, low-fat protein/iron-containing foods such as beans and legumes. This should amount to about 10% to 12% of your diet, every day.

Savory Beans

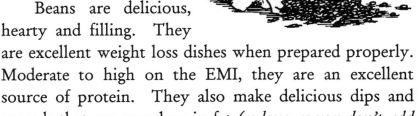

Beans are delicious, hearty and filling. They are excellent weight loss dishes when prepared properly. Moderate to high on the EMI, they are an excellent source of protein. They also make delicious dips and spreads that are very low in fat *(as long as you don't add any fats)*. If you don't have time to cook, you can get beans in a can at the supermarket or the health food store. Simply drain and use these beans as if they were cooked beans.

Unfortunately, many people stay away from beans because they can be gassy if they are not cooked or chewed properly. Gas develops when undigested protein or starch get to the large intestine, providing food for the flora that resides there. For some tips to eliminate gas, see *Dr. Shintani's Eat More, Weigh Less™ Diet*, page 197.

Beans and legumes are back in fashion. You will find many excellent bean recipes in the pages of this book. Why not start with a tasty, simple recipe for chili, such as the one that follows the cooking chart?

Cooking Chart for Beans

	Regular Pot		Pressure Cooker	
1 Cup of Beans	**Cups Water**	**Time**	**Cups Water**	**Time**
Lentils	3	30-60 min.	to cover	10-20 min.
Split Peas	2-3	30-60 min.	1/2" over	10 min.
Black Beans	4	1.5-2 hrs.	3/4" over	10-20 min.
Kidney Beans	3	1.5-2 hrs.	1/2" over	15-20 min.
Navy Beans	2	1.5-2 hrs.	1/2" over	10-20 min.
Pinto Beans	3	2-2.5 hrs.	1/2" over	10-15 min.
Chickpeas *(garbanzos)*	2	2.5-3 hrs.	1/2" over	15-25 min.
Azuki Beans	3	2-2.5 hrs.	1/2" over	15-20 min.
Soy Beans	3-4	3-4 hrs.	3/4" over	30 min.

Chunky Three-Bean Chili

3 large	Sweet onions, diced
2 C	Plum tomatoes, chopped
4 cloves	Garlic, minced
1 tsp.	Ground cumin
6 C	Vegetable broth *(or more, as needed)*
2 Tbsp.	Chili powder or to taste
1 C	Garbanzo beans, soaked and drained
1 C	Kidney beans, soaked and drained
1 C	Pinto beans, soaked and drained
1/4 C	Green chilies, canned and diced
3 Tbsp.	Low-sodium tomato paste
1 tsp.	Dried basil
	Olive oil cooking spray

Spray large pot with cooking spray. Heat 3 tablespoons vegetable broth and sauté onions, garlic, and cumin for 10 minutes. Add other ingredients, tomatoes, and remaining broth.

Boil, cover, and simmer for about 3 hours. When beans are soft and liquid is absorbed, they are done. Makes 6 portions. *(1 portion = 304.1 calories, 3.2 grams fat, 22% protein, 69% carbohydrates, 9% fat)*

Barbecue Baked Beans

1 C	Onion, diced
3 cans	Beans *(14-16 oz. kidney, black, navy, pinto, great northern, lima)*
2 Tbsp.	Blackstrap molasses
2 Tbsp.	Apple cider vinegar
1 Tbsp.	Dry mustard
1/2 tsp.	Garlic powder
1/2 C	Tomato ketchup
	Canola oil cooking spray

Heat oven to 350° F. While heating, sauté onion in an oil-sprayed nonstick pan.

Pour off half the liquid from each bean can. Mix beans and remaining ingredients in large bowl and add onion. Mix thoroughly. Put into a 2-quart casserole and bake, uncovered, for 1-1/2 hours, stirring after 1 hour. Makes 4 to 6 portions. *(1 portion = 279.1 calories, 1.6 grams fat, 18% protein, 77% carbohydrates, 5% fat)*

Zip Chili

4 cloves	Garlic, chopped
1/2 C	Onion, chopped
1-2 Tbsp.	Chili powder
2 cans	Kidney beans *(14 oz. size, with liquid from 1 can only or sauce will be too thin)*
1 can	Tomato sauce *(8 oz.)*
1/4 tsp.	Cumin

Sauté garlic and onions in water in a dutch oven. Add chili powder. Add kidney beans and tomato sauce. Simmer for 30 minutes. Makes 4 to 6 portions. *(1 portion = 159.2 calories, 1.0 grams fat, 23% protein, 72% carbohydrates, 5% fat)*

Sweet and Sour Tofu

1 lb.   Tofu, cut into 1-1/2" pieces

Sauce:

3/4 C   Water
2/3 C   Honey
2 Tbsp.   Corn starch
2 Tbsp.   Soy sauce
3 Tbsp.   Rice vinegar
          Olive oil cooking spray

Lightly spray nonstick skillet, brown the tofu until golden and textured on the outside *(about 5 minutes, watching carefully).*

Mix sauce ingredients together and pour over tofu, stirring constantly until sauce thickens.

Cover and simmer for 30 minutes. Makes 4 portions.
(1 portion = 259.2 calories, 3.3 grams fat, 12% protein, 78% carbohydrates, 11% fat)

Tomato, green pepper, pineapple chunks, cilantro, and toasted sesame seeds make excellent garnishes.

Moroccan Tacos

10 pieces Middle Eastern flatbread *(pita)*
or 10 wheat tortillas

Puree together:

3 C	Garbanzo beans, cooked *(1 cup dry)*
1 Tbsp.	Sesame seeds
1/4 C	Fresh parsley, chopped
2 cloves	Garlic
2 Tbsp.	Lime juice
1/2 tsp.	Ground cumin
1/4 tsp.	Cayenne

Purée all ingredients except pita bread, using the cooking water from the beans for moisture, as necessary. Adjust spices, to taste.

Let stand 1/2 hour at room temperature.

Lightly heat pita bread in oven, but don't let it get crisp. Cut bread(s) in half and fill "pockets" with bean mixture. Garnish with lettuce, chopped tomatoes, cucumber, onion, lime zest, parsley, or cilantro. Makes 10 portions *(1 portion = 250.0 calories, 3.2 grams fat, 16% protein, 73% carbohydrates, 11% fat)*

Broiled Falafel

2 C   Garbanzo beans, cooked *(3/4 C dry)*
1/2 C   Parsley clusters

Put in mixing bowl with:

3 cloves Garlic, pressed
2 Tbsp.   Egg replacer
1/2 tsp. Dry mustard
1 tsp.   Cumin
1/2 tsp. Chili powder
          Celery salt, to taste
          Salt and pepper, to taste
1 tsp.   Worcestershire™ sauce
2-3   Pita pocket bread

Purée garbanzo beans and parsley in blender. Mix blended beans with all other ingredients.

Place on a lightly oil-sprayed baking pan. Spread mixture on broiler pan, broil, and toss every 10 minutes.

Fill 1/2 pita pocket bread with falafel, lettuce, tomato, onion, and salsa. Makes 4 to 6 portions. *(1 portion = 206.4 calories, 2.7 grams fat, 19% protein, 69% carbohydrates, 11% fat)*

Eat More, Weigh Less™ Tip
Zing/Zapf It! ＼60／ *Save 17 gm. fat!*

Bean Dips and Spreads

WOULD YOU BELIEVE: A 2-tablespoon serving of Ranch dip can be 18 grams of fat or 95% fat.

SOME FACTS: Bean dips are one of my personal favorites because they are so versatile. I love to use them to replace high-fat dips. They are also tasty, low in fat, and can be used for snack foods as well as sandwiches. A variety of beans can be used in dips and spreads, depending on your personal taste. My favorite happens to be garbanzo bean dip. This is also known as a Mediterranean dish called hummus. If you want a bean dip that is even more convenient, use non-fat refried beans straight from the can to use as a dip or to spread on your sandwiches *(in addition to its more common use in burritos and tostadas)*.

WHAT YOU CAN DO:

- Try the following bean dip recipes.
- Try them as sandwich spreads.

EMWL Bean Dip

2	Onions, raw, chopped
3 cloves	Garlic, crushed
1 can	Tomatoes *(8 oz.)*
2 cans	Black beans *(15 oz.)*, drained
1 Tbsp.	Chili powder
1 Tbsp.	Chili con carne seasoning
2 tsp.	Cumin
2 tsp.	Coriander
1/4 tsp.	Cayenne

Sauté onions and garlic in nonstick pan with a touch of water, until soft. Add beans, heat through, move to blender and blend to dip consistency. Add spices and continue to blend until thoroughly mixed.

Use with low-fat crackers, chips, or spread onto a burrito or taco to make a bean base for your Mexican treats. You can be creative with this dip. Some people prefer to use fresh cooked beans; others like the speed of using canned. You can add chopped tomato, pepper, more onion, whatever suits your taste. Makes 6 portions.

(1 portion = 225.7 calories, 1.4 grams fat, 24% protein, 71% carbohydrates, 5% fat)

Black Bean Dip

1 can	Black beans *(15 oz.)* plus 1/2 C liquid from can
1/4 C	Tomato-based salsa
1/4 C	Onion, diced
2 cloves	Garlic, roughly chopped

Mix all ingredients together and simmer until most of the liquid has evaporated. Puree and set aside. Makes 6 portions. *(1 portion = 99.2 calories, 0.4 grams fat, 25% protein, 71% carbohydrates, 3% fat)*

Simple Hummus

1 C	Garbanzo beans, cooked
2-3 Tbsp.	Lemon juice
1 Tbsp.	Onion, minced
1 clove	Garlic, crushed
1 tsp.	Cumin
	Low-sodium soy sauce or salt, to taste
	Pepper to taste
	Water

Cook the dry garbanzo beans per package directions. *(Also, see bean cooking chart on page 318.)* You may use precooked canned beans instead, if you wish. Mash beans and mix ingredients together with enough water to keep a thick moist dip consistency. Makes 8 portions. *(1 portion = 93.5 calories, 1.3 grams fat, 22% protein, 67% carbohydrates, 12% fat)*

Eat More, Weigh Less™ Tip
Zip It!   ▽61▽   *5-minute Meal!*

Zip Burritos

Would You Believe:

- A burrito can be as high as 22 grams of fat and 540 calories *(Taco Bell® Burrito Supreme)*.

- You can make a delicious low-fat burrito in as little as 5 minutes.

Some Facts: Burritos can be an excellent low-fat way to eat beans. Unlike tacos, they have the advantage of having a "shell," a flour tortilla that is not fried. You still need to be careful of what kind of flour tortilla you use, however. Some of them are made with lard or a substantial amount of oil in them. It is preferable to use whole wheat flour tortillas with 1 or 2 grams of fat per tortilla. The fillings also play a part in making the burrito high or low in fat. The beef, sour cream, cheese, and guacamole are all high in fat content. Even the beans can be high in fat because they are "refried." The trick is to use nonfat "refried" beans or make the beans yourself *(see recipe on page 349)*.

What You Can Do: Try the "Zip Burrito" recipe that follows.

Zip Burritos

4	Whole wheat tortillas or chapatis
1 C	Nonfat refried beans
1/2 C	Fresh salsa *(see page 332 for recipe)*
1 C	Lettuce, chopped
1/2 C	Alfalfa sprouts
1	Tomato, chopped
1	Green onion, chopped

Heat the beans either in a microwave or put them in a saucepan, stirring them on the stove until heated. Spoon some of the nonfat refried beans onto a tortilla from end to end, then add fresh salsa *(if you are in a hurry, use bottled salsa)* over the beans. Next add the chopped lettuce, alfalfa sprouts, tomatoes, and green onion. Fold in the sides of the tortilla and hold it together with a toothpick. Makes 4 portions. *(1 portion = 183.2 calories, 3.0 grams fat, 15% protein, 71% carbohydrates, 14% fat)*

▽ This makes a delicious, quick burrito that you can eat any time. You can find canned nonfat refried beans in a health food store. Make sure it says nonfat refried beans rather than low-fat, because even low-fat refried beans can contain 3 to 5 grams of fat per serving. ▽

Pronto Bean and Rice Burritos

1 C	Basmati brown rice, steamed until tender and set aside
10	Whole-wheat chapatis or tortillas
1 can	Chili beans *(16 oz.)*, cooked
1	Bell pepper, diced
1	Tomato, chopped
1/4 C	Onion, chopped
1 clove	Garlic, minced
1 tsp.	Ground cumin, or to taste
1 Tbsp.	Chili powder, or to taste
2 Tbsp.	Prepared salsa
1/4 C	Green onions, chopped
1/4 C	Cilantro, chopped

Lightly warm chapatis or tortillas in oven, watching carefully so they remain soft. Reheat rice.

In the meantime, combine beans, bean liquid, bell pepper, tomato, onion, garlic, cumin, chili powder, and salsa in a saucepan. Simmer about 5 minutes.

Place a heaping tablespoon of rice and 1 to 2 tablespoons of the bean mixture in the warm chapatis or tortilla. Garnish with additional salsa, green onions, and cilantro and roll into a burrito. *Makes 10 portions. (1 portion = 238.5 calories, 3.6 grams fat, 14% protein, 72% carbohydrates, 14% fat)*

Chapati Burritos

6	Chapatis *(or more)*
2 C	Lettuce, shredded
1 C	Beans, cooked, drained *(kidneys, black, pintos)*
1	Cucumber, julienned
1 C	Broccoli florets, blanched
1/2 C	Tomatoes, diced
1/2 C	Red or green bell peppers, cut in thin strips
1/2 C	Round and green onions, sliced very thin
1/4 C	Cilantro, chopped
	Salsa, to taste

Warm chapatis *(if you use the microwave, make sure they don't get brittle)*. Place warm chapati on plate. Build burrito with above condiments, starting with lettuce and ending with the salsa. Roll and enjoy! Makes 6 portions.

(1 portion = 150.8 calories, 1.3 grams fat, 18% protein, 75% carbohydrates, 7% fat)

Fresh Salsa Caliente

1	Jalapeño or other small green chili peppers, seeded and coarsely chopped
	Cayenne pepper *(optional, to taste)*
4-6 cloves	Garlic, minced
5 small	Ripe Roma tomatoes, cored and coarsely chopped
2 Tbsp.	Fresh lime juice
1/2 med.	Onion, minced
1/2 tsp.	Cumin, ground
1 tsp.	Chili powder
1/2	Bell pepper, minced
1/4 C	Cilantro, chopped
2 Tbsp.	Parsley, minced
1/2 tsp.	Black pepper
1 tsp.	Garlic salt

Mix ingredients, marinate in refrigerator for 12 hours. Will keep, refrigerated, for 4 to 5 days. Makes 8 portions *(about 2 cups).* *(1 portion = 25.0 calories, 0.3 grams fat, 15% protein, 76% carbohydrates, 9% fat)*

Eat More, Weigh Less™ Tip
Zapf It! ⬩62⬩ *Save 10 gm. fat!*

Try "Wheat" Meat

WOULD YOU BELIEVE: Beef stew contains about 11 grams of fat per cup, which comprise 44% of its 220 calories.

SOME FACTS: While mixing beef with vegetables *(as in stew)* is an improvement over eating just the beef, the resulting food is still usually high in fat simply because the beef is usually very high in fat. For example, 4 ounces of an average cut of beef can have 30 grams of fat, which comprise 71% of its 396 calories.

One solution is to use "wheat meat" or wheat gluten, also known as "seitan." It is a product made from protein of whole wheat flour. This food can be found in your local health food store or you can make your own. Wheat gluten has the texture of meat and will be a great substitute because it absorbs flavors like meat does and has the right appearance and texture for foods such as stews and sandwich fillings.

WHAT YOU CAN DO: Try the following recipe (or page 205) which uses a "seitan" instead of beef.

Sweet and Sour Seitan Vegetables

1 lb.	Mixed vegetables *(your choice)*, cut into 1" chunks and strips
1 C	Seitan, cut into small chunks
1/4 C	Onions, chopped
1/4 C	Tomato sauce
3 cloves	Garlic, finely chopped
2 Tbsp.	Red wine vinegar
1-2 Tbsp.	Low-sodium soy sauce
2 Tbsp.	Honey
4-6	Red chili peppers, seeded and sliced *(optional)*
2 Tbsp.	Corn starch
1/2 tsp.	Salt
1/2 C	Water

Sauté garlic and onion over medium heat until golden brown.

Add seitan, brown, then add mixed vegetables, tomato sauce, red wine vinegar, soy sauce, honey, salt, and red chili peppers.

Combine the corn starch and water; blend to make a smooth paste. Stir corn starch mixture into sauce and cook 5 minutes or until vegetables are cooked and sauce is thickened. Makes 4 to 6 portions. *(1 portion = 209.3 calories, 0.8 grams fat, 27% protein, 70% carbohydrates, 3% fat)*

Eat More, Weigh Less™ Tip
Zapf It!   ▽63▽

TVP Is Better
Than Beef

TVP stands for "Texturized Vegetable Protein." This is a soy-based protein that has the texture of ground beef when cooked. It is useful for foods that ordinarily contain ground beef, such as chili, tacos, and in casseroles. TVP can be purchased in most health food stores. It is high in protein, relatively low in fat and, of course, has no cholesterol, which is the best reason to use TVP. In addition, you can eat more TVP than you can ground beef before you reach the same amount of calories and fat, because its much higher on the EMI.

Here's another chili recipe, which uses TVP, or you can add TVP to the Chunky Three-Bean Chili recipe on page 319.

TVP Chili

1 small	Onion, diced
1/2 C	Green bell pepper, diced
1/2 C	Red bell pepper, diced
1	Jalapeño pepper, minced
3 Tbsp.	Water
1 Tbsp.	Chili powder
1/8 tsp.	Garlic powder
1/3 C	TVP *(textured vegetable protein)*
1/4 tsp.	Cayenne
1/2 C	Water, boiling
15 oz.	Chili beans, canned

Soak TVP in boiling water for 20 minutes.

Water-sauté onion and pepper in nonstick skillet until onions are translucent *(about 7 minutes)*.

Add other ingredients to onions, continue cooking another 10 minutes. Serve over brown rice. Makes 2 portions. *(1 portion = 277.2 calories, 3.0 grams fat, 30% protein, 61% carbohydrates, 9% fat)*

Sloppy Jacks

1 C	TVP *(textured vegetable protein)*
1/4 C	Water
2 cloves	Garlic, minced
1 med.	Green pepper, diced *(about 1 cup)*
1 med.	Onion, minced *(about 1 cup)*
1 stalk	Celery, minced *(about 1/2 cup)*
1 small	Carrot, minced *(about 1/2 cup)*
3 Tbsp.	Tomato ketchup
1 can	Tomato sauce *(16 oz.)*
2 Tbsp.	Chili powder or to taste
1/4 tsp.	Hot pepper sauce or to taste
	Sea salt, to taste
6	Whole grain rolls
	Canola oil cooking spray

Soak TVP in water for 20 minutes.

Heat oil-spray skillet. Add vegetables and sauté until soft *(about 5 to 7 minutes)*.

Reduce heat, mix in all remaining ingredients *(except rolls)*. Cook, stirring occasionally, until heated through *(about 3 minutes)*.

Serve on rolls. Makes 6 portions. *(1 portion = 170.9 calories, 2.0 grams fat, 19% protein, 71% carbohydrates, 10% fat)*

Eat More, Weigh Less™ Tip

Zapf It!   \64/   *Save 32 gm. fat!*

Try Burger Substitutes

WOULD YOU BELIEVE: A large fast food hamburger can contain over 600 calories with 36 grams of fat?

SOME FACTS: Hamburger patties contain so much fat *(a 3-ounce patty is 260 calories, 19.2 grams of fat or 68% fat by calories)*, they should be called "lard burgers."

BRAND		CALORIES	FAT (gm.)
McDonald's®	Big Mac®	560	32
Jack in the Box®	Jumbo Jack®	551	29
	with cheese	628	35
Burger King®	Whopper®	630	36
	with cheese	740	45
Wendy's®	"Single"	511	27
	with cheese	580	34

- Some fast food chicken sandwiches are actually worse! They contain between 575 calories *(with 36 grams of fat at Jack in the Box®)* and 685 calories *(40 grams of fat at Burger King®).*

- Even fast food fish sandwiches contain between 442 calories *(with 26 grams of fat at McDonalds®)* and 554 calories *(32 grams of fat at Jack in the Box®).*

- Add a slice of cheese *(106 calories, 9 grams of fat)*, and the problem gets even worse.

WHAT YOU CAN DO:

- Try a meatless burger such as Garden Vegan™ or Garden Burger® *(total sandwich equals 3 to 4 grams of fat).*

- Heap tomato, lettuce, onions, and other high EMI foods onto your "burger" and you'll move the sandwich ever higher on the EMI scale.

- Avoid the mayo – use mustard or ketchup instead.

- Try one of the burger recipes below.

Potato Beanburgers

1-1/2 C   Brown rice, cooked
1 med.   Potato, cooked and mashed
1-1/2 C   Garbanzo beans *(or one 15 oz. can, drained)*
1 tsp.   Garlic powder
1 tsp.   Onion powder
1 tsp.   Salt, or to taste
2 tbsp.   Nutritional yeast flakes
2 stalks   Celery
1 small   Onion *(optional)*
          Canola oil cooking spray

Steam the brown rice according to directions on page 62. Pierce raw potato with a fork in half a dozen places, then microwave, according to your microwave's directions *(usually about 5 minutes)*.

Place beans in blender, pulse until coarsely chopped *(about the texture of finely chopped nuts)*. Add the potato, pulse again until well mixed. Add other ingredients, blending well. The mixture should stick together with about the same texture as thick cookie dough. Form into patties. Spray a nonstick skillet with canola oil spray, brown patties, then place in toaster oven and bake until they're firm yet moist. Delicious on a bun, or covered with one of the EMWL gravies. Makes 6 to 8 portions. *(1 portion = 132.3 calories, 1.5 grams fat, 16% protein, 74% carbohydrates, 10% fat)*

▽ SPECIAL TIP: If the mixture is too thin to form into patties, you can add whole grain bread crumbs until you get the right texture. If too thick, add water *(a tiny bit at a time)* until you have them perfect for you. ▽

Lentil Burgers

A 7-ingredient, 30-minute recipe

1 large	Onion, chopped fine
2 cloves	Garlic, minced
1 large	Tomato, diced
1/8 C	Vegetable juice
2 C	Lentils, pre-cooked
1 Tbsp.	Fresh basil *(or pinch of dried)*
	Salt, to taste
	Pepper, to taste
	Olive oil cooking spray

Spray skillet with olive oil, heat and sauté onions and garlic. Stir often. Cover and reduce heat to low, add tomato and vegetable juice, simmer for 5 minutes. Take off stove and add cooked lentils. Add seasonings. If mixture isn't dry enough, add whole grain bread crumbs until the mixture has a firm, almost pliable texture. Form into moist patties, place on cookie sheet in preheated *(350° F.)* toaster oven and cook another 10 minutes on each side. The texture will be between a Sloppy Joe and a burger. Serve on whole grain buns with salad and/or American Fries. Makes 6 portions. *(1 portion = 96.9 calories, 0.5 grams fat, 26% protein, 69% carbohydrates, 5% fat)*

Eat More, Weigh Less™ Tip
Zapf It! \\65/

Better Than Chicken

WOULD YOU BELIEVE:

- Chicken has about as much cholesterol as beef *(85 mg. compared to 91 mg. for a 3-1/2 ounce portion).*

- A 3-1/2-ounce portion of broiled chicken thigh has 15.5 grams of fat or 55% fat by calories. If skinless, it still has 10.9 grams of fat and 49% fat by calories.

- A 3-1/2-ounce portion of broiled chicken breast is 196 calories, with 7.8 grams of fat. If skinless, it is 165 calories with 3.6 grams of fat *(but it still has 85 mg. cholesterol).*

SOME FACTS: Chicken isn't as healthy as some would have you believe. It has nearly as much cholesterol and fat as beef. And skinless chicken is lower in fat, but is still a relatively high-fat product.

One substitute is to use tofu as if it were chicken. A recipe follows. It turns out to be like chicken nuggets, but the cholesterol is 0 and the fat content is about 75 calories and 4.8 grams of fat per 3-1/2 ounces – much less than the 239 calories and 13.3 grams of fat in 3-1/2 ounces of chicken "nuggets."

Another excellent substitute is a new meatless chicken produced by Wholesome & Hearty Foods, Inc. called GardenChick'n™. It looks like shredded chicken, has about 3.5 grams of fat per 3-1/2 ounces, and has no cholesterol.

You can use either GardenChick'n™ or Tofu Nuggets as a sandwich filler or add the chicken substitutes to vegetable dishes, such as stir-frys. You can even use it to top baked potatoes. Experiment and enjoy it!

WHAT YOU CAN DO:

- Try "GardenChick'n™."
- Try the following recipe for "Tofu Nuggets."

Tofu Nuggets

1 blk.	Firm tofu, cut in 3/4" cubes
1/3 C	Nutritional yeast
1 tsp.	Spike® seasoning
1/2 tsp.	Black pepper
1-1/2 Tbsp.	Soy sauce or tamari
1/4 tsp.	Olive or sesame oil *(or cooking spray)*

Slice or break tofu into approximately 3/4" cubes. Coat nonstick pan with oil or cooking spray and heat at medium-high. Add tofu cubes and brown. Turn heat to low and drizzle soy sauce on each piece of tofu. Add yeast, Spike®, and pepper and toss, coating the pieces of tofu evenly. Cook until golden brown. Makes 2 to 4 portions. *(1 portion = 118.2 calories, 3.6 grams fat, 45% protein, 29% carbohydrates, 26% fat)*

Marinated Tofu

1 lb.	Tofu, extra firm
1/2 C	Vegetable broth
1 Tbsp.	Soy sauce
1/2 tsp.	Garlic powder
1/2 tsp.	Onion powder
1 tsp.	Sage, dried
2 tsp.	Nutritional yeast
2 Tbsp.	Lemon juice
1/4 tsp.	Black pepper

Mix all ingredients except tofu. Cut tofu into 1/4"
slices and marinate in the mixture for 1 hour.

Heat oven. Broil tofu on a lightly-oiled baking sheet
just until golden, about 10 minutes; turn and broil
10 minutes more. Remove from broiler, cool, add to sub-
marine sandwiches and serve. Makes 4 to 6 portions.
*(1 portion = 66.5 calories, 2.0 grams fat, 48% protein, 27% carbohy-
drates, 26% fat)*

Eat More, Weigh Less™ Tip

Zapf It! $\triangledown$ 66 $\triangle$ *Save 13 gm. fat*

What Is Tempeh?

WOULD YOU BELIEVE: Tempeh is not a city in Arizona.

SOME FACTS: Tempeh, a soy-based product, is another good substitute for meat. It is made from soybeans which are packed into flat patties and then lightly fermented so that the beany flavor of soybeans is eliminated and its gassiness is reduced. Tempeh can be used like gluten in a number of different dishes, such as in stews, side dishes, and for sandwich fillings.

Tempeh can be found in your local health food store in the refrigerator or freezer section. For a 3-ounce portion, it is 169 calories and 6.5 grams of fat compared to 260 calories and 19.2 grams of fat in a 3-ounce hamburger patty.

WHAT YOU CAN DO:

- Try tempeh in a sandwich.

- Try the following recipes for delicious entrées.

Tempeh Cutlet

1 piece	Tempeh, 1/4" to 1/2" thick piece
1 Tbsp.	Low-sodium tamari
1 tsp.	Ginger juice
2 Tbsp.	Water
1-1/2 tsp.	Honey
1 clove	Garlic

Place tempeh in a bakeware dish that has a cover, marinate in the tamari mixed with ginger juice, water, honey, and garlic.

Bake at 350° F. for about 25 minutes. Makes 1 portion *(1 portion = 279.7 calories, 8.8 grams fat, 31% protein, 43% carbohydrates, 26% fat)*

▽ Can be served as a simple bean dish with rice or potatoes or can be delicious if used in a sandwich. ▽

Marinated Tempeh

1 lb.	Tempeh, sliced in strips
6 Tbsp.	Low-sodium soy sauce
1/4 C	Apple concentrate, frozen
1 tsp.	Dry mustard
2 cloves	Garlic, crushed
1 small	Ginger root, grated
1/4 C	Mirin
2 tsp.	Sesame seeds, toasted
1 Tbsp.	Corn starch in 1/4 cup water

Place sliced tempeh strips in shallow baking dish. Blend soy sauce, apple concentrate, mustard, garlic, ginger, and mirin together for marinade. Pour marinade over tempeh to cover. Sprinkle sesame seeds on top. Bake at 350° F. for 20 to 30 minutes or until brown. Use corn starch and water to thicken sauce. Makes 4 portions. *(1 portion = 333.4 calories, 9.7 grams fat, 27% protein, 49% carbohydrates, 25% fat)*

More Bean/Protein Recipes

Cuban Black Beans

1 C	Cuban black beans, dried
2	Tomatillos, sliced in half
2	Bay leaves
1 Tbsp.	Parsley flakes *(optional)*
1 Tbsp.	Chili powder

▽ Cuban black beans are small and very black. If you cannot find, you may substitute conventional black beans or other small beans, such as pinto beans. ▽

Soak beans in cold water overnight. Drain and put in cooking pot. Add 5 cups of water, tomatillos, bay leaves, parsley, and chili powder. Bring to a boil, then reduce heat. Cook on low until the beans are very tender *(about 2 hours)*. Keep covered with liquid. Discard the tomatillos and bay leaves *(unless combining with Cuban Salsa recipe)*. Makes 4 to 6, 1/2 cup portions. *(1/2 cup = 55.20 calories, 0.594 grams fat, 23% protein, 68% carbohydrates, 9% fat)*

▽ This bean recipe can be combined with the Cuban Salsa recipe that follows to make a new dish. DON'T TAKE OUT THE BAY LEAVES AND TOMATILLOS YET! See next recipe. ▽

Cuban Salsa and Beans

1 large	Onion, finely chopped
4 cloves	Garlic, minced
1\2 C	Dry white wine
2 tsp.	Ground cumin
1 med.	Tomato, chopped
2	Jalapeño peppers, seeded and finely chopped
1 C	Cilantro, chopped
1 C	Green onion, chopped
	Salt, to taste
	Black pepper, freshly ground, to taste
	Fresh parsley, chopped
	Olive oil cooking spray
2-3 C	Cuban black beans, cooked *(recipe on previous page)*

Sauté onions until softened in an oil-sprayed, nonstick skillet over medium heat *(about 5 minutes)*.

Add wine, cumin, tomatoes, jalapeño peppers, cilantro, and green onions. Simmer for 10 minutes, stirring frequently.

Stir the salsa mixture into hot, cooked beans and continue cooking an additional 45 minutes to 1 hour, or until the beans are very soft. Remove the bay leaves and tomatillos *(from bean recipe)*. Salt and pepper to taste, garnish with additional cilantro or parsley, and serve. Makes 6 portions. *(1 portion = 87.9 calories, 1.1 grams fat, 19% protein, 71% carbohydrates, 10% fat)*

Navy Beans on Rye

1 C	Navy beans, cooked and drained
1 clove	Garlic, minced
1 Tbsp.	Fresh chives, chopped
1 Tbsp.	Fresh cilantro, chopped
1 Tbsp.	Round onion, minced
1 Tbsp.	Green onion
2 Tbsp.	Lime juice
1/4 tsp.	Salt
1/8 tsp.	White pepper
8 slices	Pumpernickel bread
1	Cucumber, peeled and thinly sliced
	Boston lettuce
	Mung bean or alfalfa sprouts

Place everything but bread, lettuce, cucumber, and sprouts in a food processor. Use your S Blade to blend until smooth. Add seasonings and lime juice to taste.

Spread bean mixture on four slices of pumpernickel bread. Cover the remaining four slices of bread with a layer of cucumber. Top with sprouts and lettuce, add onion slices if you wish, or other delicious vegetable sandwich fillings. Slice sandwiches in quarters. Makes 4 portions. *(1 portion = 235.1 calories, 2.5 grams fat, 17% protein, 73% carbohydrates, 9% fat)*

Black Beans With Carrots and Cabbage

1 C	Napa cabbage, sliced thin
6 large	Carrots, diced
2 large	Onions, sliced thin
2 tsp.	Onion salt
2 cloves	Garlic, minced
1 Tbsp.	Chili powder
1 tsp.	Oregano
1 tsp.	Dried basil
3 tsp.	Marjoram
1	Bay leaf
2 cans	Black beans with liquid *(16 oz.)*
2 cups	Spinach, chopped
6 plum	Tomatoes, diced
	Olive oil cooking spray

Spray a large pot with olive oil and sauté onions and garlic over medium heat until translucent. Mix in cabbage, carrots, salt, spices, and herbs. Sauté until the carrots are soft. Stir in beans with liquid, add spinach, then tomatoes. Cook until the tomatoes are heated through and spinach is tender. Makes 6 to 8 portions.

(1 portion = 252.6 calories, 1.7 grams fat, 22% protein, 73% carbohydrates, 6% fat)

▽ Cook a day in advance for better blended flavors. ▽

Hearty Red Lentil Soup

2 C	Red lentils, rinsed and drained
2 med.	Potatoes, cut in even-sized chunks
2 med.	Carrots, diced
5-6 C	Vegetable broth
2 cloves	Garlic, minced
1 large	Onion, thinly sliced
1 stalk	Celery, sliced
1 can	Tomatoes *(15 oz.)*
1	Bay leaf
1 tsp.	Thyme, dried
1 Tbsp.	Low-sodium soy sauce
	Salt, to taste
	Pepper, to taste
1/2 tsp.	Paprika
10 oz.	Peas and carrots, frozen
1 C	Mushrooms, small and thinly sliced
	Olive oil cooking spray

Sauté onions and garlic in a nonstick skillet, lightly oiled. Add vegetable broth, vegetables and spices. Simmer until vegetables are tender. Add peas and mushrooms just before serving. Makes 4 portions. *(1 portion = 324.3 calories, 1.8 grams fat, 24% protein, 72% carbohydrates, 5% fat)*

Eat More, Weigh Less™ Tip
Zapf It! $\sqrt{67}$

Aw Nuts!

WOULD YOU BELIEVE: A single whole cashew nut contains nearly 1 gram of fat *(about 0.9 gram)*.

SOME FACTS: Nuts are a non-cholesterol source of protein, as are beans. However, I do not advocate using nuts as a primary source of food, or even as a snack. Nuts are much too high in fat to fit well into your *Eat More, Weigh Less™ Diet*. The average nut is somewhere between 75% to 80% fat by calories. Therefore, I recommend using nuts simply as condiments. For example, you may want to sprinkle some nuts onto a salad or use some in a stir fry. One ounce of nuts contains:

Nut	Calories	Fat Grams	% Fat
Peanuts	156	13	73%
Cashews	164	15	73%
Walnuts	178	15	77%

WHAT YOU CAN DO: Use nuts sparingly, e.g., as a condiment. Aw nuts!

FOODS NOT NECESSARY

FOR HEALTH

Earlier, I mentioned that the optional foods group at the bottom of the Inverted Food Pyramid is separated from the rest of the food groups because we would generally be healthier without them. We certainly do not need them on a daily basis. This is why I have classified these foods as "FOODS NOT NECESSARY FOR HEALTH."

Low-fat Fish/ Poultry/Meat Protein Iron Foods

These foods are low in EMI — that is, low in bulk value. They induce the consumption of more calories, and are generally high in fat. In

Nonfat Dairy Calcium Foods

the section on non-dairy calcium, we talked about dairy foods and why you don't need to eat them. In the "Non-Cholesterol Protein/Iron Foods section, we talked about meat, fish, and poultry. Now, a few more words about the "Fats/Oils/ Sweets" section. The following *Eat More, Weigh Less*™ Tips will explain in more detail why you should always be cautious when using these foods, and why you should stick to the *Eat More, Weigh Less*™ *Diet*.

Fats/Oils/ Sweets

I would, however, like to repeat a bit of advice:

> For those who have health conditions that might affect their digestion, absorption, metabolism or otherwise affect their nutrition, please consult your own physician while making your decision about using or giving up these foods.

Eat More, Weigh Less™ Tip
Zapf It! \68/

Avoid Animal Products

WOULD YOU BELIEVE:

- The leading cause of death of animals in America is human beings – because we slaughter them by the millions.

- The leading cause of death of human beings in America is animals - because we eat them.

SOME FACTS: The leading cause of death in America, cardiovascular disease *(including heart attacks and strokes)*, and the second leading cause of death, cancer, are related, in part, to the consumption of animal products. High serum cholesterol is directly related to the leading cause of death in this country, heart disease and the third leading cause, stroke. For every 1% increase in serum cholesterol, there is a 2% increase in risk of heart attack. What causes high cholesterol? In general, a high saturated fat, high cholesterol, high total fat diet. In general, animal products have all three. High fat diets and high animal protein diets are also associated with high rates of certain cancers. Consider these facts:

- An average cut of beef is between two-thirds and three-fourths fat *(71% fat from calories)*, and most of the fat is saturated.

- All animal products *(including poultry and fish)* contain cholesterol. No plant products do.

- High fat diets are associated with cancer of the colon, breast, and prostate.

- High animal protein consumption is associated with cancer of the colon and breast.

WHAT YOU CAN DO:

- Try a vegetarian diet *(i.e., a strict Eat More, Weigh Less™ Diet for three weeks)*.

- Then switch to it for the rest of your life.

Eat More, Weigh Less™ Tip
Zapf It! 69

The #1 Diet Destroyer

WOULD YOU BELIEVE: Lard, animal fats, olive oil, canola oil, and other vegetable oils all have the same amount of calories: 9 calories per gram or about 13.5 to 14 grams of fat and 120 calories per tablespoon.

SOME FACTS: Fats and oils promote obesity, whether these are found in saturated form, as in meat, poultry, and fish; or in vegetable oil such as corn, sesame, and flaxseed oil. Or in even the "healthier" oils with monounsaturated such as olive and canola oil.

Of course, with respect to heart disease, monounsaturated oils seem best, especially "extra virgin olive oil" *(which is actually unprocessed olive juice).* This may be more because of the high antioxidant content of the olive juice rather than solely because of the oil.

In any case, they're all 9 calories per gram, and in terms of weight loss, it's best to keep all of them to a minimum.

What You Can Do:

- Elipidate™ your diet.

- If you must use oil, use as little as possible *(e.g., oil sprays such as PAM)*.

- Use applesauce or other fruit purées when baking, instead of oil. *(See Tip #20.)*

- When stir frying, use the following in place of oil:

  - Vegetable broth
  - Cooking or other wine
  - Water
  - Mirin (vinegar)

Eat More, Weigh Less™ Tip
Zapf/Zing It! ▽70▽ *Save 20 gm. fat!*

The "Mayo" Clinic

WOULD YOU BELIEVE: Mayonnaise is 98% fat by calories and 11 grams of fat per tablespoon. That makes it about 100 calories per tablespoon.

SOME FACTS: What's wrong with mayonnaise? It is an easy way to make a good sandwich bad and a bad sandwich worse in terms of health. The reason for this is that most people use a tablespoon or two or even more in making sandwiches. In doing so, one can add 200 calories or more to a sandwich, and increase the fat intake by 22 grams which may be your entire day's allotment of fat *(if you want to keep a 10% fat diet on a daily intake of 2,000 calories).*

WHAT YOU CAN DO: Mustards of various kinds are a great substitute. They contain only 1 gram of fat per tablespoon and 18 calories. One of my favorites is "Dijon mustard." It has a rich but mild flavor and is excellent to use in sandwiches. And if you use 2 tablespoons of it to replace mayo, you'll save 20 grams of fat.

Eat More, Weigh Less™ Tip
Zapf It! $\overline{\diagdown 71 \diagup}$

Margarine Is Not
a Better Butter

WOULD YOU BELIEVE: Both margarine and butter are 99-100% fat by calories, and are both about 11 to 12 grams of fat and 100 to 108 calories per tablespoon.

SOME FACTS: For years people have been promoting margarine as a better alternative to butter. This was based on research that indicated that while the high saturated fat content of butter raised serum cholesterol, polyunsaturated fats, found in margarine seemed to lower cholesterol. What the promoters of margarine never tell you is that margarine is 99% fat and whether it is saturated or polyunsaturated fat, it promotes obesity just the same.

What's worse is that recently, it has been discovered that margarine isn't even as good for cholesterol control as was once thought. This is because the oil in margarine is partially hydrogenated when margarine is being manufactured.

This process produces "trans" fatty acids which are just as bad as saturated fat in terms of raising serum cholesterol and the risk of heart disease. In addition, studies on mice suggest polyunsaturated fats are even worse that saturated fat in terms of promoting certain cancers, such as breast cancer.

WHAT YOU CAN DO:

- If you want to eat more, weigh less, and stay healthy, I suggest not using butter or margarine at all.

- Instead, use one of the many types of spreads I described in *Eat More, Weigh Less*™ Tip 21.

Eat More, Weigh Less™ Tip
Zing It! ▽72▽

Natural Substitutes for Sugar

Most people are used to something sweet with their morning meals. Sugar on cereals, syrup on hotcakes and waffles, jam on toast. It's okay to have something sweet for breakfast. But try to avoid refined sugar. And when I suggest use substitutes for sugar, I don't mean change to artificial sugar substitutes. These may be worse than sugar itself.

If you have a morning sweet tooth, I recommend that you use partially refined sugar products, such as: maple syrup, brown rice syrup, barley malt, and blackstrap molasses. These will probably affect your blood sugar level as much as regular sugar does. However, because they are somewhat diluted in that they are not totally refined *(as is white sugar)*, the calorie density is a little less and its EMI value is slightly higher. In addition, foods such as blackstrap molasses contain other redeeming qualities. Blackstrap molasses has a high calcium content as well as a high iron content. These are two nutrients that are commonly deficient in poorly planned vegetarian diets.

An even better suggestion is to use dried fruit for your sweetening. At least these foods are whole foods. The use of the above sweeteners should be considered a significant compromise from the *Eat More, Weigh Less™ Diet* principles, and if used at all they should be used only on rare occasions and in limited amounts. But you can adapt these sweeteners and still make the diet work for you without giving up on sweets altogether.

You can also be creative. For example, I like to use a handful of raisins to sweeten oatmeal, rather than using a couple of teaspoons full of sugar. Come up with your own variations, and make this diet your own. For an especially tasty breakfast recipe that will satisfy your sweet tooth and enhance your health, try whole grain, fruit-juice sweetened muffins. They're a delicious way to start the day.

SMART SNACKING

All your life you've probably had people telling you that you shouldn't snack between meals, that it's bad for you, that it will cause you to gain weight.

They're wrong. It's not snacking that's bad for you, but rather the foods that are usually eaten as snacks that are the problem. Most of them are high in fat and low on the EMI scale. Snacking actually helps keep your body fueled, so you won't get hungry and do something foolish like go on a binge of foods that are bad for you. Keep the following snacks handy, at home, work and play. Encourage your family to trade their old snacks in for these improved forms of snacking food. You'll find that the following snacks are fast and easy to prepare. Eat all of them you want, at any time.

Eat More, Weigh Less™ Tip

Zapf It! ▽73▽ *Save 9 gms. fat!*

Smart Snacking

WOULD YOU BELIEVE:

- Potato chips are 58% fat by calories or 10 grams per ounce.

- Corn chips are 53% fat by calories or 9 grams per ounce.

- Pita bread chips are 2% fat by calories or 0.7 grams per ounce.

SOME FACTS: One of the greatest advantages of the *Eat More, Weigh Less™ Diet* is that it allows you to eat all you want, including snacking. This helps keep you satisfied so you won't be tempted to "binge."

WHAT YOU CAN DO:

- Cut whole wheat pita bread into eighths and toast in a toaster oven or in a regular oven on a cookie sheet. Eat them like chips, especially with dip such as the Simple Hummus *(garbanzo)* dip on page 327.

- Try these additional snack ideas.

  1. Air-popped popcorn *(see Eat More, Weigh Less™ Tip 53)*

  2. Corn on the cob *(see Eat More, Weigh Less™ Tip 4)*

  3. Oven roasted potatoes

  4. Baked "new potatoes"

  5. Steamed sweet potatoes *(see Eat More, Weigh Less™ Tip 31)*

  6. Rice cakes with spread

  7. Bagels with spread *(see Eat More, Weigh Less™ Tip 18)*

  8. Chapati bread with spread *(see Eat More, Weigh Less™ Tip 60)*

  9. Whole grain pretzels

  10. Slices of fresh fruit

  11. Veggies and dips *(see Eat More, Weigh Less™ Tip 45)*

  12. Zip pizza *(see Eat More, Weigh Less™ Tip 41)*

  13. Zip burritos *(see Eat More, Weigh Less™ Tip 61)*

  14. Brown rice balls wrapped in nori

  15. Fat-free chips

SOME FINAL EAT MORE,

WEIGH LESS™ TIPS

Weight gain and weight loss are multifaceted problems. In the companion book, *Dr. Shintani's Eat More, Weigh Less™ Diet,* I describe exactly why this diet works so well and delve into the principles behind it in far more detail. There are both social and physical factors involved, and this cookbook has focused almost entirely on the physical/dietary aspects, by guiding you to the proper way to eat. In this final brief section, I'd like to introduce you to a few of the most important concepts that you will find in greater depth in the parent book, to better round out your understanding of this unique diet. The first tip shows what you're doing by following the diet. The final three tips address other aspects of the diet, and encourage you to adopt them so the diet will work best for you.

Eat More, Weigh Less™ Tip
Zing It!   \74/

Chew the Fat Away

WOULD YOU BELIEVE: Chewing can help you lose weight.

SOME FACTS: There are two simple ways in which chewing can help you lose weight. The first way is direct: chewing sends messages to the brain through nerves around the mouth and throat that the act of eating is taking place and it helps to satisfy hunger.

The second way is indirect and is related simply to the fact that chewing takes time. It is natural for the body to take a certain amount of time to enjoy the food, fill up its stomach and ultimately send messages to the brain to make it feel satisfied. These hunger satisfaction messages are partly chemical *(nutrient and hormones)* and partly sensory *(stretching of the stomach, taste, swallowing)*. Nature seems to have timed these messages to the brain during eating.

Chewing allows time for these messages to reach the brain so that they can shut off the hunger drive before excessive calories are consumed. This is one of the fundamental factors addressed in the *Eat More, Weigh Less™ Diet.* With foods that are medium to high EMI, it takes additional time to chew, which makes the act of eating more enjoyable, which in turn allows you to feel satisfied.

WHAT YOU CAN DO:

- Choose medium- to high-EMI foods, i.e., whole foods above the dotted line on the Inverted Pyramid *(page 27)*.

- Chew your food 25 to 50 times per mouthful.

Eat More, Weigh Less™ Tip
▽75▽

Play Your Fat Away

Would You Believe: One of the best ways to *Eat More, Weigh Less™* is to *play!*

Some Facts: One of the reasons people gain weight as they get older is because they don't play the way they did when they were younger.

Imagine a bunch of children running around, playing on a playground or at recess in grade school. Perhaps you were one of those children. Being physically active is fun – literally child's play.

So, since when did it become "exercise," almost as if it were a chore? Instead, I like to recommend that everyone play regularly. Find something that is physically active "play" that you enjoy doing and do it 4 times per week for at least 30 to 40 minutes. Make sure it is something you enjoy *(if you like watching TV, get an exercise bike and watch your favorite show).*

To help you ensure that the activity is vigorous enough, try to get your heart rate up to "training heart rate" *(if okay with your doctor)* or 60% to 80% of maximum heart rate. Maximum heart rate is estimated at 220 minus age. Thus, the calculation of your training heart rate is as follows:

$$220 - age = maximum\ heart\ rate$$
$$this\ number\ x\ 60\%\ to\ 80\%$$
$$= training\ heart\ rate$$

And if you think of any excuse, think of my radio show co-host, Ruth Heidrich, who is in her 60's, a grandmother, and still competes in triathlons! Also, with exercising, you can eat more because your body will burn calories faster even when you sleep and you can "Play Your Fat Away."

WHAT YOU CAN DO:

- "Play" 4 to 7 times a week for at least 30 to 40 minutes.

- Get your heart rate up to your "training heart rate" or 80% of your calculated maximum, i.e., 220 minus age times 80%.*

- Play your fat away.

---

* Provided it's okay with your doctor.

Eat More, Weigh Less™ Tip

76

Relax, God's In Charge

WOULD YOU BELIEVE: Saying mealtime grace, a prayer, or meditation anytime helps relieve stress and may help us maintain our health.

SOME FACTS: Most of us are under a great deal of stress these days because we're trying to keep up with the fast pace of society. In such a setting, it's more important than ever to keep a perspective on things in order to keep our stress level down. This helps prevent stress-related bingeing. Saying grace, a prayer, or meditating helps us keep our priorities straight and tap into a Power greater than we are to help deal with daily problems. To *Eat More, Weigh Less™* is important. To "give more and need less" is also important. Even more important is to "pray more and worry less."

WHAT YOU CAN DO:

- Say your grace, pray, or meditate daily.
- Do your best at your job and in working to fulfill God's plan.
- Relax, God's in charge.

Eat More, Weigh Less™ Tip

Share This Book
With Your Friends

WOULD YOU BELIEVE: What you do affects everyone and everything else in the world.

SOME FACTS: In Hawaii, we have a number of universal concepts that are keys to health. I'll share two of them with you now.

Lōkahi: The first concept is known as "Lōkahi." Lōkahi literally means "consensus," but in its deeper sense means "oneness." It means that we are all connected within and without, with each other, and with all beings and things. It means that our health is related to our inner "oneness" spiritually, mentally, emotionally, and physically. It also means that we are "one" with our food. And if our food is whole, fresh, in harmony with the environment, and full of life-force, then we will be in harmony with our environment and full of life. It also means that you are connected to everyone around you, and when you share with others, it comes back to you.

Aloha: This brings us to the second principles known as "Aloha."   "Aloha" is known around the world as the friendly greeting people receive when they visit Hawaii. In its true sense, however, it means much more than that.   It means universal unconditional love for everyone and everything.   It means giving endlessly and sharing with others. If you do this, by the principle of "Lōkahi," it will eventually come back to you.

WHAT YOU CAN DO:

- Try to see the spirit of God in everyone and everything, and understand the concept of "Lōkahi."

- Send your "Aloha" to everyone you meet.

- Be generous to all your friends with your new-found knowledge about how to *Eat More* in order to *Weigh Less*, and your generosity will come back to you. After all, it's more fun to do things with friends, and they, in turn, will help you support your own way of eating for life.

CONCLUSION

Some Final Thoughts

Whole Person

While this book is primarily about diet, for your maximum health it is important to deal with the whole person, rather than just the diet or exercise. The root word of health is "hal," which means whole. The word "health" in and of itself means to be whole. In other words, true health includes all aspects of a person, including the spiritual, mental, emotional and physical. Diet and exercise deal primarily with your physical aspects, and now I want to remind you about the other elements of total health.

The true spirit of the *Eat More, Weigh Less™ Diet* is to focus on your health and in maximizing your health, the weight comes off automatically. I encourage you to continue to make efforts to become even healthier than you already are in all aspects of your life, including mental, emotional, and spiritual aspects.

Whole Community

Community standards help mold our dietary choices. We are stuck with the supply of food that is available to us in the supermarkets and restaurants, and we do not have a choice as to what kinds of foods are advertised on television. We are immersed in a social environment in which food choices are often dictated: hot dogs at ball games, hamburgers at fast food places, barbecue beef at picnics, roast turkey at Thanksgiving — the list goes on and on. However, we can make choices now that affect our health and influence the community to change.

At the same time, the whole community is at risk for the diseases that I've mentioned in this book. If for no other reason than that alone, we all need to adopt healthier diets and lifestyles. Ultimately, you will influence your family and friends. In my practice, many people adopt healthier ways of eating after seeing the effects of the diet. You may indeed save lives in the years to come, by serving as an example. By preparing *Eat More, Weight Less™* meals and sharing them, by letting others see the wonderful results in you, you'll be doing your part to help the whole community improve.

Whole Earth

What we do with our own health can ultimately affect the world. We live in a smaller and smaller world. Communications, transportation and commerce is much more rapid and convenient. The concept of a global community is not far from us and may become reality within this generation. What we eat affects us not only in terms of our health and our community's health, but it affects the health of the world.

Diet For A New America

For example, by avoiding the use of animal products, we save a lot of wasted resources in terms of energy and natural resources. John Robbins, author of *Diet for a New America*,[27] points out that in order to conserve water resources you could either refrain from eating one pound of beef, or refrain from taking a shower for an entire year. That's how much water is used in producing that one pound of beef! If you doubt these figures, please read his book. He has dozens of well-documented examples of environmental, health, and moral reasons for avoiding animal products.

Diet For A New World

Another example of how our diets can affect the world is described in *One Peaceful World* by Michio Kushi.[28] This book describes, among other things, how eating animal products can increase the likelihood of war and how diet may be the key to world peace.

These are just some aspects of the greater influence you may have, toward improving things for all of us. We often forget that we do not live in a vacuum. Everything you do in this world affects someone else. By changing your diet, you're certain to influence your family, close friends and others in your immediate circle. Your change to a better diet will have implications far, far beyond just the pounds you eliminate.

But you don't need to become a crusader or go out looking for a soapbox. Just follow the *Eat More, Weigh Less™ Diet*, let it do its natural work for you, and tell others what you're doing and why. The rest will take care of itself, even as the pounds drop off. You've finally found a weight loss plan that works, because it's nature's way. Dieting is dead. Eating is alive and well. Enjoy the recipes in this book, and *bon appetit!*

Suggested Reading List

Harris, William. *The Scientific Basis of Vegetarianism*, Hawaii Health Publishers, Honolulu, HI; 1995.

Heidrich, Ruth, *A Race for Life*, Hawaii Health Publishers, Honolulu, HI: 1991.

Heidrich, Ruth, *A Race for Life Cookbook*, Hawaii Health Publishers, Honolulu, HI: 1993.

Kushi, Michio, et al. *One Peaceful World*, St. Martin's Press, New York, NY: 1987.

Kushi, Michio. *The Cancer Prevention Diet*, St. Martin's Press, New York, NY: 1983.

Lappé, Frances Moore. *Diet for a Small Planet*, Ballantine Books, NY: 1982.

McDougall, John, M.D. *A Challenging Second Opinion*, New Century Publishers, Inc., Piscataway, NJ: 1985

McDougall, John, M.D., et al. *The McDougall Plan for Super Health and Life-long Weight Loss*, New Century Publishers, Inc., Piscataway, NJ: 1983.

Ornish, Dean. *Dr. Dean Ornish's Program for Reversing Heart Disease*, Ballantine Books, New York, NY: 1991.

Pinckney, Neal, Ph.D. *Healthy Heart Handbook*, Healing Heart Foundation, Makaha, HI: 1994.

Robbins, John. *Diet for a New America*, Stillpoint, Walpole, NH: 1987.

Shintani, Terry. *Eat More, Weigh Less™ Diet*, Halpax, Honolulu, HI: 1993.

Turner, Kristina: *The Self-Healing Cookbook*, Earthtones Press, Grass Valley, CA: 1989.

Bibliography

1 Dr. Marian Apfelbaum, Professor of Nutrition, University of Paris, as quoted by Sue Pleming, Reuter's, 1993.

2 Dr. Jean-Paul Deslypere, Professor of Human Nutrition, Ghent, Belgium; as quoted by Sue Pleming, Reuter's, 1993.

On Population Studies

3 Whittemore AS, et al. JNCI 1990;82;11:915-26.

4 Romieu I, et al. Am J Clin Nutr 1988; 47:406-12.

On Clinical Intervention

5 Shah M, et al. Am J Clin Nutr 1994;59:980-4.

6 Shintani TT, et al. Am J Clin Nutr 1991;53:1647S.

7 Kendall A, et al. Am J Clin Nutr 1991;53:1124-9.

8 Buzzard IM, et al. J Am Dietetic Assn 1990;90(1):42-53.

9 Dreon DM, et al. Am J Clin Nutr 1988;47:995-1000.

10 Lissner LL, et al. Am J Clin Nutr 1987;46:886-92.

11 Duncan KH, et al. Am J Clin Nutr 1983;37:763-67.

12 Weinsier RL, et al. Int J Obes 1983;7:538-48.

13 Weinsier RL, et al. Br J Clin Nutr 1982;47:367-79.

On Fat Calories

14 Acheson KJ, et al. Am J Clin Nutr 1988;48:240-7.

15 Danforth E. Am J Clin Nutr 1985;41:1132-45.

16 Acheson KJ, et al. Am J Physiol 1984;246 (Endocrinol Metab 9): E62-E70.

17 Center for Science in the Public Interest, Nutrition Action Health Letter, May 1994.

Studies of Low-Fat Diet

18 Ornish D, et al. Lancet 1990;336:129.

19 Snowdon DA. Am J Clin Nutr 1988;48:739-48.

20 Salmon DMW. Intl J Obes 1985;9:443-449.

On Animal Protein

21 Havala S, et al. J Am Dietetic Assoc 1993;11:1317.

22 Harris W. *The Scientific Basis of Vegetarianism*, Hawaii Health Publishers, Honolulu, HI; 1995.

On Calcium

23 Weaver C and Plawecki K. Am J Clin Nutr 1994;59(suppl):1238S-41S.

24 Abelow BJ. Calcif Tissue Int 1992;50:14-8.

25 Bowes & Church. *Food Values of Portions Commonly Used*, LB Lippencott Co.; 1985,

26 Recker R. Am J Clin Nutr 1985;41;254.

Peaceful World

27 Robbins J. *Diet For A New America*, Stillpoint, Walpole, NH; 1987.

28 Kushi M. *One Peaceful World*, St. Martin's Press, New York, NY; 1987.

Type I Diabetes or Juvenile Diabetes

29 Dahl JK. Diabetes Care 1991;14;1081.

Arthritis

30 Welsh C. Int Arch Allergy & Appl Immunology 1986;80:192.

31 Panush R. Arthritis Rheum 1986;29:220.

Glossary

Agar Flakes: Also called agar-agar, this is a mineral-rich seaweed processed into a form that can easily substitute for gelatin.

Arame: A high-calcium food *(like almost all seaweeds)*, this Japanese seaweed is a "stringy" sea vegetable like hijiki.

Azuki Beans: Tiny, hard red beans from Japan with a faintly sweet flavor. Also mistakenly called "Aduki."

Basmati Rice: This is a rich and aromatic grain from India. It is known as the "King of Rice" and is eaten by India's elite. *(Best when eaten in the brown variety.)*

Brown Rice: This applies to any type of whole rice wherein the germ and the bran are intact. White rice, by contrast, is devitalized — with germ and bran removed — which means that brown rice is always the preferred form of rice, no matter what specific subtype of rice you prefer. Brown rice has a chewy, nutty flavor that is much better than the bland flavor of white rice.

Buckwheat: This is a plant seed from the buckwheat plant, which is related to rhubarb. The iron and mineral content is especially high, and this food has been a staple in Russia, Eastern Europe, and China for centuries. It may be prepared in a variety of ways, such as breakfast "cereal" *(though is it not technically a cereal grain)*, pilafs, and other tasty treats. Roasted buckwheat is also known as Kasha, and this grain is increasingly popular in health food cereals.

Bulgur Wheat: A true grain, this is popular in the Middle East. When you purchase it, this soft grain is usually already steamed, cracked, and toasted. You can soak it, then use it as a base for delicious Mediterranean salads, such as Tabouleh *(a mixture of bulgur, raisins, herbs, oil, lemon juice, onions, and tomatoes)*.

Chapati: An East Indian unleavened flat bread that is much like flour tortillas, and which make an excellent sandwich.

Curry: A combined form of East Indian spices which ranges from very mild to very hot. Be careful, when purchasing, to get the type that is just right for your personal taste.

Elipidate™: A word coined by Dr. Shintani, derived from the word "eliminate" and "lipid," which means to eliminate fats, oils, and cholesterol from a food, recipe, or diet.

EMI: Dr. Shintani's Eat More Index, a table which lets you see at a glance just how much bulk and nutritional value each food has. The suggestion of the EMWL diet is that you should always eat as high as possible on the EMI scale.

Empty Calories: The kind of calories found in foods that supply energy but little or no actual nutrients. Usually unhealthy, fat-laden foods.

Fatty acids: The specific molecules that make up fats and oils.

Fat Finder Formula: A simple mathematical device which allows you to find the actual percentages of fat and oil in packaged foods *(see page 21).*

Fiber: There are two types of fiber: Soluble, which dissolves in water, such as gums and pectins and insoluble, which does not dissolve in water, such as cellulose.

Garbanzo Beans: Also known as chickpeas, these are highly popular in the Middle East. There are many healthy foods derived from Middle East cuisine. These are high in protein, can be mashed into paste with a bit of lemon oil and fresh garlic, and eaten as a dip for pita bread or used as a sandwich filler. They are also sometimes ground into flour.

Hijiki: A high-calcium food which is a stringy Japanese seaweed similar to arame.

Inverted Food Pyramid: Dr. Shintani's modification of the USDA's Food Guide Pyramid. It optimizes the percentage of healthy foods, and emphasizes the problems with Optional, Occasional, or Special Conditions foods.

Konbu: A broad, thick seaweed also known as kelp or laminaria that is used both as a high calcium food as well as the basis of soup stock.

Lipids: A category of substances that are not water soluble including including fat for example fats, oils, and cholesterol.

Mirin: A sweet Japanese cooking wine.

Miso: A fermented soy paste product which has a savory flavor often used in soups and sauces.

Mung Beans: These green or yellow beans are highly popular in Asia, where they are used in vegetable dishes or are sprouted and eaten as sprouts.

Nutritional Yeast: This golden-colored condiment is also sometimes used as a dietary supplement. It has a distinct but pleasant flavor that adapts itself well to a variety of dishes, from nutty to cheesy. It is available in flaked or powdered form in natural food stores and some supermarkets. Don't mistake it for the ordinary form of baking yeast. It's altogether different.

Pilaf: A pilaf was initially a Persian dish made of rice and raisins, with meats or fowl and a variety of light sauces. Today, pilafs have been adapted to showcase every great cuisine in the world. These dishes are simple to make, are easily adaptable to your own taste, and should be used often in the EMWL diet — but without the meat, of course.

Pita Bread: A flat, round bread that when cut in two, forms two pieces of pocket bread that can be stuffed to make sandwiches.

Quinoa: Pronounced "keen-wah," this fluffy tiny grain was a staple of the Incan civilizations, and was actually worshipped by them at one time. It has a rich nutty flavor, and is excellent in pilafs, casseroles, as a cereal and in a variety of other ways.

Rice Milk: Milk made by blending rice and water.

Salsa: A thick Mexican sauce that is akin to a relish. Salsas are traditionally made from tomatoes and chili peppers. Today, adaptations abound, and it's not uncommon to find pineapple salsas, mango salsas, and other types of salsas at nouveau cuisine restaurants. Here, we generally stick to the traditional sauce, but if you want to spice up your foods, try some of the newer versions of salsa.

Seitan: A chewy, high-protein food made from boiled or baked wheat gluten mixed with water and seasonings. Seitan has the chewy texture of meat and is used as a meat substitute. Available in natural food stores.

Soba: Long, thin buckwheat noodles, used in a variety of Asian salads and soups.

Shiitake Mushroom: A delicious Japanese mushroom, sold in either fresh or dried form. The dried is easily used by soaking in water.

Sushi: A traditional Japanese food based on rice flavored with vinegar. It is usually served with nori seaweed, wrapped around rice and other ingredients.

Soy Milk: This is a whitish creamy drink is made from soybeans.

Soy Sauce: A dark, salty, tasty sauce made from soybeans, water and salt. This is usually thin, like water, but can be found in thicker variations.

Tahini: Sesame butter, used in a variety of foods, including desserts. This is a high-fat food, so use sparingly if at all.

Tamari: Genuine tamari is soy sauce made naturally without wheat as a by-product of miso making. However, it is commonly used as a term simply describing naturally brewed soy sauce.

Tarragon: French tarragon is the preferable kind of this spice. Other brands tend to be tasteless, so look for the "French" name on the label.

Tempeh: A whole soybean food that is a good meat substitute. It is fermented, which minimizes its "beany" flavor and gassiness.

Texturized Vegetable Protein (TVP): Usually referred to by the abbreviation of "TVP." A fibrous-textured soy product made from extruded soy flour. Used for making sauces have the texture of ground meat. Available at natural food stores in minced, granule, and chunk form.

Tofu: Fermented soybean curd.

Umeboshi: A Japanese pickled plum which has a strong tart and salty flavor. In Japan, it is used as a condiment as well as a folk medicine.

Wakame: A tender, leafy Japanese seaweed, high in calcium as are just about all other seaweeds.

Vegan diet: A diet which eliminates all animal products, such as meat, poultry, fish, eggs and dairy products.

Vegetarian "Chicken" Seasoning: A powdered product that is made from vegetable products and spices, that has a chicken flavor. It is used for soup bases and gravies.

Wild Rice: This is actually a grain, from the grass family of foods, rather than rice. But it resembles rice and is used in much the same way, and therefore is always referred to as rice. It is highly nutritious, and has a light, subtle taste. Excellent in pilafs, or combined with other types of rice.

Zapf: Dr. Shintani's word for "Zap the Fat," a synonym for "Elipidate™."

Recipe Credits

I would like to thank the following people for their contributions to the recipe section of this book.

First, thanks to go to the Family and Consumer Science teachers who make up such a creative and hard-working team. Credit and thanks belong to:

Lynne Lee — recipes contributed: Mung Bean Surprise, Sekihan, Golden Whole Wheat Rolls, Automatic Whole Wheat Bread, Buckwheat Banana Muffins, Cinnamon Raisin Muffins, Apricot Cranberry Tea Bread, Gingerbread, Cinnamon Apple Bread, Tomato Vermicelli, Lentil Leek Soup, Spicy Tofu with Cabbage, Hearty Red Lentil Soup, Cuban Black Beans, Savory Gravy, Honey Almond Fruit Cocktail, Fresh Salsa Caliente, Barbecue Baked Beans, Apple-Strawberry Jel, Green Apple Pastry Pie, Pronto Bean and Rice Burritos, Ginger Mustard Cabbage with Konbu, Cabbage-Wrapped Watercress, Thousand Island Dressing, Amber Dip, and Clear Dip.

Carol Devenot — recipes contributed: Apple Raisin Pancakes, Waffles, Potatoes with Horseradish Sauce, Asian Pasta Salad, Honey Oatmeal Cookies, Mulligatawny Soup, Peking Hot and Sour Soup, Fennel Bulgur Salad, Hawaiian Savory Stew, Local Style Curry Stew, Garden Pizza, Spicy Szechwan Eggplant, Peach Crisp, Broiled Falafel, Sloppy Jacks, Zip Chili, Navy Bean on Rye, and Potato Beanburgers.

Jenny Choy — recipes contributed: Mushroom-Broccoli Noodle Soup, Potato and Corn Chowder, Simple Whole Wheat Bread, Whole Wheat Honey Bread, Seitan Ginger Stirfry, Mushroom Marinara Sauce, Chunky Three-Bean Chili, Quick Apple Pie, and Black Beans with Carrots and Cabbage.

OTHERS who also contributed recipes and advice are:

Ann Tang, a home cookin' expert, kindly shared some of her delicious and novel recipes — recipes contributed: Oriental Salad Dressing, Garden Dumplings, Fried Rice Roll-ups, Vegetarian Raviolis, Marinara Sauce, Pasta with Eggplant Sauce, Pasta with Roasted Vegetables, Portuguese Bean Soup, Butternut Squash with Stuffing, and the Salsa recipe for Baked Potatoes with Salsa.

Dick Allgire, Honolulu TV personality, crusader in the field of nutrition — recipes contributed: Chickenless Bouillon, Bow-tie Pasta with Miso Sauce, Papaya Seed Dressing, and California Sunshine Dressing.

Ruth Payne, another a home cookin' expert — recipes contributed: Vegetable Barley Soup and Potato Bean Barley Soup, two hearty and much-needed dishes.

Neal Pinckney, author of *The Healthy Heart Handbook*, allowed me to use his recipe for Crispy Onion Rings.

Ruth Heidrich, author of *A Race for Life Cookbook*, contributed Texas Fries.

Paul Onishi contributed the Pineapple Ginger Dressing recipe.

Janice Miller contributed the pizza recipe, the Pronto Potato Soup recipe, and several stir-frys.

Nathan Hina, a Honolulu chef, contributed the recipe for Sweet Potato Salad.

Karen Kumada, Family and Consumer Science teacher, contributed the dressing for the Sweet Potato Salad.

Thanks to the people at Country Life Vegetarian Cookbook *(available through Family Health Publications, 13062 Musgrove Highway, Sunfield, Michigan, 48890)*, who allowed me to use their excellent recipe for Corn Bread, and who also inspired a few other of these recipes.

Recipe Index